D0886839

Diplomacy During The American Civil War

AMERICA IN CRISIS

A series of eight books on American Diplomatic History

EDITOR: *Robert A. Divine*

Empire and Independence:
The International History of the War of American Independence
RICHARD VAN ALSTYNE

Diplomacy During The American Civil War
D. P. CROOK

A Nation on Trial:
America and the War of 1812
PATRICK C. T. WHITE

When the Eagle Screamed, 1800–1860
WILLIAM H. GOETZMANN

America's Road to Empire:
The War with Spain and Overseas Expansion
H. WAYNE MORGAN

The Great Departure:
The United States and World War I, 1914–1920
DANIEL M. SMITH

The Reluctant Belligerent:
American Entry into World War II
ROBERT A DIVINE

American Diplomacy during the Second World War, 1941–1945
GADDIS SMITH

America, Russia and The Cold War, 1945–1975, Third Edition
WALTER LAFEBER

Diplomacy During The American Civil War

D. P. CROOK
University of Queensland, Australia

John Wiley and Sons, Inc., New York • London • Sydney • Toronto

Library of Congress Cataloging in Publication Data:
Crook, David Paul.
Diplomacy during the American Civil War.

(America in crisis)
Based on the author's The North, the South, and the powers, 1861–1865.
Bibliography: p.
Index.
1.   United States—Foreign relations—1861–1865.
2.   Confederate States of America—Foreign relations.
I. Title. II. Series.
E469.C75   973.7'2   75–25678
ISBN 0–471–18856–5
Printed in the United States of America

10 9 8 7 6 5 4 3 2 1

For my brothers Arthur and Phillip.

Foreword

The eight original volumes in the "America in Crisis" series all dealt with foreign wars, ranging from the eighteenth-century struggle for independence to the twentieth-century cold war with the Soviet Union. The omission of the Civil War, often viewed as the gravest of all American crisis, has now been remedied by Professor Crook's study. Based on his larger work, *The North, the South, and the Powers, 1861–1865,* this book deals comprehensively with Civil War diplomacy by placing it in an international setting. Avoiding the partisan bias for North or South that has marred many of the earlier accounts, Professor Crook stresses the unstable nature of the European political system in explaining why England and France refrained from intervention in the American conflict. Yet he also examines the internal workings of both the Union and Confederate governments to trace their conflicting diplomatic strategies and to appraise the relative success and failure of their efforts. The result is a critical but balanced narrative that provides a long-needed overview of Civil War diplomacy.

In analyzing the impact of the Civil War on America's world role, the author finds that the internal struggle failed to displace the traditional idea of America's imperial mission. He sees Seward as the embodiment of expansionism, operating out of a deep-seated belief in the beneficence of the republican ideal and bent on fostering American commercial and territorial growth. Thus, even in the midst of grave internal crisis, the fulfillment of the nation's destiny remained at the core of American diplomacy. The trauma of reconstruction and the distraction of industrialization, coupled with a postwar distaste for more violence, slowed the imperial impulse until a new generation brought it to fruition in the 1890s.

Robert A. Divine

Preface

The American Civil War has never been accorded its just place in the international history of our times. It threatened to break up the entire balance of power in the western hemisphere, and beyond. But that promise was betrayed and, in world history, the ordeal of the Union was soon overshadowed by the drama of Germany's rise to power. Nevertheless, the American crisis contributed its legacy to the new world being born in the later nineteenth century. The simplest, and most fundamental, outcome of events was that the United States was enabled to continue its headlong rush into superpowerdom. Men spoke in the 1860s of a globe divided between American and Russian spheres of influence; and they knew that a battle in the Wilderness, or at Gettysburg, might hold the key to that future. Also, the war marked a turning point in "Atlantic history," diverted the career of American imperialism, and bore upon the great debate on Democracy's future that rent the developed world. The animosities that developed between Britain and the American contestants during the Civil War hastened a process of economic and cultural disengagement which had been gradually taking place within the Anglo-American connection. Thereafter, the relationship of Britain and the United States became more frankly a matter of power. The War Between the States also put a stop, for a time, to American expansionist activity, so conspicuous a feature of the preceding generation. Secretary of State Seward's abiding achievement was to deflect expansionist energy into the Unionist war effort. In the south, it went into the struggle for survival. Yet the idea of American imperial mission proved to be highly resilient, despite the national firestorm. Geopolitical ambitions featured persistently in

9

the foreign policy outlook of both sections. Those who view the so-called "new imperialism" of 1898 as an aberration from American tradition would be well advised to look again at the neglected 1860s. Finally, that decade witnessed the travail and crisis of American democracy. The course of events seemed of epochal significance for the politics of Western Europe. There the American image had long been ideologically symbolic. It is not the least of history's ironies that victory for the north gave impetus abroad, not only to Abraham Lincoln's liberal ideals but also to militarism, centralist nationalism, and monolithic capitalism.

This volume abridges the interpretation and themes of my more detailed study, *The North, The South and the Powers, 1861–1865,* * which is recommended to those who desire a fuller documentation of events. To the acknowledgments made in that work, I add renewed thanks to my editor, Robert A. Divine, and to Wayne Anderson and Wiley's helpful, competent staff. Spencer Routh, Reference Librarian at the University of Queensland, erudite and ever-suffering in the cause of sweetness and light, deserves my gratitude for helping to overcome the problem of researching the Civil War from Brisbane, Australia. The warm encouragement of Professors Richard W. Van Alstyne and L. C. F. Turner was much appreciated. So too was the contribution of my wife Monica, who helped with proofs, index, and morale.

David Paul Crook

---

*Wiley, 1974.

Contents

MAPS

ABBREVIATIONS OF SOURCES CITED IN TEXT

AEJ	*Albany Evening Journal*
AHR	*American Historical Review*
B. M. Add. Mss.	*British Museum Additional Manuscripts*
BSP	*British Sessional Papers*
CWH	*Civil War Histroy*
EDA	Ephraim Douglass Adams, *Great Britain and the American Civil War* (N.Y., 1926, repr. Gloucester, Mass., 1957)
EHR	*English Historical Review*
JMH	*Journal of Modern History*
JSH	*Journal of Southern History*
MHSP	*Massachusetts Historical Society Proceedings*
MVHR	*Mississippi Valley Historical Review*
NYDT	*New York Daily Tribune*
NYEP	*New York Evening Post*
NYH	*New York Herald*
NYT	*New York Times*
NYW	*New York World*
ORN	Official records of the Union and Confederate Navies, in the war of the Rebellion (29 Vol., Washington, 1894–1922)
PRO	Public Records Office (London)
WDMC	*Washington Daily Morning Chronicle*
WNI	*Washington National Intelligencer*

Diplomacy During The American Civil War

CHAPTER I

The Eve of War

AT SWEET SULPHUR SPRINGS IN SEPTEMBER 1856 four southern Congressmen approached the British consul resident in Virginia, and asked him whether England would support the south in the event of American disunion. It was the time of the Presidential election which put James Buchanan, a Democrat, in the White House, thus postponing for four years a sectional reckoning. The consul, G. P. R. James, the novelist, believed that many American politicians considered "a war with some European power—England of course —would be the only remedy for the internal dissentions of the States, by rallying all parties against the common enemy."[1] Politicians such as Stephen A. Douglas, Caleb Cushing, Jefferson Davis, and William H. Seward were commonly believed to be among those hostile to England. In 1860, after the Democratic party had smashed itself to pieces, a Republican, Abraham Lincoln, was elected President. He promptly installed as his Secretary of State-elect William H. Seward—perhaps the most articulate of the American "warmongers." The Presidential victory of the Republicans in 1860 proved obnoxious to the south and the prelude to a national holocaust. Seward's "foreign war panacea" for America's ills would soon be put to the test.

As the shadows of war lengthened over the North American continent, the great powers of Europe watched and waited. As the documents show, the first reactions of the British Foreign Office and the French *Quai d'Orsay* were fretful and defensive rather than predatory. There were good reasons for this: the situation

---

[1]Laura A. White, "The United States in the 1850's as seen by British Consuls," *MVHR,* XIX, No. 4 (March, 1933), 531–534.

was complex, and there were deterrents against avidity, or reck-lessness. In the eighteenth and nineteenth centuries, as the Americans had elbowed their way to the Pacific coast, thrust south and southwest into the old domain of the Spanish empire, claimed the western hemisphere as their sphere of influence, whitened the seven seas with their sails and sought for control of trade routes vital to their commerce, they had encountered the competitive interests of European nations. American expansionism was part of a struggle for mastery against imperialist rivals, a fight not merely for territory but for resources, commercial leverage, and strategic advantage in the larger world.[3] The "scramble for America" was not over by 1860; but to all appearances its most aggressive phase was completed. The strongest rival in the hemisphere to the domi-nating United States was Great Britain. The British were firmly installed in Canada (British North America) and the West Indies, strategically placed in Central America, commercially strong in Latin America, almost impregnable in world trade because of their industrial power, colonies, and maritime supremacy. Spain, enjoy-ing a minor economic renaissance under the moderate one-party system of the veteran general O'Donnell, held Puerto Rico and Cuba, the "Jewel of the Caribbean," and nourished other ambi-tions in the region. France, after losing its eighteenth century American empire, tried with indifferent success in the nineteenth century to reassert itself in the hemisphere, most notably in Texas and Mexico. Under Napoleon III, the Second Empire continued to compete with Britain and the United States in the Isthmus of Panama, the Pacific, and Asia. The likeliest hemispheric trouble spots appeared to be Mexico, partitioned by the American army in the 1840's, and Cuba, a ripe tropical fruit ready for plucking.

On the eve of the Civil War, something of a detente existed between the United States and its competitors in the American sphere, a detente based on mutual recognition of reality. American power dominated the hemisphere; and European governments came to see that it was prudent, even profitable, to come to terms with it. As Lord Palmerston, the British Prime Minister, com-plained: "These Yankees . . . are on the Spot, strong, deeply inter-

---

[3]See William H. Goetzmann, *When the Eagle Screamed: The Romantic Horizon in American Diplomacy* (Wiley, New York, 1966). The great pioneering study is Rich-ard W. Van Alstyne, *The Rising American Empire* (Oxford, 1960).

ested in the matter, totally unscrupulous and dishonest and determined somehow or other to carry their Point; We are far away, weak from Distance, controlled by the indifference of the Nation as to the Question discussed, and by its Strong commercial Interest in maintaining Peace with the United States."[4] In turn, many Americans accepted the need to stabilize the region, in recognition of the fact that worsening sectional tensions threatened to disable the Republic's effectiveness abroad.

In the 1850's Britain and the United States reached a shaky accommodation over the envenomed question of Central America, a matter not merely of colonies but of geopolitical control. Nineteenth century statesmen persistently dreamed of building, and owning, canals across the isthmuses of Panama and Suez. Whoever commanded a Central American canal route also commanded the lucrative trade between California, no longer Mexican, and places to the east and would also enjoy invaluable strategic advantages. The Clayton-Bulwer treaty, signed in 1850, proposed that Britain and the United States jointly renounce colonial ambitions in Central America, and promote in partnership an Isthmian canal project. It is instructive to note how doggedly the British pursued a lasting settlement along these lines. A compromise proved no easy task to obtain from the Americans, with complications arising from filibustering adventures and party politics. But a settlement meant long-term benefits for the British and relief from imperial difficulties.[5] English merchants wanted stability in Latin America and easy transit between the Atlantic and Pacific oceans. The Clayton-Bulwer treaty also offered protection to the British West Indies against American encirclement. Perhaps most important, good relations with America would relieve pressure upon Canada. Canada's border defenses were vulnerable to an American land thrust. They could be improved only by massive expenditure on fortifications and troops. That was unlikely from a miserly British treasury, while Canadians themselves were notoriously reluctant to shoulder their share of defense burdens.

Preoccupied with their far-flung commercial and imperial inter-

---

[4]Lord Palmerston to Lord Clarendon, December 31, 1857; q. R. W. Van Alstyne, "Anglo-American Relations, 1853–1857," *AHR*, XLII, No. 34 (1936–7), 500.

[5]R.W. Van Alstyne, "British Diplomacy and the Clayton-Bulwer Treaty," 1850–1860," *J. Mod. Hist.*, XI, No. 2 (June, 1939), 149–183.

ests, determined to keep their hands free for dealing with major European issues, the British were, on the whole, willing to accept the existing balance of power in the western hemisphere. In the mid-century, that seemed a good bargain. It should be remembered that, prior to the Civil War, many Englishmen privately expected their North American colonies—still not confederated—to slide peacefully into the great Yankee empire. Nor did it seem improbable that Caribbean countries like Cuba, Haiti, or Santo Domingo would also be absorbed into the United States. The Great Disruption put an end, for a time, to "those inordinate dreams of 'manifest destiny' and unapproachable imperial grandeur which used to inflate the American imagination."[6] Whether it would also signal the death of the detente arrived at in the antebellum years was the central issue of civil war diplomacy.

Historians have been, perhaps, too ready to imply that the Civil War extinguished the assessments of the 1850's. It would be rash to jump to the conclusion, for instance, that Britain necessarily welcomed a breakdown in the hemispheric power balance or the onset of an era of instability and foreign meddling in the American theater. The humbling of an arrogant rival may have presented superficial attractions; but the balance of advantage to be won in the obscure situation created by the south's rebellion could not be easily struck. The Union appeared likely to dissolve into two or more federations without any action from jealous onlookers. Intervention, depending on its form, would have costs as well as benefits. Foreseeably, no outside power could afford to move on America without consulting its full range of international interests, inspecting its alliances, and the security of its European standing. During the prelude of great changes in the old European balance of power, that scrutiny produced cautionary views.

The British Prime Minister in 1861 was Lord Palmerston, whose schoolbook image is that of a blustering, interventionist John Bull, a womanizer with ginger sideburns and a gunboat approach to diplomacy. Palmerston was indeed capable of saying that "Diplomats and protocols are very good things, but there are no better peacekeepers than well-appointed three deckers." Nevertheless, his biographers reveal him as a realist statesman, aware of the

---

[6] *Leeds Times*, April 29, 1861.

limits of British power, skilled in applying it to maintain national prestige, defense capability, and a competitive edge internationally; and capable of exercising discretion when necessary. He opposed "crusades of conquest" that saddled England with debts, and was an antislavery zealot. His great pride was that he had helped to crush the international slave trade. Under Palmerston, Britain stood basically for a settled international order, although it occasionally made gestures in support of such causes as constitutional reform of autocratic regimes.

A fluid party situation, and the vagaries of public opinion, constituted domestic constraints upon diplomacy. The Corn Law crisis of 1846 had fragmented British politics for a generation. Although a Liberal party was cobbled together in 1859 from the Whigs, reformist and Irish radicals, and a scattering of able ex-Tories—old followers of Peel, William Ewart Gladstone at their head—conflict between cliques still dominated politics. Palmerston arbitrated, rather than dominated, over his patchwork administration. Palmerston himself had been a strong Foreign Secretary in previous Whig administrations, including one led by Lord John Russell. Now Russell served as Foreign Secretary under Palmerston, who tactfully refrained from meddling unduly in foreign policy. Some said, unkindly, that Richard Cobden, great free trader and pacifist, was England's real Foreign Secretary. Cobden certainly reflected a strong mood in the country at large against adventurist policies abroad. The Crimean War and the Indian Mutiny had shaken national confidence. "No more Crimeas" was the slogan of the day. The Liberals had a tenuous parliamentary majority, and indifferent party discipline; while both sides of the House of Commons contained a great variety of stubbornly held views on foreign affairs. In those circumstances, a prudent cabinet sought to win bipartisan support on vital diplomatic questions. Only too often the politics of "consensus" turned out to be safe but indecisive.

America, and American democracy, had always evoked a great range of attitudes from British public opinion. The spectrum of issues raised by the Civil War—slavery, states rights, the use of force in a democracy, etc.—complicated the English response, which varied with the enormous heterogeneity of economic, ideological, and group interests involved. Traditionally, support for

American liberties and universal suffrage came from radical and reformist groups. Those alienated from the political and religious establishments still appealed to America as an argument against aristocracy, status and establishments.[7] Traditionally again, the friends of America were recruited from professional and middle-class people, Nonconformists, and politically conscious artisans. However, interest in parliamentary reform had lapsed in the prosperous 1850's, and with it the urgent need to use the American example. American expansionism alienated even ardent admirers of American institutions and economic system, such as Richard Cobden. Among radicals, some fierce anticapitalists deplored America's exploitative industrial system and competitive ethic, criticisms also made by anti-industrialists within the rural aristocracy. The violence and corruption of American politics, the crudities of transatlantic culture, invited censure. The breakdown of the Union shocked the radical partisans of American democracy and bolstered their conservative opponents. But a significant and intelligent part of British opinion, especially people of the center, did not fell deeply committed. Either ambiguous about, or healthily sceptical of the war aims and propaganda of north and south, subject to conflicting pressures of humanitarian, liberal and nationalist sentiment, they molded their attitudes according to what was happening.

Across the channel, Napoleon III firmly managed his authoritarian Second Empire, supported by army, church, and business. The French economy flourished during the mid-century years of expansion, Haussmann rebuilt Paris, and republicanism lived underground. But by 1860, disenchantment was growing over Napoleon III's leadership, and in particular over his adventurist foreign policy, based on contempt for the treaties of 1815 imposed on post-Napoleonic Europe. Just concluded was the war of 1859 against Austria, begun with élan by Napoleon III, ending in all-round disappointment. Hatched by Napoleon and Cavour, the war was fought in the name of Italian liberation from Habsburg

---

[7]See D. P. Crook, *American Democracy in English Politics, 1815–1850* (Clarendon Press, Oxford, 1865), arguing that British ideas on the United States were accommodated into a gradualist tradition and existing values. To Benthamites America vindicated utilitarianism; to Whigs, Whiggery; to free traders, the dogmas of the Manchester School; to Tories, the need for heirarchy and standards of excellence.

Austria. While the campaign proved unpopular with conservative and clerical groups, generally pro-Austrian, the outcome displeased the Italian patriots, their French friends, and the British. Napoleon's claim to be the savior of Italy weakened when he agreed to the armistice of Villafranca, which maintained Austrian rule over Venetia. Henceforth the emperor's consuming passion was to win Venetia for Italy. By annexing Nice and Savoy as the price of his alliance with Piedmont, Napoleon almost destroyed the foundation of his European policy: the "understanding" with England reached in 1854. The Anglo-French alliance survived strictly through self-interest on both sides, self-interest tempered by mutual suspicion. Napoleon attempted to repair the accord after the strains of the Italian war by means of the Cobden-Chevalier treaty, signed in 1860. The treaty outraged traditionally protectionist French industry and business, among Napoleon's chief supporters. Their anger underlined the political difficulties facing the Second Empire, and it put limits to future liberties that Napoleon might take with the economy. If Napoleon intervened in the American theater—and he was slow to consider the possibility—he would need to ensure two things: intervention must not endanger the English accord; nor must it endanger economic equilibrium in France. These were tricky requirements. Napoleon showed little inclination to meet them, at least until he was driven toward Mexico by his Austrian diplomacy and colonial ambition. Meanwhile the breakup of the United States threatened to deprive France of a counterweight to British seapower.

The American upheaval coincided with a revival of liberal opposition in France. In 1860 Napoleon broadened the basis of government, providing at least the trappings of a parliamentary system, and mitigated press censorship. Political journalism received an infusion of life, with voices of dissent emerging from liberal Catholics, Saint Simonians, socialists, and Protestants as well as from republicans, Orleanists, and legitimists. Political exiles were permitted to return home. As far as the "left" was concerned, it was not a time to abandon the ideals offered by the republican democratic experiment in America; not, as in England, an apt moment for liberal doubts and reappraisal concerning the relevance of the American experience. "Liberal Europe," proclaimed Eugene Forcade, in the Orleanist *Revue des Deux Monde*, "cannot balance

between these two sides: its wishes will accompany the cause of
the North, the cause of human liberty and emancipation against
the cynical and violent party of slavery."[8] While the court and the
enemies of democracy sympathized with the south, the ideological
battle was joined in France itself; in the trial of American democracy, the future of republicanism in Europe also seemed at stake.

* * *

The diplomacy of an independent southern Confederacy had
been in the making at least half a decade before secession became
a reality. The assumptions, logic, and strategy underlying southern
foreign policy may be seen in evolution during the catastrophic
events that led from the Kansas-Nebraska conflict, the Dred Scott
case, John Brown's Raid, and the division of the Democratic party
to Lincoln's election and South Carolina's secession from the
Union. The secession debates that raged in the cotton states during
the fateful winter of 1860–1861 discussed, intermittently, what
posture a sovereign south should adopt before the world at large.
In a move to ward off any fears that a filibustering south would
gasconade aggressively in the Caribbean and Central America, the
south's leaders insisted on the rebellion's limited ambitions. They
showed obvious faith that the European powers must regard as
irresistible bait the chance to snap up spoils and reassert European
influence in an unprotected hemisphere. Secessionists expected
quick recognition, or judicious intervention, by European countries, acts sealing the rebellion's success. At a stroke, Yankee continental might and commercial power would be diminished, the
south's right to independence—all that it asked—gained, while its
friends abroad profited from the eruption of the American power
balance.

Another foundation of Confederate diplomacy rested upon cotton's dominating role in Atlantic trade. Cotton manufacturing had
been a vital industry, the pacemaker of change, in the world's first
Industrial Revolution. America's slave states and Lancashire, Britain's cotton workshop, became virtually interdependent econo-

---

[8]Cited Serge Gavronsky, *The French Liberal Opposition and the American Civil War*
(New York, 1968), p. 28. For the reaction in other European countries, see D. Jordan
and E. J. Pratt, *Europe and the American Civil War* (1931; repr. New York, 1969).

mies after Eli Whitney's invention of the cotton gin in 1793. Between 1820 and 1860 Britain obtained over three-quarters of its raw cotton from America. In 1860, after a bumper crop in Dixie, the figure was 85 percent. British shipping waxed fat on the cotton trade, importing the raw staple from America, exporting finished cotton wares to hungry, and ever-expanding, world markets. The British cotton industry was a heavy employer of labor, while cotton exports made up about half of British exports across the 1850's. Cotton also dominated United States' exports, often totalling over half the value of all exports in the antebellum years.

Such statistics bred two effects in the antebellum south: encouraging ire at the north's capitalist exploitation of southern agriculture, but also begetting a complacent confidence that secession could be carried out peacefully. Antitariff sentiment grew strong in the antebellum south, many complaints arising that the expanding sections of the north and northwest combined to force protectionist policies upon the nation, thus benefitting northern industry at the cost of the planters. Although cotton was the backbone of American trade, exorbitant profits seemed to accrue to entrepreneurial northerners, who stifled the use of natural outlets from Dixie to world markets. The south felt outraged when the 1857 depression, which left the cotton industry unscathed, aroused cries for more tariff protection from northeastern industry. Let the south secede, said southern editors, and grass would grow in the streets of New York. Cotton logic of this type nourished southern complacency: secession would not cause war, because war would dry up trade between north and south. If the Republicans tried to coerce the rebels, there would be a revolt of the northern middlemen and merchants whose wealth was built upon the south's bulk exports.

Nor, it was claimed by King Cotton advocates, would the outside world permit a war upon cotton. A cotton famine would raise the spectre of revolution over the aristocratic regimes of Europe. The powers must intervene to wedge open their lines of supply, even if they dispersed the Union fleet to do so. The effect of a decade's pamphleteering and speechifying on that text is sufficiently illustrated in a story told by William H. Russell, famous military correspondent for the London *Times*. Scenting war, Russell was in the Carolinas a few days before the bombardment of Fort Sumter, and there encountered cocky farmers in full army regalia, complete with swords:

I inquired of a fine, tall fair-haired young fellow whom they expected to fight. "That's more than I can tell" quoth he 'The Yankees aint such cussed fools as to think they can come here and whip us, let alone the British.' 'Why, what have the British got to do with it?' 'They are bound to take our part: if they don't we'll just give them a hint about cotton, and that will set matters right'. This was said very much with the air of a man who knows what he is talking about, and who was quite satisfied 'he had you there'. . . .[9]

The south also offered the lure of a free-trade south as a vital new market for British and French goods. After the Cobden-Chevalier treaty, Western Europe seemed on the brink of becoming a free-trade area. The Confederacy might join that world, once it had detached itself from the monopolist grasp of the northerners. In December 1860 Robert Barwell Rhett, arch-secessionist and part owner of the *Charleston Mercury,* approached Robert Bunch, the British consul at Charleston, revealing that a cotton federation was to be set up within sixty days. The southern states, said Rhett, preferred an alliance with England: "they would be Her best customer; . . . free trade would form an integral portion of their scheme of Government, with Import duties of nominal amount and direct communication, by steam, between the Southern and British Ports."[10] Rhett persisted in urging an active foreign policy upon the South. At the Montgomery convention, held in Alabama in February, 1861, to organize a Confederate government, Rhett became chairman of the Committee on Foreign Relations, and interrupted the leisurely constitution-making to urge that a mission be sent to Europe to offer treaties of commercial alliance. The signatories would enter "reciprocal obligations offensive and defensive for twenty years or more." In return the south would impose no import duty higher than 20 percent ad valorem, "and would permit European parties to the treaty to enjoy the privileges of the coasting trade free." A 10 percent discriminatory duty would be levied on all nations refusing to sign. Rhett alienated

---

[9]W. H. Russell, *My Civil War Diary* ed., Fletcher Pratt (London, 1954), p. 61.

[10]Bunch to Russell, December 15, 1860, F.O. Ser. II,, v. 745, printed in *AHR,* XVIII (July, 1913), 784–787. Also Laura White, *Robert Barnwell Rhett: Father of Secession* (Gloucester, Mass., 1965).

Jefferson Davis, the convention's choice as President of the Confederacy, and the plan lapsed. Davis did, however, appoint a European mission, headed by William Lowndes Yancey, a strong aspirant for the Presidency, and including Ambrose D. Mann and Pierrre A. Rost. Bunch sent an unflattering portrait to London: Yancey was able but "impulsive, erratic, and hot-headed; a rabid Secessionist, a favourer of a revival of the Slave-Trade, and a 'filibuster' of the extremist type of 'manifest destiny'." Mann he dismissed as having "no special merit of any description."[11] Rost, a Lousiana judge, was chosen for his French origins. The commissioners' dispatch bag carried a treatise on states rights, a lecture on King Cotton, and a prospectus on market opportunities. Rhett told Yancey contemptuously "you carry no arguments that Europe cares to hear. My counsel is . . . to stay at home, or to go prepared to conciliate Europe by irresistible proffers of trade."[12]

What the new Confederate leadership at Montgomery did not fully appreciate was that economics by no means entirely favored the south. Ties of mutual self-interest bound segments of British and French business to largely northern partners. The prospect of a civil war in America, or of Anglo-American or Franco-American conflict arising from the crisis, threatened to destroy the whole complex, and profitable, network of transatlantic trade.

Britain and the United States, in particular, were yoked together in a close economic embrace, virtually a single Atlantic economy. In the post-Revolutionary era, the general North American region assumed a vital role in Britain's world commercial empire, as market and supplier of raw materials. Britain supplied capital, labor, tools and technology which the Americans needed to develop their huge natural resources.[13] Heavy British investment, a great deal of it in the north, went into American canals, railroads, land, banking

---

[11]Bunch to Russell, March 21, 1861, *MHSP,* XLVIII (Jan. 1915), 208–210.

[12]J. S. Du Bose, *Life and Times of Yancey* (Birmingham, Ala., 1892), 588–9. See also J. Preston Moore, "Lincoln and the Escape of the Confederate Commissioner," *Illinois State Hist. Soc.,* LVII, 23–27. Mann insisted on sailing from New York, where the State Department planned to arrest him. However Lincoln, wanting to calm tempers, allowed Mann to embark.

[13]See F. Thistlethwaite, *The Anglo-American Connection in the Early Nineteenth Century* (Philadelphia, 1959), esp. Ch. 1; J. Potter, "Atlantic Economy, 1815–1860" in A. W. Coats and R. M. Robertson eds., *Essays in American Economic History* (London, 1969).

and public securities. Northern commerce was long sustained by an intricate transatlantic credit network, with a prominent role played by Anglo-American banking houses such as Barings, Peabody's, and Brown-Shipley. To cite but one statistic of economic interrelationship: between 1815 and 1860 roughly one-quarter of British exports went to the United States, while almost half of American exports went to Britain—each was the other's best customer. If commerce within the "Atlantic Triangle," Britain, Canada and the United States, is treated as a unit, the figures are even more impressive. Although cotton still dominated the trade statistics, the 1850's saw a massive expansion in British imports of grain and foodstuffs from the American prairies.

By 1860 this, the most intimate phase in the history of the Atlantic economy, was ending. In retrospect the signs of realignment are obvious: steady diversification of the British economy, a trend to heavy industrialization in the American northeast, the growth there of strong local money markets, an American preoccupation with continental development at the expense of transatlantic trade. Textiles, and thus slave cotton, had lost central importance in the British system by mid-century, superceded by heavy coal and iron industries. Again, as Yankee textile, iron, and railroad industries boomed, British business faced an increasingly difficult struggle to maintain position in American markets and enterprises.

In that context the firebrand secessionists were rash in forecasting inevitable British intervention to secure a cotton supply, or to cripple a rival maritime power. At the least, a vindictive British stand against the Union must jeopardize investments and markets, invite commercial retaliation by northern business, and threaten to accelerate the growth of a rival industrial system behind tariff walls. Similarly, the French risked vested interests if they supported the rebellion. A string of industries catered to markets in the American north: Lyons silk, Limoges luxury goods, Rochechouart china, Montbeliard clocks, Normandy woolens, French shipbuilding, wines, hat-making, glass, lace and embroidery trades.[14] Cotton manufacturing depended upon southern supply

---

[14]See Lyn M. Case znd Warren F. Spencer, *The United States and France: Civil War Diplomacy* (Philadelphia, 1970), Chs. 4, 5; Henry Blumenthal, *A Reappraisal of Franco-American Relations, 1830–1871* (Chapel Hill, N.C., 1959), Ch. 4.

almost entirely, but the industry was localised in Normandy, Alsace and the Nord, and, as with Great Britain, was conveniently oversupplied with stock from 1860's bumper crop. In neither Britain nor France did the abiding economic anxiety provoked by the events of 1861 concern cotton alone, or even primarily. Hostilities in America threatened to disrupt oceanic trade, and to reduce the buying power of Americans: shocks likely to reverberate in the economies of Western Europe. Ultimately, a protracted civil war would strike at the very foundations of the Atlantic economy.

With much reason, and some self-delusion, the rebellious south anticipated political sympathy abroad for the underdog in a struggle between empire and nationalism. Had not Italy just broken free from Habsburg dominion, to the joy of the enlightened world? Did not southern Americans enjoy the same right of an oppressed people to independence? Moreover, the south's self-image was romantic and conservative, expected to appeal to the aristocratic ruling classes of the old world: the south constituted a coherent civilization, its values distinct from those of the restless, money-grubbing, hectoring, abolitionist north. Southern culture was leisured and oligarchic. Levelling and utilitarian doctrines were rejected in favor of agrarian elitism. Slavery, obnoxious to most Europeans, was defended as a natural feature of planter society: upon the slave-run plantation rose a social system that exhibited the benefits of paternalism and the hierarchy. The planters drew parallels between their condition and that of the English manorial system. Cavalier origins were assigned to southern gentlemen, Puritan beginnings for the Yankee. The south symbolized stability and order, the north disreputable radical principles.

On both sides of the Mason-Dixon line there were prophecies in 1861 of a quick strike by Europe's "frightened despots" against the Union—their purpose to impress upon the masses everywhere the unfeasibility of Yankee-style democracy. Such prophecies gave exaggerated priority to the role of ideology in international affairs, assumed that European governments wanted confrontation with reformist movements within their own countries, and ignored complex realities. The south potently invoked the rights of small nations. But among European liberals there was a countervailing, historic commitment to the idea of the American democratic experiment. Men who rallied to the cause of Hungarians and Italians against the Austrians, or Poles against Tsarist Russia, might also be antislavery radicals, seeing malevolence in the south's reactionary revolt, or progressives who deplored heirarchic social theory and the archaism of chattel slavery. Free traders approved the idea of open markets in the south; but the most illustrious free traders of the age, Cobden and Bright, were conspicuous apologists of American democracy, and noted opponents of big power intervention in the affairs of other countries. Nor could genuine imperialists condone the principle of nationalist emancipation, pursued by insurrection. As we shall see, the American Civil War evoked complex crosscurrents in world opinion. Much would depend upon the dynamics of domestic politics in individual countries.

It cannot be gainsaid that misconceptions and wishful thinking handicapped early Confederate diplomacy.[15] One fetter was fatal ignorance of European conditions, a result of the cultural isolation in which the south had sought redemption from sectional tensions. The defense of slavery, W. J. Cash tells us, "not only eventuated . . . in a taboo on criticism; in the same process it set up a ban on all analysis and inquiry."[16] Hence, perhaps, the ingredient of credulity so marked in despatches of southern diplomats, the hugging to comforting ideas, the spurning of unpleasant facts. The south might have won if it had taken a diplomatic offensive in the fluid early stages of the war, one exploiting its limited strengths and recognizing the odds facing the rebellion. That offensive never took place.

Small nations need allies at the hour of their birth. History should have taught that lesson in 1861. The United States in the 1770's, the Italians in 1859, survived by means of a French alliance. On the other hand, diplomatic isolation explained many abortive endeavors, including nationalist revolts of 1848, and those other "lost causes" of the 1860's, the Poles and Danes. Southern self-assurance was itself a stumbling block to a decisive search for allies. Bred on states rights theory, most southerners believed that their states were entitled to withdraw peaceably from a federal compact to which they had given only provisional allegiance.

---

[15]See Henry Blumenthal's brilliant indictment, "Confederate Diplomacy: Popular Notions and International Realities", *JSH,* XXXIII (May, 1966), 151–171.

[16]W. J. Cash, *The Mind of the South* (Vintage, 1960, 1st ed. 1941), 101.

They hardly conceived that the north would fight a war against brother-whites for abolitionism, or the chimera of republican unity. In any case a war would be short. The south's generals and statesmen were superior, Johnny Reb's military flair greater than that of Yankee townsmen. The Confederate armies enjoyed the advantage of interior lines of defense; their commanders, like Robert E. Lee, were masters of the tactical offensive. The people were determined in defense of their homeland, their war aim simple and nonaggressive: the right to self-existence. Optimism seemed justified, for the past provided few examples of imperial success over a rebellious people so well situated.

Less appreciated was the northern will to win, the north's strength in men and money, its resolve to mobilize its resources to keep the Union intact. The north held over three times the south's value of real and personal property, four times the capital of incorporated banks, ten times the value of products manufactured annually. The northern economy proved strong, capable of massive wartime expansion, of sustaining a war effort unseen in modern times without exorbitant inflation. The southern economy proved lopsided and fragile, cracking under the strain of war, the Richmond government finding it increasingly difficult to finance its army and tiny navy as credit eroded and inflation ran higher.

A critical disparity in maritime resources existed between the sections. At the beginning of the war the south hardly disposed of a notable ship, and its naval facilities were negligible. Stephen R. Mallory, Confederate Navy Secretary, brilliantly improvised a program to buy and equip a navy abroad—an example of using southern power to the limit that was worth emulating in other arenas. But the odds always strikingly favored the Union navy. It had more money to build ships, well-appointed yards for their construction and repair, no foreign complications attached to shipbuilding, more trained officers to man ships. The north's ports were unblockaded, while southern commerce-raiders lacked bases or prize harbors, their movements constantly reported home by United States consuls and agents. The south's problem is sufficiently stated in the fact that by 1865 Union Navy Secretary Gideon Welles administered the world's largest navy.

The southern rebels labored under rebellion's classic disadvantages: unrecognized by the family of nations, the Confederacy began life with no diplomatic corps, archives, tradition; nor would it ever afford to match the Union in the *materiel* of diplomacy, including spies, agents and special missions abroad. Not until Judah P. Benjamin became Confederate Secretary of State—a post with little appeal to fighting southerners—did a man of stature rival the dominating figure of Union Secretary of State Seward.

A wiser Richmond would have recognized earlier the weaknesses in its international position. Its foe had vast commercial strength, applicable at points of global pressure. The United States, a long-established power, sought only to maintain the status quo. It asked to be left alone to quench a local conflagration. "A nation," said Seward, "has a right and it is its duty, to live." Clearly, states like Russia and Austria agreed: they were themselves ever-fearful of revolt from the subject peoples living within their own ramshackle empires. But neither the British nor Napoleonic empires dared treat lightly the principle of legitimacy, despite their ostensible regard for nationalist and independence movements. Americans, of north and south, disliked begging favors from Old Europe, accustomed as they were to barter from a position of strength in the hemisphere. But it was the Confederacy which needed to induce action from the powers—even the action of acknowledgement—when as a proud nation it preferred to demand acceptance as a right.

CHAPTER II

The Opening Phase

THE UNION WAS SHATTERED, and the Confederate States of America formed, during the last, "lame duck" months of James Buchanan's presidency. During that appallingly tense secession winter, Abraham Lincoln, the President-elect, stayed in voluntary retreat in Illinois, hoping thereby to calm the south. The mantle of Republican leadership fell on Seward, the Secretary of State-elect, who worked tirelessly for a national compromise. Americans knew Seward better than Lincoln. Ex-governor of New York—commonly referred to as "Governor" Seward—magnate of the old Whig party and founder of its Republican successor, a born politician with support from eastern business, antislavery and Irish voters, Seward ran Lincoln hard for his party's presidential nomination in 1860. In that struggle the press, which Seward cultivated assiduously, backed him, but he was harmed by an uncertain image on the slavery issue: his abolitionist language alarmed southerners, while radicals like Charles Sumner and Gerrit Smith knew Seward to be a moderate, willing to accommodate abolition to national needs. Lincoln chose a cabinet of strong men, of "all the talents," many of them opponents of Seward and his New York machine. But Seward was still widely expected to be the power behind the throne.

He was in his sixtieth year, slightly built, but endlessly energetic, beaknosed, a careless dresser, immoderately fond of cigars, brandy, good talk, and political intrigue, keeping one of the best tables in Washington—a salon for men of all camps. Seward was a curious mixture, and is still an enigma: a man of vision and ideals, also a political animal, earthy, vain, cynical. Superficially he and Lincoln had little in common, one the close associate of eastern business, the other a frontier lawyer. In fact both were consummate politicians with fundamentally compatible views on the Negro question—the mediating approach of the old Whig party, of which both had been stalwarts, rather than that of the "iron-back" radicals who formed a core of the Republican party. Their partnership, despite early difficulties, proved highly fruitful for the Union. Lincoln, not versed in foreign affairs, permitted Seward to be a strong Secretary of State, occasionally curbing Seward's impetuosity and defending him from partisan critics.

His stature obscured by Lincoln hagiology, Seward has long been one of the forgotten men of American history, often dismissed as a rash and expedient Secretary of State. Yet during his nation's greatest trial, he demonstrated a superb understanding of American nationalism, and he knew, better than his critics, the need to connect diplomacy with public opinion. Seward has recently been rediscovered: his vision of America's global role is now presented as being in the mainstream of American tradition; his foreign policy no longer seems aberrant. "New Left" historians, in particular, judge Seward to be the most brilliant articulator of the idea of imperial mission in the middle period, a precursor of the so-called "new imperialists" of the 1890's. Closely involved with northeastern business, Seward understood expansionism as the Janus-face of America's nascent industrial capitalism. William Appleman Williams discerns two controlling assumptions in Seward's world view.[1] Disturbed by the stagnation that followed the 1837 depression, he insisted that American manufactures and commercial agriculture must have a constantly expanding market. He emphasized, not territorial expansion outside the continent, but control of bases and trade routes needed to protect and develop commerce and investment. Second, Seward wanted peaceful expansion, since war consumed democracies. Above all, he hated the idea of a sectional war that would kill the dream of national destiny. Ironically, Seward is remembered in the schoolbooks as the freesoil politician who spoke of the antislavery principle as

---

[1]Writings that stress Seward's view of empire include William A. Williams, *The Contours of American History* (Chicago, 1966, first edition, 1961), 292, 318; Walter La Feber, *The New Empire: An Interpretation of American Expansion, 1860–98* (New York, 1963), 24–39. For a splendidly researched biography from a more traditional stance, see Glyndon G. Van Deusen, *William Henry Seward* (New York, 1967).

"higher law" and forecast the "irrepressible conflict." His deeds show that he fought to the last to avert civil war and to arrange a compromise between the sections. He did so in the confident belief that slavery would disappear peacefully as America became an industrial economy geared to worldwide markets. The preoccupation of men like Seward with America's imperial frontier in the antebellum era has been interpreted as their way of evading economic and sectional problems within the nation. When the sectional crisis became unavoidable, Seward and others naturally appealed for unity by reference to America's grander destiny. He threatened foreign war, of welding the north and the south together in a swoop upon Cuba and other spoils. These were not inexplicable gestures or signs of madness. His threats were the desperate extension of prevailing logic.

Whether the new Republican administration would ever assume office was uncertain. Seward labored prodigiously to forestall a rebel *coup* in Washington, to ensure Lincoln's inauguration, prevent an exodus of the border states from the Union, and generally to head off the crisis until the new regime settled in to power. However the numerous peace and compromise schemes of the new year broke on the rock of slavery's supposed right to expand into the territories. The Republican party opposed the westward expansion of slavocracy into the newly organized portions of the old Mexican empire, spoils accruing to the United States after the Mexican War. Lincoln made his name, especially during the Lincoln-Douglas debates, defending his party's founding plank—exclusion of slavery from the territories. The south demanded its rights, denouncing northern attempts to "contain" a rival society and economy. Seward, as usual, was flexible: he was convinced that slavery would die naturally in noncotton areas west of Texas because of the superiority of the free labor system. Seward's views reflected common northern attitudes which underestimated the determination of the secessionists, believed the dispute was negotiable, or trusted that time would cool tempers or spur to action the inert Unionists in the south. But these hopes soured, and Seward's credibility fell, as Mississippi, Florida, Alabama, Georgia, Louisiana, and even Sam Houston's Texas joined the rebels at Montgomery. A discouraged Seward threatened to resign on March 2, upset when his friends were outmaneuvered in the contest for cabinet places by a powerful rival faction led by radical Treasurer-elect Salmon P. Chase. Lincoln, characteristically, mollified Seward but kept Chase in the cabinet. Lincoln was duly inaugurated, in the gravest circumstances known to American history.

The issue which threatened to make or break the administration, and America, was whether to relieve or evacuate Fort Sumter in Charleston harbor, a major symbol of federal authority in rebel domain. Sumter had hardly six weeks supplies and was menaced by South Carolinian troops under General Beauregard. Its commandant reported the fort to be indefensible, and implied that it should be evacuated. Lincoln's inaugural speech promised to maintain forts that had not yet fallen into rebel hands, a position from which retreat was difficult without placing unbearable pressure on loyalist opinion in the north. However the seceded states swore resistance to Sumter's relief as an invasion of states' rights. Virginia—which had so far resisted secession—opposed the use of Federal force against any of the departed states. Any aggressive move by Lincoln risked the loss of the whole "upper south," something he desperately wanted to avoid.

Seward favored a Union concession in the interest of reconciliation. To southern commissioners, in Washington seeking recognition of the Confederacy, he intimated, confidentially, his belief that Sumter would be evacuated: a typical gamble, based on military advice and cabinet discussion, and aimed at warding off any reckless move against Sumter by the South Carolinians. As well, time would be gained in which to negotiate. The gamble failed when Lincoln, responding to rising war fever in the north, decided on March 29 to supply Sumter. Whether the president expected war, and preferred it now, started by the south, is a moot point in Civil War historiography. Whatever the case, Seward's peace plan lay in ruins. In a move that has re-appeared in later American history, Seward attempted to discharge explosive domestic emotions by directing their energies into foreign channels.

Stoking up the hysteria of late March, Britain adopted a menacing stance on the question of a possible northern blockade of the long rebel coast. Anxious to protect British trade, especially cotton trade, with the south, the Palmerston ministry sought to impress upon the Lincoln administration the perils of excluding British merchantmen from rebel ports. At the same time, wary that Seward might contrive a war against interventionists abroad, Britain and France agreed to act together in the North American theater. British interests tugged in opposite directions on the blockade issue. Acting as restraints upon Lord John Russell, Britain's Foreign Minister, were Britain's historic use of blockade as a war weapon and Admiralty determination to affirm and expand aggressive blockade usages. By mid-March Russell had come to accept that a Union blockade of the rebel coastline could hardly be repudiated by England, if enforced according to international law. Russell instructed Lord Lyons, his minister at Washington, to this effect; but before Russell's despatch reached him, Lyons abruptly warned Seward that Britain might well retaliate against any blockade by recognizing the Confederacy. Lyons, normally unimpulsive —an earnest bachelor of forty-one, he was fond of Americans, sorry over secession, but above all a dutiful defender of British interests—had made an impulsive move, a sign of the times. British recognition policy required that states that claimed independence from their previous rulers must demonstrate a viable political organization; and be able to show that their former government had abandoned—at least *de facto*—its effort to restore its dominion. The last condition was notably absent in the American case. Lyons stood on sounder ground in opposing Union talk of closing rebel ports by proclamation, or by light naval investiture, moves amounting to a "paper blockade" forbidden by international law. Lyons' threat cast Seward into a highly cantankerous mood. So also did the attitude of the French minister in Washington, Henri Mercier, who regarded rebel independence as virtually a *fait accompli.*

Close on the heels of these developments came news that Spain, dreaming of imperial restoration in the Americas, had invaded the Caribbean island republic of San Domingo. Unstable and badly governed, San Domingo might long since have reverted to Spanish rule or some other "foreign protection" but for the checks of international rivalry and the operation of the Monroe Doctrine.[2] Following negotiations with Spain, the Dominican President San-

---

[2] C. C. Haunch, "Attitudes of Foreign Governments towards the Spanish Reoccupation of the Dominican Republic," *Hispanic American Hist. Rev.,* XXXVII (1947), 248ff.

tana announced on March 18 the island's wish to be ruled by Madrid. On March 23 Spanish troops sailed for San Domingo from Havana: France had been neutralised in return for French freedom of action in Mexico, Britain by a guarantee that forebade slavery in Spain's new colony. The United States, Spain hoped, lay crippled by the sectional crisis. In an editorial headlined "The Gathering of the Vultures," the *Boston Daily Journal* declared: "The terror of the American name is gone, and the Powers of the Old World are flocking to the feast from which the scream of our eagle has hitherto scared them."[3]

Seward was ready to provide the vigorous measures against Spain demanded by newspapers such as *The New York Times.* Two schools of thought existed on the Dominican crisis. The "coercionists" favored first use of the mailed fist against the traitors of the south, arguing against foreign diversions on the ground that the south welcomed them and would exploit them to win Confederate independence. The "conciliationists"—Seward at their head—appealed to blocs of opinion in both sections, people who, out of interest, conscience, or politics, abhorred bloody civil war. Seward wanted dramatically to highlight the overriding need for American unity in the face of an outside emergency. By threatening war against Spain over San Domingo, he intended to invoke the tattered flag and the Monroe Doctrine, hoping that loyal men in the border states and deep south would respond to their country's call. Even fire-eaters might be shamed back into their senses. Seward's was, in fact, a desperate last-minute peace scheme in the tradition of the Crittenden Plan and the Virginia Peace Congress. As a reward for staying in the Union, it offered southern expansionists the chance of acquiring Cuba, the long-coveted jewel of the Caribbean, with the living space that Cuba promised for the slave power. Would not the south find that prospect more pleasing than a career as a miniature republic, tied to the aprons of European powers and exposed to their contempt and ambitions? Indeed, could the cotton states stand by while the abolitionist north conquered Cuba and freed her slaves, or while Britain and France contrived the same end by diplomacy? In any respect, if the south

---

[3] *Boston Daily Journal,* April 3, 1861; also *NYT,* March 31, 1861.

abstained, "then the U.S. would at least gain a great island base for operating against the Confederates, and for closing the Gulf . . . If France entered the war, the U.S. would also seize the French islands."[4]

As new documents come to light, the close connection between the Sumter and Caribbean crises, and Lincoln's leadership challenge, becomes clearer. Seward proposed more than a Spanish war. He proposed to lead the campaign as *de facto* president. In the process he intended to defuse the explosive Sumter issue. Those were the ingredients making up his famous, or notorious, "April 1 Program." Lincoln's performance in office had come under widespread northern criticism, not least from *The New York Times,* controlled by Henry J. Raymond, one of Seward's campaign managers in 1860. Raymond's paper also played a key role in spreading alarmist rumors on San Domingo, Mexico, and Anglo-French fleet maneuvers in American waters. On April 1, Seward presented Lincoln with a memorandum which pressed for the abandonment of Fort Sumter, urged an onslaught on the predatory European powers so as to revitalize southern Unionism—and then plainly invited Lincoln to step down in favor of Seward. At the same time Henry Raymond and Thurlow Weed, Seward's political manager and editor of the *Albany Evening Journal,* readied themselves to launch an instant press campaign designed to win over public opinion to Seward's peace program.[5] Answering an urgent request from Seward, Raymond arrived *post haste* in Washington around midnight on Sunday March 31. He gave instructions to his Washington correspondent, James B. Swain, to hold open the telegraph to New York; he expected to send by telegram explosive news, that is, "the reply of the President, which it was thought by Messrs. Seward and Weed, could not fail to be in accord with the suggestion of the Secretary."[6] No such telegram was sent. "I pre-

---

[4]Alan Nevins, *War for the Union I, The Improvised War 1861–1862* (New York, 1959) pp. 62–63.

[5]Patrick Sowle, "A Reappraisal of Seward's Memorandum of April 1, 1861, to Lincoln," *JSH,* XXXIII, No. 2 (May, 1967), 234–239.

[6]Illumination is shed on the whole episode by a recently discovered letter, James B. Swain to John Hay, February 21, 1888 (Illinois State Historical Library), printed in Sowle, p. 236. *The New York Times* was to prepare a "vigorous pronunciamento that Seward alone could fill the measure which Seward had outlined."

sume," recalled Swain in 1888, "Raymond had in New York received from Seward the substance of Lincoln's response, and had reached the conclusion that 'that cat wouldn't raise'." Swain was right. Lincoln, uninterested in a Caribbean war and immovable on the need to supply Fort Sumter, affirmed his intention to lead the Union.

Extended analysis of Seward's April 1 memorandum as a guide to his foreign plans may well be wasted effort, for it is likely enough that the document's dominant purpose was crudely political, to stampede Lincoln. The memo raised the possibility of war with France as well as Spain, advised a minatory tone with Britain, and spoke of raising the hemisphere against European intervention. But there was no obvious pretext for a French war, which would nullify Spain's diplomatic isolation in the Caribbean. Goading the British—even as revenge for their high-handedness on the blockade—risked creating a foreign coalition against the United States. More discreetly Seward kept open the option of Anglo-American cooperation in guaranteeing Dominican independence and ending the Cuban slave trade. Seward's real *idee fixe* was a Spanish war. First, such a war would enable Seward, firmly installed after the April 1 *coup* as a northern leader more amenable to the south than Lincoln, to give up Fort Sumter, thus postponing a reckoning. Second, war with Spain over San Domingo would allow Seward uncontroversially to reinforce Union forts on the Gulf of Mexico claimed by the rebels. This, he hoped, would protect Union prestige without affronting southern pride. In particular Seward wanted to secure Fort Pickens, controlling Pensacola Bay, against "all attacks foreign and domestic." The situation at Pickens had built up almost as dangerously as that at Sumter. Union troop carriers had been anchored off Pensacola Bay since February, but refrained from landing soldiers in response to Florida's pledge of nonaggression. Lincoln ordered the reinforcement of Fort Pickens on March 12, but a misunderstanding over orders prevented the plan's execution. On March 31, the day before his planned *coup*, Seward obtained presidential permission for another naval expedition to Pickens. The expedition's orders were to secure the Federal fort, then set up a main base of operations at Fort Jefferson in the Dry Tortugas—a mere hundred miles striking distance from Havana. Cuba was obviously Seward's target. Pickens' reinforcement would presumably be accepted by the Confederates in a deal with a new northern leader, Seward, as security against Spanish aggression.

Even after Lincoln vetoed Seward's takeover bid, the Secretary of State plunged on with his Pickens plan. He protested stiffly to Spain over its armed intervention in the Dominican Republic. Perhaps a Spanish war might yet break out before the die was cast over Sumter. Seward used all his influence—and perhaps some skulduggery—to gain top priority for his Pickens expedition, simultaneously pressing for a compromise over Fort Sumter. There seemed still a chance that Lincoln might backtrack on his decision to provision Sumter if by doing so Virginia stayed within the Union. At the worst Seward thought his scheme would bring civil war at Pensacola and not at Sumter, over which he had made too many promises. The Pickens expedition commandeered the warship *Powhatan* without the knowledge of the Navy Department, causing immense confusion when Welles earmarked the vessel as flagship for the Sumter relief flotilla. Before the confusion lifted —with Seward playing an unhelpfully obtuse part—the *Powhatan* hastily sailed as a troopship to the Gulf of Mexico. Welles came to suspect Seward of conniving with men of suspect loyalty to jeopardize the Sumter relief project. Rancor persisted between the two ministers for the duration of the war.

By March 6 the Davis government at Montgomery guessed from intelligence received from Washington that Pickens was to be reinforced, and ordered additional troops to join General Bragg's Confederate forces deployed around Pensacola. Seward's "peace plan" was building up to war, with each side secretly determined to break the "truce." Jefferson Davis refused to tolerate a "foreign garrison" at Pickens even in return for Sumter's evacuation. Bragg had orders to reduce Pickens at first opportunity—he hesitated only for military reasons—and would have reacted to reinforcement as an act of war. So much for Cuba as a diversion, for Seward's "Spanish war panacea." On April 12 Bragg was unable to prevent federal troops taking Pickens. By then however Lincoln's relief expedition had been sent to Sumter, the fort shelled by shore batteries at Charleston, and the Civil War had begun.

* * *

On April 15 Lincoln called for 75,000 volunteer militia, an act swiftly followed by Virginia's secession and a desperate struggle to preserve Maryland, Kentucky, and Missouri for the Union. Riots in Baltimore cut off the capital from the north, while the rebels took possession of the federal naval yards at Norfolk and arsenal at Harper's Ferry. Seward's first diplomatic steps were taken in this distraught atmosphere. His policy before Bull Run has been variously described as crude warmongering, still aiming for a divertive external war, or as skilled brinkmanship, designed to make foreign warhorses skittish. Seward's diplomacy was often baffling: indeed it is possible to argue that his unpredictability deterred the powers rather than any profundity of design. But the facts best fit the theory of brinkmanship. The south's enthusiastic mobilization for war rendered hollow the idea of any "foreign war panacea." A slender hope remained that the south might be persuaded, or forced by diplomatic isolation, to come to terms with the north. Seward blustered in order to block any quick *fait accompli* by the powers that might seal the Union's fate. But he did not push bluster to the point of war: that would have defeated his purpose. He strove not for war with Britain or France, but to stave off their recognition of rebel independence—or even of the rebels' belligerent status. Thus, on April 10—two days *before* Sumter— Seward drew up his instructions for his English minister, Charles Francis Adams, warning that recognition of southern independence by other countries would be regarded as a *casus belli.*[7] That policy endured for the duration of the war.

Seward insisted on the Union's sovereign rights, even to the point of unreality. He demanded, for instance, that the world regard the Confederates as engaged in minor insurrection, yet proposed to crush the gnat of rebellion by the full force of northern might. Seward wanted international respect for a massive naval blockade of rebel coasts, but denied the assumption on which such respect

---

[7]Seward to Adams, April 10, 1861. Adams had not yet left for England, Seward giving him permission to linger for his son's wedding. Seward's penchant for viewing diplomacy in propaganda terms is shown when he took the extraordinary step of reading the dispatch to W. H. Russell of the London *Times* nineteen days before it got to Adams: no doubt he wanted London to know his hard line as early as possible, via the *Times.*

must rest, namely the existence of a state of war. By demanding that the powers turn a blind eye to realities, Seward invited legal wrangles. On the other hand, he held out rewards for a policy of friendship to the Union; he invoked the ties of kinship that bound America and Britain, those of historic friendship that joined America and France; and warned that peace was essential to the health of the whole Atlantic economy.

On the critical issue of the blockade—and here there was a war for the picking with Britain—Seward was anything but reckless. On April 19 Lincoln declared his intention to blockade the ports of South Carolina, Georgia, Alabama, Florida, Mississippi, Louisiana, and Texas; on April 27 the blockade was extended to the ports of Virginia and North Carolina. The blockade was a centerpiece in the north's grand strategy, designed to deny the unindustrialised south the sinews of war and to stop the export of cotton. Union strategists such as General Winfield Scott planned to crush the life from their antagonist by the combined pressures of blockade, a military advance along a broad Virginian front, and an amphibious invasion of the Mississippi basin. As with other phases of the grand plan, the blockade proved easier to expound than to implement. Navy chief Welles faced the task of welding an effective force from an antiquated fleet, which had been scattered to the four corners by secessionists in Buchanan's cabinet. Welles was required—as Lyons sceptically observed—to close over 3000 miles of coastline from Chesapeake Bay to the Rio Grande. A carelessly declared, or weakly enforced, blockade would offend against international law, and give the powers a pretext for intervention. Seward passed the first test of his statesmanship when he ensured that the navy punctiliously notified and set up the blockade. In tedious negotiations dragging into June between Lyons, the State, and Navy Departments, Seward's prudence shone forth. Whether England—habitually a naval belligerent—would tolerate a less than perfect Union blockade, a precedent likely to benefit the Royal Navy, remained an abiding uncertainty in 1861.

By instituting a full-scale blockade, the Union forced the question of neutrality upon the powers, who must ask themselves if they were obliged to recognize the existence of a state of war in America. The threat of both sides using privateers raised a similar dilemma. In retaliation against Lincoln's call for volunteers, Jefferson Davis invited privateers to sail under the Confederacy's commissions of marque and reprisal. Adopting a defensive strategy on land—Europe should see that aggression stemmed from the imperialistic north—the south expected to take some offensives at sea. The use of privateers and specially-constructed commerce destroyers might offset the Confederacy's inferior naval capacity and facilities. Both sides lived in the past, remembering 1812, and forgetting the vulnerability of wooden vessels against the firepower of iron-armored steamers. Seaboard maritime interests took grotesquely exaggerated alarm at Davis' proclamation, and plied Lincoln with pleas for protection. On April 19 Lincoln proclaimed that the government would punish as pirates persons who molested northern ships under the pretended authority of the rebels.

The major sea powers had renounced their right to privateering in the Declaration of Paris, 1856, when the victor nations at the Crimean peace talks laid down a new code of maritime law. America did not sign, refusing to relinquish privateering unless general protection was afforded to all noncontraband private property at sea. The Paris declaration gave immunity to enemy goods on neutral ships, and neutral goods on enemy ships, if noncontraband; but none to enemy property on enemy ships. The American proposal would drastically have circumscribed warfare at sea, and was unacceptable to Britain. Nonsignatories to the Paris convention retained the right to issue letters of marque to private citizens. In international law, privateers normally acquired a belligerent status that protected them from hanging as pirates. However the case of authorities whose sovereign rights were unrecognized, or who had not been granted belligerent rights, was confused. The United States now proposed to disregard letters of marque issued by the Confederacy. Even Lyons thought that English warships might seize privateers "which sail under a flag we do not recognize."[8] This dilemma became one major incentive that, as we shall see, pushed England into a prompt—the north thought premature— recognition of southern belligerency.

On April 24 Seward instructed his agents abroad that the United States now offered to sign the Declaration of Paris. The plan had logic, and promised advantages to the Union—too obvious for the

---

[8]Lyons to Russell, April 23, 1861, *MHSP*, XLVIII, p. 225.

powers to accept. The code of 1856 set forth an advanced and civilized set of rules for maritime war, attractive to neutrals. Under it the United States would renounce privateering, accept that blockades must be effective, and agree to the rules governing neutral and enemy noncontraband property at sea. Seward hoped for two gains: the powers would be obliged to indict southern privateering, and to accept his doctrine that southerners were internal rebels, not belligerents. The second goal was as important as the first. No nation had yet conceded southern belligerency, and Seward determined to block the blow. By tendering his country's adherence to the Paris convention he offered safety for neutral ships and property. In return they must acknowledge American unity, for he insisted that the agreement was "to be obligatory equally upon disloyal as upon loyal citizens."[9] The Union navy could then suppress southern privateering as piracy, for it would be executing domestic laws making privateering by disloyal subjects piracy. The plan however became outpaced by events. It lost its point when the powers accepted southern belligerency, and then later denied their ports to privateers. Protracted negotiations took place between the United States, Britain, and France, but they were clumsily handled, creating confusion and mutual suspicion. The talks were called off in August when the powers insisted that any agreement should have no bearing on "the internal differences now prevailing in the United States."[10] The United States nevertheless adhered for the rest of the war to the code laid down in 1856.

April and May were months of intense frustration for Seward and the north. The rebellion, far from subsiding, won popular support from the southern people, who ratified the Confederate constitution. Energetically the Confederacy prepared for war. Confederate Vice-President Alexander H. Stephens flatly declared the futility of peace talks between the sections when he spoke with the Bremen minister, Rudolph Schleiden, who visited Richmond with Seward's blessing (April 24–27). As Seward's peace

---

[9]Seward to Dayton, July 6, 1861, *Foreign Relations* (*For.Rels.*), 1861, 233.
[10]The subject is exhaustively covered in: C. F. Adams Jr, "Seward and the Declaration of Paris" *MHSP*, XLVI, 23–81; E. D. Adams, I, Ch. 5; Case and Spencer, Ch. 3; Ferris, Ch. 5.

schemes faded, he also struck trouble in Canada. Canadian emotions tugged in conflicting directions over the civil war in their giant neighbor, but the question of Canadian survival overshadowed all other issues and dictated a stance of strict neutrality.[11] Victory for either section posed perils for Canada: an independent Confederacy would destroy the power balance on the American continent, and make Canada a tempting prey for vengeful northern armies. A win for the Union might spur annexationist designs on the part of an overweening and ambitious neighbor. The war, in any case, created mighty armies in North America, a prospect feared by the militarily insecure Canadians for half a century.

Seward managed to inflame these raw nerves. His tactics were probably piecemeal: to probe at British weakness in North America, to keep the British worried about the consequences of rashness, to test the quality of Canadian neutrality, to squash any Confederate operations north of the great lakes. One effect was to hasten the military reinforcement of Canada.

Friction first arose when the colonial authorities, sticking to their Militia Act, refused to sell arms to Ohio, Illinois, New York, and Massachusetts, mustering forces in answer to Lincoln's call to arms. Yankees expected Canada, long a refuge for runaway slaves, to prove a more reliable ally in the contest against slavery. Seward sent to Quebec a special agent, George Ashmun, a friend of Lincoln's, to plead the northern cause to Canadians and secretly to exchange views with the Canadian Governor-General, Sir Edmund Head. The move backfired when the *New York Herald* leaked details of the mission. The Colonial Office ordered Head "quietly to discourage all missions whether from the United States or from the Southern Confederacy." But the most serious scrape arose over the *Peerless* affair. Late in April the State Department received intelligence that the Canadian vessel *Peerless,* then at Toronto, had been sold to the rebels, and would pass down the St. Lawrence with British papers to be delivered to a pirate commander on the open seas. Seward bluntly warned Lyons that the United States intended to seize the ship, regardless of British flag or papers, unless the Canadians moved against the vessel. The

---

[11]See Robin W. Winks, *Canada and the United States: The Civil War Years* (Baltimore, 1960), a definitive study. Chapter 4 for this period.

Union would not tolerate the fitting out of "piratical vessels" in Canadian waters. Although Seward ordered seizure with the proviso that evidence be found of rebel ownership, he acted on flimsy grounds. It turned out that federal, not southern, sympathizers had purchased the ship.[12] Luckily for Anglo-American relations, the *Peerless* escaped interference. The incident was soon forgotten amidst more momentous events taking place in London.

* * *

The slaveholding rebellion at first evoked little public sympathy in Britain; the growth of romantic admiration for the gallantry of southern arms against great odds came later.[13] Antislavery sentiment was traditionally strong in Britain and, although polite society relished no love for the bumptious, expansionist Yankee Republic, much of educated and propertied British opinion tended to view secession as indeed a "great conspiracy" by disaffected planters: "The game went against them, so they threw up their cards and kicked over the table."[14] What eroded British patience with the northern cause was the disenchanting march of events that led to Sumter: the vacillating of northern politicians, the seeming ineptitude of Lincoln and his government, the fear of a futile war that was going to disrupt the comfortable commercial arrangements of the Atlantic world. The passing of the Morrill tariff by the Republican rump in Congress, dominant after the departure of southern representatives, seemed to herald an era of "new protectionism," to be both a piece of sectional vengeance and an economic error. After hostilities had begun at Sumter, armchair strategists in England enjoyed a field day; one school

---

[12]Van Deusen, *Seward*, p. 296. It is likely that southern sympathisers intended to buy the ship but lacked funds and that northern sympathizers privately purchased the vessel. (Information from Robin Winks, 1972).

[13]For closer study of this topic see D. P. Crook, "Portents of War: English Opinion on Secession," *J. American Studies*, IV, No. 2 (February, 1971), 163–179; and more extended account in D. P. Crook, *The North, the South, and the Powers, 1861–1865* (Wiley, 1974), hereafter *North, South, and Powers*, esp. Chapters 2, 4. As in the present volume I lack space to do more than touch briefly on the vexed issue of British public sympathies during the Civil War, the reader is referred to the literature on the subject listed in "Suggestions for Further Reading," found at the close of this book.

[14]*National Review*, July 1861.

holding that a southern militia defending its own territory, with internal lines of defense, must be irreducible; the other agreeing with Walter Bagehot that "a wealthy and free population of twenty millions cannot but conquer in the long run in a contest with a poor free population, numbering at most seven millions."[15] Few denied the right of the Union to use coercion—the contractual, federal language of the secessionists had a quaint eighteenth century ring in nineteenth century Europe. But many questioned the wisdom of solving the American problem at the bayonet-point. Humanitarian and pacifist feeling recoiled from the vision of bloody, fraticidal war; liberals displayed a reasonable foreboding that militarism and repression of American liberties would be the bitter fruits of civil war; no matter what the verdict of arms, the end result must be merely to increase hatred and division. Common sense dictated that groups whose way of life was so abrasively different should live apart.

On May 14 Queen Victoria proclaimed British neutrality in the American Civil War. The Queen's proclamation shook the north, where it was denounced as maliciously premature, a deliberately unfriendly act that amounted to recognition of the slave confederacy, an act that kept the breath of life in an otherwise transient mutiny. After the war an immense superstructure of hysteria was raised by angry Americans, including Charles Sumner, John L. Motley and Bancroft Davis, on the foundation stone of the Queen's proclamation. It became the basis for astronomic damages, claimed by the United States against Britain for loss of life and national expenses incurred because of that country's "prolongation" of the war. The proclamation was a major item in Charles Sumner's calculation of $2,125 million as the British bill for dereliction of its international obligations (significantly, about the going price for Canada in 1869!) The American barrage contained a great deal of emotion, confused law and warped facts. The British possessed a reasoned case for seeking the protection that neutrality afforded, but they handled it poorly. When the French, after prudent delay, produced a lucid apologia for their own declaration of neutrality, they helped their cause in Washington. What em-

---

[15] *Economist,* March 2, 1861. The young Bagehot had been recently appointed editor of the *Economist.*

barassed the British was the unexpected onset of a period of "phony war" before the battle of Bull Run in July, giving color to Yankee complaints that England acted before armies had clashed or a rebel navy existed. Sinister implications were read into the timing of the proclamation, for Russell proclaimed neutrality before Lincoln's new envoy had arrived at his post—Adams landed in London on May 14—and just after the rebel envoys Yancey, Mann, and Rost had been received at the Foreign Office.

A case can be made that Russell allowed himself to be stampeded by swift-moving events. News of Sumter, Lincoln's call for volunteers, and the southern threat of privateering arrived simultaneously with the arrival in England of Yancey and Rost. (April 27). Parliamentary friends of the south, having given notice of a motion in the Commons favoring recognition of the Confederacy, arranged an unofficial meeting between Russell and the rebel mission. As with other events in this hectic fortnight, Russell anticipated no hostile reaction in America over what was a common diplomatic practice in such cases. He was later astonished at the hornet's nest he had disturbed. At the interview (May 3), Russell listened noncommittally to Yancey's justification of secession, plea for recognition and assurances of rebel military strength. The envoys made a "delicate allusion" to the consequences for England of being cut off from its southern cotton supply. Russell promised to place the matter before cabinet as soon as possible. Reporting home, the commissioners expressed confidence that England and France would grant recognition as soon as the Confederate army had won a decisive victory.

Russell had already (May 1) ordered the reinforcement of the British North American fleet under the experienced Vice-Admiral Alexander Milne, and learned (May 2) of Lincoln's blockade proclamation. The Union fleet clearly proposed to exercise what was tantamount to a right-of-war to search and seize foreign vessels testing the blockade. The issues of blockade and privateering demanded that the question of neutrality be resolved. Russell sought his Attorney-General's advice on the propriety of recognizing southern belligerency, and was told that it was the south's right to issue letters of marque. The Attorney-General suggested a deal: recognize the south's belligerency on condition that it promised to wage war according to the rules of the Treaty of Paris. Russell ignored the suggestion: negotiations with the south would protract the affair, while the question of belligerent status should be a question of fact, not something to be traded for a price. But he accepted the view that the European nations must treat the American situation as a "regular war." Cabinet approved his reasoning. On May 6 Parliament was informed, Lyons sent notice of the decision, and Paris approached to concert with Britain on the matter. As the French had already agreed to follow the British lead, their concurrence was prompt.

The cabinet had acted swiftly but not, as claimed later, on inadequate information or provocation. The Confederacy existed, had adopted a constitution, federal legislature, executive, and judiciary, begun to raise an army of 100,000 men, appropriated over two million dollars for a navy, and commenced hostilities. The Union was raising an army of 75,000, and had admitted a *de facto* state of war by proclaiming a full-scale blockade that would be strictly enforced according to international usage.[16] The cabinet knew such facts. The cabinet received a copy of the blockade proclamation on May 5, sent by the British consul in New York. The paper itself was officially communicated to Russell by the American embassy on May 11, three days before the Queen's proclamation was gazetted. The need for regularization emerged promptly enough, when on May 21 the British schooner *Tropic Wind* was captured for breach of blockade.[17]

The Queen's proclamation conferred belligerent status upon the south, but it did not recognize southern sovereignty. As the French government soon argued:

. . . to be called belligerent, it is enough that a portion of a people in revolt have possession of only enough force to create, in the eyes of neutrals, a doubt as to the final outcome. In such a case modern international law

---

[16]The American Supreme Court in March 1863 justified Lincoln's use of the war power in proclaiming the blockade by declaring that act conclusive evidence that a state of war existed. The court, strengthened by Republican nominees, decided by five to four.

[17]*Case Presented on the Part of the Government of Her Brittanic Majesty to the Tribunal of Arbitration* (Geneva), in *House of Representatives Documents*, 2nd sess., 42 Cong., 1871–2, I, pp. 11–18.

requires that foreign powers, without prejudice to the final results of the clash of forces, keep an attitude of impartiality toward the two contestants.[18]

Belligerency gave the south a status within its own jurisdiction similar to that enjoyed by sovereign powers, and granted practical rights for purposes of war:

to solicit loans, contract for arms, and enlist men abroad, except when forbidden to do so by neutrality laws; to send commissioned cruisers to sea, exercise belligerent rights of search and seizure, and make use of prize courts; and to have the Southern banner and commissioners recognized as representing a quasi-political community.[19]

Neutrality conferred obligations as well as rights upon the powers. For this reason, English friends of the north accepted, even welcomed, its arrival. The Bradford liberal, W. E. Forster, saw neutrality as a means of deterring Englishmen from enlisting in the Confederate cause or equipping rebel privateers.[20] Perhaps most important, and least appreciated in the north, the world's greatest seapower had given practical recognition to the Union blockade, a fact to temper severely Confederate joy over their achievement of limited international status.

The documents shed no light on the question whether Russell deliberately rushed the cabinet into neutrality before Adams arrived to bear official weight against the move. Britain certainly achieved the advantage of presenting Adams with a *fait accompli*—Adams considered but rejected an immediate withdrawal—but it was at considerable cost: Adams was outraged, his mission begun on a disastrous note, while northern resentment outlasted the decade. Adams' New England conscience kept him at his post when hurt pride might have excused him asking for his passports. But the signs pointed to early recognition of the south by England, and that Adams determined to prevent at all costs. Seward's pa-

---

[18]Thouvenel to Mercier, May 11, 1861.

[19]Stuart L. Bernath, *Squall Across the Atlantic: American Civil War Prize Cases and Diplomacy* (Berkeley and L. A., 1970), 19–20. The British proclamation prohibited enlistment of British nationals in the war.

[20]D. G. Wright, "Bradford and the American Civil War," *J. British Studies,* VIII, No. 2(May, 1969), 69–85. Bradford worsteds sold to a large American market.

tronage had sent his old friend and political ally, the son of John Quincy Adams, to the court of St. James, and historians have justly endorsed his choice. Charles Francis Adams proved to be Seward's loyal and statesmanlike, if not always most perceptive, agent abroad.[21]

Russell soothed the new minister's ruffled feelings by arranging an early presentation at court. Adams avoided offence to Queen Victoria by wearing stockings and lace instead of the republican black assumed by previous representatives. But Adams and Russell conducted a stormy first interview. Adams complained that Britain's impetuous declaration of southern belligerence gave unnatural encouragement to a cause lacking military and naval might. It smacked of a sinister plot to injure the United States. Obeying an irascible dispatch sent by Seward on April 27, Adams spoke of withdrawing if England gave comfort to the Union's foes. Russell, caught off balance, answered that England acted out of legal necessity, a sense of reality, and a wish to bring the war "within the rules of modern civilized warfare." The exchange cleared the air, and the principals—Adams, stiff, correct, cautious, principled; Russell, diminutive, cold, punctilious; both members of famous political families—discovered respect for each other. Adams did not know it but he had won a victory for the north: henceforth Russell kept southern commissioners at arms length; and he showed new respect for the intense animosity with which northerners regarded foreign interference.

France proclaimed its neutrality on June 10, a lead soon followed by other European governments. These proclamations, far from heralding recognition of the Confederacy—as its agents were prone to believe—in effect pronounced its remoteness. The western powers committed themselves to fixed positions of "impartiality" until emphatic military changes should occur. Napoleon III, as he realized later, had lost his best chance of intervening, when the Union was weakest. The Union gained time to mobilize its industrial and military capacities, while the passing of time weak-

---

[21]For detailed account of Adams first year in London, see Norman Ferris, *Tempestuous Mission, 1861–2: The Early Diplomatic Career of Charles Francis Adams* (Unpub. D thesis, Emory, 1962); and briefer coverage in M. B. Duberman, *Charles Francis Adams, 1807–1886* (New York 1961.)

ened the legal basis for recognizing the south or rejecting the blockade.[22] However, it is worth remembering that Napoleon's thinking on America was not so predatory in early 1861 as it would become. The retiring American ambassador, Charles J. Faulkner, a Virginian who requested his own recall, noted in March that Napoleon did not share the virulent anti-Yankee sentiments of his court circle: "He looks upon the dismemberment of the American Confederation with no pleasure, but as a calamity to be deplored by every enlightened friend of human progress."[23] The same outlook was taken by Napoleon's foreign minister, Antoine Edouard Thouvenel, a liberal pro-Italian diplomat who replaced the conservative Walewski in January 1860. Thouvenel adopted a tactful, and rewarding, policy towards Washington. In interview with the incoming American minister—William Dayton, New Jersey's favorite for cabinet, whom Lincoln sent to France, although he spoke no French—Thouvenel said that France would require the Confederacy to survive for perhaps three or four years before considering recognition. The secret record of French policy in 1861 shows that it was less minatory towards the north than northerners realized.

Solid reasons underlay this vital French caution. The emperor's officials reported an unwarlike spirit from the French people, tired of a decade of foreign escapades. The specter of a cotton famine existed, but there was no immediate danger in 1861: cotton imports did not fall sharply until winter, while surpluses from the 1860 crop still lay in reserve. The American disruption threatened greater economic damage by undermining French export markets, and by dampening commercial activity generally in western Europe. A Franco-American war, fought to raise the blockade, might suit French textiles, but risked a wider depression within the economy. Merchant and manufacturing circles generally favored nonintervention in 1861.

Strategically, a unilateral and aggressive French move in the civil war theater would entail high risks at a time when Europe was being transformed by changes associated with the unification of

---

[22]Henry Blumenthal, *A Reappraisal of Franco-American Relations, 1830–1871* (Chapel Hill, 1959), p. 124.

[23]Faulkner to Jeremiah Black, March 19, 1861; q. Case and Spencer, p. 24.

Italy and Germany. France, in any sober appraisal, needed to be able to apply maximum military and diplomatic pressure in the European heartland. The Italian Intervention had tended to isolate France in Europe, the acquisition of Nice and Savoy in particular angering the British. Napoleon, his efforts focused on pacifying his British allies, regarded a lone move on America as likely to rouse British suspicion concerning French good faith. Mutual distrust suggested that Britain and France move in harness in American, as well as European, affairs. In 1861 France followed the British lead, most notably in accepting the Union blockade, even though it was assailed by Jefferson Davis and many neutrals as a "paper" blockade. Britain tolerated the blockade largely because British naval policy favored strong belligerent rights; Napoleon because his European needs dictated a consolidation of the English entente.

The traditional French desire to maintain an American counterweight to the British empire still exerted influence. Many Frenchmen viewed the American navy as auxiliary to the French fleet. Even if the United States should be partitioned, a case existed for salvaging as much as was possible of northern power, naval and political. Count Mercier, Napoleon's envoy at Washington, took this view. A realist, not a crude southern sympathizer, Mercier thought the giant American Republic to be finished. But French interest lay in maintaining a powerful state composed of the northern and western sections, the future centers of American vitality. Mercier wanted France to keep on friendly terms with even a defeated United States, for it would have, like England, "a huge merchant marine, iron like hers, coal and cotton, the same aptitudes, the same greed, the same bumptious roughness, . . . it will be her real rival in the world, and since its field of action will not be Europe, by the same token it will be our ally."[24]

Yankee friendship was worth having for France on three assumptions: that America desired no European role; that American naval power did not exceed parity with the British, thus creating a new disequilibrium; and that the geopolitical interests of France and the United States were compatible in the hemisphere. The first two conditions were fulfilled in 1861. (However European enmity to

---

[24]Daniel B. Carroll, *Henri Mercier and the American Civil War* (Princeton U.P., Princeton, 1971), p. 75, & *passim*.

the north might cause the Americans to take a retaliatory role in Europe at some later date, while the war promised to create a massive Union navy within years.) The last was the sorest point. Napoleon resented the Monroe Doctrine and intended to challenge it. He scented strategic and economic gains to be made in Mexico, and hoped to barter the Mexican crown for an alliance with Austria (see Chapter 8). But the Mexican affair was only a storm cloud on the horizon in 1861, and it suited neither Napoleon nor Lincoln to have a headlong clash about it.

*　　*　　*

Seward's diplomacy aimed to stave off a joint Anglo-French demarche on America by dividing the allies. He emphasized their divergent interests in the hemisphere: France intended to supplant British influence in Central America; Britain wanted to entangle Napoleon in America in order to weaken his power in Europe. In a remarkable concession to European-style diplomacy, Seward recognized the validity of the balance of power concept in Europe, and claimed that it would survive only if there were equilibrium in the American hemisphere. Could the great empires of Britain, France, Austria, Russia, or Spain suppress internal rebellions, or survive the "wars of ambition" which must inevitably break out "if this continent of North America, now, after the exclusion of foreign interests for three-quarters of a century, is again to become a theatre for the ambition and cupidity of European nations"?[25] Using boldly sweeping economic and political arguments, Seward exploited the "peace factors" in the Anglo-French-American world. These three nations, he said, were in effect "one great society or commonwealth," one economic community exchanging resources, food, and manufactures. The overriding interest of that community lay in the swift return of peace before irreparable damage was done to the pattern of international trade.

Seward's behavior came closest to the textbook version of panic, overreaction, and warmongering when he learned of the impending neutrality of Britain and France. His program of "quarantine" for the south lay in ruins. Their emissaries were already entering European audience chambers. Seward swore to give the British

---

[25]Seward to Dayton, April 22, 1861, *For. Rels.,* 1861, 195–201.

hell. They seemed to be aiding and comforting the rebels for the sake of cotton; if not careful they would "drive us to make war" against them as allies of the traitors. Congress was about to meet, and Seward's bellicosity was also a political response to widespread war talk, common even in business circles of the northeast.

His notorious dispatch Number 10 (May 21) proposed breaking off relations with Britain if it continued to communicate—officially or otherwise—with Davis' commissioners. He spoke in provocative terms of being forced into war with Britain if it recognized Confederate independence (a threat he had made before.) Seward's draft dispatch provoked Lincoln into one of his rare interventions into foreign policy. The President countermanded Seward's order that the message be read to Lord Russell, and blue-pencilled the Secretary's more warlike phrases. The dispatch still had teeth. The north insisted upon international respect for its blockade, and promised to react with hostility against any nation recognizing, or even treating with, the Union's rebellious subjects. Adams' tact in presenting the kernel of Seward's instruction to Russell without its offensive husk did much to avert an unnecessary alienation of the English.

Although some of Seward's subsequent maneuvers bordered upon comic opera, they are understandable in two regards: he wanted to stress that the United States rejected the "proto-recognition" offered by the powers to the south in the form of belligerent status; and he was determined to discredit the Anglo-French entente in the eyes of the American public. When Lyons and Mercier sought to interview Seward jointly on the subject of southern belligerency (June 15), the Secretary jokingly admonished them, refused a joint encounter and arranged separate interviews. The incident was blown up in the press, and Seward spoke in later life with excessive pride of his dexterity in the matter. Again, he read but refused to receive "officially" documents assuming the Confederacy's belligerent rights. As talks on the Paris Declaration touched on the same prickly issue, Seward transferred the negotiations to the European capitals, allowing time for passions to cool in the north. Meanwhile, he promised northern cooperation in observing the Paris rules respecting private property at sea: surprisingly moderate behavior.

The eagerness of the neutral powers to have the sea war conducted with maximum security for their shipping precipitated the

"Bunch affair." The British and French consuls at Charleston were charged by their governments to conduct discreet negotiations with southern officials, in order to obtain Confederate adherence to the Paris Declaration. The need for discretion was essential. The north was averse to open dealing with the rebels, although international law permitted states to communicate with *de facto* governments to protect neutral property and persons. Seward hinted that he would turn a blind eye unless forced to take offical notice of foreign intercourse with the Confederate government. The consuls bungled. Instead of following orders and working quietly through the Governor of South Carolina (whose legal status at least predated the rebellion), they approached Jefferson Davis through W. H. Trescott, who had been Buchanan's assistant Secretary of State before defecting from the Union. In August the Confederate Congress approved Articles 2 to 4 of the Paris Declaration, thus giving Europe its guarantee of immunity for noncontraband trade. By refusing to sign Article 1, the south kept its right to use privateers; but that right had been much weakened since June when Britain and France declared their ports closed to rebel privateers. A result satisfactory to Britain was spoiled when their consul, Ralph Bunch, foolishly confided details of the negotiations to a friend, whose correspondence on the subject fell into Federal hands. Seward felt obliged to ask for Bunch's removal from office, and a diplomatic storm blew up between London and Washington. Tempers had not been calmed by the Union army's humiliation in battle at Bull Run in July, a rout that occasioned sneers throughout Europe and raised to dizzy heights rebel hopes of recognition. Lord Russell, however, denied that the "Bunch affair" was a pretext for accepting southern independence. He refused to recall Bunch. Seward revoked Bunch's accreditation (Foreign consuls in the south were still legally accredited to the Union, much to southern indignation.) The squall subsided when Seward toned down his protests. He played on Anglo-French rivalry by rather obviously ignoring France's role in the affair. When asked to support the British stand, the French were unresponsive.

By the autumn of 1861 a secret deal seemed possible between France and the Union, a deal by which—if Seward's game paid off —France would renounce its recognition of southern belligerency in return for special access to cotton sources. Initiatives began with Mercier and Thouvenel; Seward in turn sent a negotiating mission to Paris headed by the Catholic Archbishop of New York, John Hughes, and including Thurlow Weed. This was a gambler's move, depending on the Union navy's ability to establish beachheads on rebel coasts from which cotton might be funnelled overseas. But it offered the hope of splitting the allies if Napoleon accepted the deal, leaving England in the cold. An abrupt end was put to all such speculation when in November occurred the war's most alarming international incident, the *Trent* affair.

CHAPTER III

The "Trent" Affair

The *Trent* affair, although often treated as an isolated incident, was in fact a symptom of the increasing tensions created by the maritime war. As this case showed, the pressures of war continually forced the United States further away from its historic position of attachment to neutral rights. Britain, as the world's greatest sea carrier, now played the unfamiliar role of a key neutral, its pride and economic interests exposed to the "high-handedness" of the Union navy. Ambivalence existed aplenty on both sides as habitual attitudes, and considerations of long-term national advantage, clashed with immediate interests.

The Confederacy precipitated the clash by upgrading their diplomatic representation abroad. Appointed as special commissioners to London and Paris respectively, James M. Mason of Virginia and John Slidell of Louisiana ran the blockade to Cuba in a specially chartered river steamer. Pro-southern Havana gaily welcomed the envoys, who made no secret of their intention to sail to Europe under the protective British flag. On October 31 the Union steam-sloop *San Jacinto* arrived in Havana, captained by the flambuoyant Charles Wilkes, veteran naval scientist and explorer. Wilkes determined upon the capture of the commissioners and their dispatches, for, as he wrote in his journal, "I know of no act that would so effectually [despoil] their diabolical scheme."[1] Soon after noon on November 8, in the Old Bahama Channel, 300 miles east

---

[1] See *North, South and Powers,* pp. 99–102 for speculation that authorities in Washington ordered the seizure of Mason and Slidell by Wilkes. While inconclusive on that issue, the documents do show that Wilkes acted on his own initiative, before orders had time to arrive in Havana. The claim that Richmond deliberately contrived the arrest of their envoys is dismissed, *ibid,* p. 106,n14.

of Havana, the *San Jacinto* stopped the British mail-packet *Trent,* en route to Danish St. Thomas and carrying as passengers Mason, Slidell and their entourage (Map 1). The Union boarding party had orders to arrest the envoys and their secretaries, to take possession of their baggage and any dispatches found aboard, and—very importantly—to make a prize of the *Trent.* Fulfilment of these orders would greatly have helped the American case. However Wilkes' first lieutenant failed to locate any dispatches (they had been hastily entrusted to the British mail agent aboard); and he deliberately avoided confiscating the ship, fearing that such a course would goad Britain into war. Using a token display of force, the Americans transferred the envoys and their secretaries to the *San Jacinto,* ignoring the indignation of the *Trent's* passengers and the protests of her master. Wilkes released the *Trent,* as he was impressed by arguments that its detention would inconvenience numerous passengers and require a large prize crew, thus weakening the fighting capacity of his vessel. The *San Jacinto* subsequently took its prisoners to Fort Warren at Boston, and its captain to a Roman triumph.

The affair stirred jubilation in a north hungry for victories after a season of military and naval reverses, but there was also an undercurrent of apprehension over Britain's reaction. In the British Isles, the incident provoked extraordinary hysteria, "every sword leaping from its scabbard, and every man looking about for his pistols and his blunderbusses."[2] The *Trent* affair was never about purely legal rights and wrongs, but even those were not clear cut. The mail packet carried Confederate dispatches, and the British proclamation of neutrality listed dispatches as contraband of war, liable to capture by a belligerent vessel. A strong view of belligerent rights might hold that a ship carrying dispatches relating to the war's conduct, likely to give succor to the enemy or to foment foreign conspiracies against the integrity of the United States, might be confiscated even though it sailed to a neutral destination. On the same lines, it could be said that diplomats forfeited their claims to inviolability—might even, as Wilkes had vaguely understood when meditating the capture, be classified as

---

[2]Rochdale Address by John Bright, Dec. 12, 1861, in J. E. Thorald Rogers ed., *Speeches on Questions of Public Policy by John Bright M.P.* (London, 1868), I, p. 191.

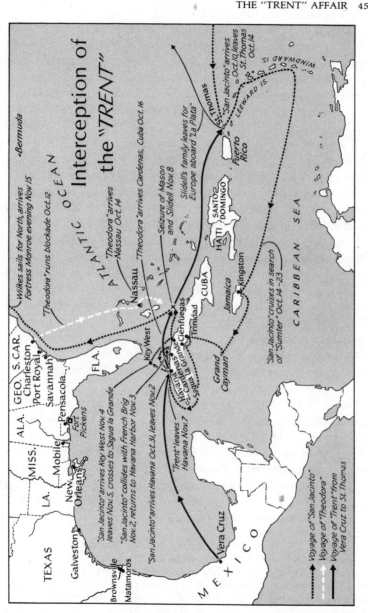

Interception of the "TRENT"

Wilkes sails for North, arrives Fortress Monroe evening Nov.15

"Theodora" runs blockade Oct.12

•Bermuda

ATLANTIC OCEAN

"Theodora" arrives Nassau Oct.14

"Theodora" arrives Cardenas, Cuba Oct.16

St. Thomas

"San Jacinto" arrives Oct.10, leaves St. Thomas Oct.14

WINDWARD IS.

LEEWARD IS.

Seizure of Mason and Slidell Nov.8

Slidell's family leaves for Europe aboard "La Plata"

•Puerto Rico

SANTO DOMINGO

HAITI

Nassau

Kingston

CUBA

Jamaica

Cienfuegos

Trinidad

CARIBBEAN SEA

"San Jacinto" cruises in search of "Sumter" Oct.14-23

Key West

Havana

Grand Cayman

Cardenas

Sagua la Grande

S.CAR.

GEO.

Charleston

Port Royal

Savannah

ALA.

FLA.

Pensacola

Fort Pickens

"San Jacinto" arrives Key West Nov.4 leaves Nov.5, crosses to Sagua la Grande

"San Jacinto" collides with French Brig Nov.2, returns to Havana Har-bor Nov.3

MISS.

Mobile

"San Jacinto" arrives Havana Oct.31, leaves Nov.2

LA.

New Orleans

"Trent" leaves Havana Nov.7

TEXAS

Galveston

Brownsville

Matamoros

Vera Cruz

M E X I C O

Voyage of "San Jacinto"

Voyage of "Theodora"

Voyage of "Trent" from Vera Cruz to St. Thomas

a type of contraband—if their passage on a neutral ship was of clear material aid to a belligerent's war operations. This was to compare the role of envoys with that of military or naval persons in enemy service, for no dispute existed that carriage of such personnel exposed a ship to condemnation. What vastly weakened an American case based on such views was Wilkes' failure to confiscate the *Trent* and its contents, so that the issues might be adjudicated before a competent prize court. Such a court was the only proper authority to decide, from the ship's papers, captured documents, etc., whether unneutral activities had occurred. Instead, men who claimed the rights of embassy had been unceremoniously removed from the protection of a neutral flag without trial and at the mere mandate of a navy officer.

When news of Wilkes' perfidy reached London on November 27, five days of crisis politics followed. The blockade, the Bunch affair, high Union tariffs, Britain's "premature" neutrality, and Canada's reinforcement already bedevilled Anglo-American relations. Northern warships hovered off British coasts, ready to harass rebel commerce-raiders and, possibly, British commercial shipping. With their neutral rights at threat, Englishmen placed the worst possible construction upon the *Trent* incident. Anger blossomed under the assumption that the act had been deliberately planned, and was regarded as legal, by Washington.

The British Cabinet met on November 29, after its law officers had declared illegal the *San Jacinto's* action, and justified a claim for reparation. Individuals, not officers in the Confederate army or navy, had been taken by force from a neutral merchantman pursuing a lawful and innocent voyage. The *Trent* (according to the law officers) had not been carried into an American port for adjudication as a prize and could not, under the circumstances, be considered as having breached international law.[3] The cabinet soon

---

[3]Curiously, the Crown law office had given an almost identical opinion some two weeks earlier (Nov. 12) when Foreign Office intelligence suggested that an American warship, the *James Adger*, intended to intercept the British mailpacket plying the St. Thomas-Southampton run, and to extract from her Mason and Slidell (if aboard). They opined that the warship might take the packet as a prize, but would have no right to remove the envoys while leaving the ship to continue her voyage. Palmerston apparently misinterpreted this verdict in a letter to the editor of the *Times*, causing a considerable historical controversy: See *North, South and Powers*, pp. 121–124.

agreed that a demand must be made for American disavowal of Wilkes' action, together with restoration of the prisoners and an apology. Armed preparations were set in train to back up this stand. Gladstone urged that the American side be heard, "for I could not feel sure that we were at the bottom of the law of the case."[4] He was overridden. With the aplomb appropriate to the world's most powerful executive, the ministers simply declared that "a gross outrage and violation of international law has been committed."Palmerston, in a bellicose mood, supported an embargo on arms to the United States, and seemed willing to dispatch the Channel fleet immediately to American waters. He was deterred from this provocative move, it seems, by the persuasions of Richard Cobden, who called personally at Downing Street while the meeting was in progress.

Before they could begin sword-rattling in earnest, the British needed to insure French neutrality. It was possible that Seward had premeditated an insult to Britain, and was offering bait (the French province of Canada perhaps?) for a French alliance, reminiscent of the American War of Independence. "Mr. Seward figures in the British imagination as a Giant Blunderbore, thirsting day and night for the blood of Englishmen:" thus judged *The New York Times.*[5] And even sober diplomats like Lyons in Washington, and Cowley in Paris, feared that north and south would "shake hands over a war with us."[6]

Paris swiftly reassured London of French reliability. France and America had stood firm in the past for neutral rights: for restricted concepts of contraband, immunity of enemy persons covered by a neutral flag unless they were combatants, and safety of cargo and passengers carried between neutral ports. The Union's violation of these principles shocked French opinion and posed a threat to French shipping. Napoleon soon showed that he wanted to act the peacemaker, supporting the British in any protest but maintaining neutrality. If possible he would persuade the north to retreat, vindicate the rights of smaller neutrals, and even maneuver Britain into accepting French principles of maritime law. Above all, the emperor hoped to repair the shaky alliance, while gaining as a

---

[4]Gladstone to Argyll, Dec. 3, 1861, q. Morley, *Gladstone,* pp. 73–4.
[5]*NYT,* Dec. 24, 1861.
[6]Cowley to Russell, Dec. 2, 1861, q. *EDA,* I, p. 214.

reward greater freedom of action in Mexico, where international intervention was just starting.

Amidst rumors of war and a stock market panic, the British Cabinet met (on Saturday, November 30) to draft an ultimatum. The *London Times* of that morning adopted a calm voice, one of the few newspapers to do so; it suggested that Wilkes may have acted without authorization but spoke also of upholding "our strict rights."[7] Lord Clarendon expressed the ominous sense of the occasion when he wrote to Cowley: "I have a horror of war and of all wars one with the U.S. because none would be so prejudicial to our interests, but peace like other good things may be bought too dearly and it never can be worth the price of national honor."[8]

Cabinet's draft ultimatum to Washington condemned "this act of violence against a neutral and friendly nation," and proposed the return of the captives to British protection with an apology "for the insult offered the British flag." Should the Americans refuse compliance, Lyons was to withdraw his embassy. The proposals went at once to Windsor Castle for Queen Victoria's approval. During Saturday night and the early hours of Sunday, the Prince Consort—the Queen's trusted adviser on state affairs—painfully devised a draft that he thought was less likely to offend the Americans while still exacting atonement. He was suffering from heavy catarrh and insomnia, symptoms of typhoid, from which he was to collapse on December 2, and to die on December 14. Historical folklore is substantially sound in praising his dying effort to preserve Atlantic peace, which he believed to be essential to British interests. Prince Albert's memorandum—the last he wrote, and one the Queen revered in her husband's memory—reflected the influence of the *Times,* and possibly of Gladstone, who had dined with the royal family on preceding evenings. It was largely at the Prince Consort's instigation that the cabinet on December 1, in a new dispatch, professed a willingness to believe that Wilkes' act was unauthorized or the result of a misunderstanding of orders,

---

[7] See N. Ferris, "The Prince Consort, the 'Times' and the 'Trent' Affair", *CWH,* VI (1960), pp. 152–6.

[8] Clarendon to Cowley, Nov. 29, 1861, F.O. 519/178, q. Kenneth Bourne, *Britain & the Balance of Power in North America, 1815–1908* (London, 1967).

referred to Anglo-American amity in the past, and hoped that the Americans, of their own accord, would make the required redress.

In separate instructions Lyons was empowered to offer the Americans time to consider, "not exceeding seven days." But if no answer were given, or any answer except that of compliance with the British demand, Lyons and the whole legation were to repair at once to London. Russell privately advised Lyons to prepare the ground tactfully before reading the dispatch to Seward, and to "abstain from anything like menace." Lyons was not openly to threaten withdrawal of the legation. If Seward asked the results of an American refusal "I think you should say that you wish to leave him and the President quite free to take their own course." The cabinet, concluded Russell, was disposed "to be rather easy about the apology" but were immovable on restoration of the envoys: "The feeling here is very quiet but very decided. There is no party about it: all are unanimous."[9] On December 2 a special messenger carrying the dispatches embarked on the Europa for America.

Across the Atlantic the *Trent* affair had been intensely debated. Patriotism lent an edge to the "support Wilkes" school: the captain had dealt an exhilarating smack in the eye to the south, and to the old enemy Britain. How could the latter complain, when her record was one of high-handedness against American shipping during the Napoleonic Wars? Other voices, at first muted, warned that, in their eagerness to defend Wilkes, northerners verged on the brink of seriously weakening their nation's historic commitment to neutral rights. Moreover, to press Britain into war would be a capital blunder when the north's whole energies were devoted to subjugation of the south. Amidst the clamor and joy over the exploit, one finds expressed surprisingly often the confident belief that any dispute would be readily settled by negotiation, or arbitration. Right from the start, the northeastern newspapers—even the pugnacious and anti-British *New York Herald*—conceded that a government disavowal of Wilkes' act, reparation, even an apology might become expedient. Radical Republicans and loyalist Unionists who put highest priorroty on the war against slavery, and for the Union, suspected the rapid anti-British posture taken by the Copperhead and Peace Democratic press: the secessionists

---

[9]Russell to Lyons, Dec. 1, 1861, in Newton, *Lyons*, I, pp. 62–63.

clearly wanted to pitch the north into a war on many fronts. Whatever the fluctuations of opinion—and men veered crazily during these weeks—the "one war at a time" school proved most basic.

The politicians shared the passions and uncertainties of the day. Of Lincoln's cabinet only Postmaster-General Blair denounced Wilkes' act immediately. Seward was noncommittal, treating the matter with such scant urgency that he delayed for two weeks before sending Adams the news that Wilkes had acted without orders. Senator Charles Sumner, head of the Senate Foreign Relations Committee, reputedly saw at once that the emissaries must be given up.[10] Accounts vary as to Lincoln's first reaction, one press report indicating that he argued in cabinet for restoration of men who would only be liabilities to the Union.[11] But before long the administration adopted a policy of inaction, avoiding commitment, and hoping for the best. Any case that the Union government seriously maintained the option of war with England is difficult to sustain. Only feeble gestures were made toward fortifying the border with Canada, and not even an elementary contingency plan for war seems to have been prepared.

The arrival of the British demand, conveyed by Lyons to Seward on December 19, faced the administration with stark reality, and the opportunity for statesmanship. Not without pain and fumbling, the chance was finally accepted. Lyons' prudence, and the British cabinet's concern not to humiliate the Lincoln administration, eased the path to settlement. According to his brief, Lyons withheld the formal demand, first "preparing" Seward unofficially, and allowing a breathing space for Lincoln and his cabinet to deliberate alternatives. Not until pressed by Seward did Lyons tell him confidentially of the seven days time limit. Lyons agreed to delay formal presentation of the note—an "unofficial" copy of which he gave Seward—for two days: this would give Seward, Lyons thought, time to maneuver, and also permit the arrival of a dispatch from Paris to Mercier, adding French pressure on the

---

[10]David Donald, *Charles Sumner*, p. 31, takes this view. More sceptical of the claim is V. H. Cohen, "Charles Sumner and the *Trent* Affair," *JSH*, XXII, No. 2 (May, 1956), pp. 205–219.

[11]*NYDT*, Dec. 31, 1861.

United States to conciliate. So that the Americans should not mistake British courtesies for weakness, Lyons made it plain that England would tolerate no evasions, no failure to surrender the men. This proved a timely caution, as the primary danger was of war by miscalculation. The British habitually distrusted the American capacity for litigation and vacillation, and knew that England must be seen to be in deadly earnest. As every edition of the newspapers carried details of British mobilization, of troops, arms and supplies hastening to Canada, of fleet movements, vulnerable seaboard defenses, and a weakening New York stock exchange, the message should have been clear. Britain was ready for war, if the Yankees were not.

In the week before Christmas intense pressures built up for conciliation. War panic in the world's money markets, and the onset of a crisis in the northern shipping industry alarmed commercial interests. Businessmen and grain merchants received messages from their overseas agents not to ship goods in American vessels in case of war. The price of imports rose astonishingly; the sale of cotton goods ceased. Bankers and investors, already worried at the erosion of confidence caused by Federal military reverses, feared that the *Trent* scare would sabotage all efforts to raise the huge loans required for the civil war. The financier Jay Cooke, the man whom Lincoln most heavily depended on to raise Union loans, urged upon Seward, Treasurer Chase, and other politicians the overriding need for peace abroad.[12]

Lincoln, however, balked at returning the prisoners. Seward, according to one version of events, insisted that no other safe course existed than to bow to the demand: if Lincoln refused to yield the men, the President would have to write the reply to the British government himself, for Seward would not do it.[13] Lincoln devised a compromise: Seward should draft the case for, and he the case against, immediate release, the papers to be compared before the cabinet met.

Ironically the "warmonger" Seward engineered the final settlement, while the apostles of Atlantic peace labored during these

---

[12]See M. P. Claussen, *The U.S. and Gt. Britain: Peace Factors in International Relations* (Unpub. Ph. D. thesis, Illinois, 1937), pp. 99–104.

[13]N. B. Ferris, "Lincoln and the *Trent* Affair," *Lincoln Herald,* LXIX (1967) p. 132.

crisis days on an impractical and risky peace plan to which they almost converted Lincoln. Sumner almost certainly showed to Lincoln a peace plan sent to him by John Bright, for Lincoln's draft reply to the British demand incorporated Bright's ideas and even reproduced his language.[14] Lincoln proposed as a possible solution that the dispute be put before international arbitration—a remedy already pressed upon him by Sumner, and recommended in the Paris Conference of 1856 as a way of avoiding the use of force in world politics. Lincoln's wide terms of reference would certainly have confirmed Lord Russell's worst fears about the litigiousness of the Americans. Alternatively, the Americans proposed to argue their counter-case before the British government, the latter alone to determine what reparation, if any, was due. The Union would accept the ruling, provided it did not surpass the present demand and that "the determination thus made shall be the law for all future analogous cases."[15] The President's plan proposed a dangerous policy of procrastination. Should the Confederates not be restored by the time limit (now seven days from December 23), Lyons must obey his instructions and withdraw. Seward, and presumably Lincoln, knew these plain alternatives. What they did not know was that Russell had not entirely ruled out further negotiations if Washington tried delaying tactics. Nevertheless Lincoln's plan would have caused the withdrawal of the legation and the creation of a tinderbox situation.

In the end good sense prevailed. Lincoln did not present his peace plan to the Cabinet when it met on Christmas Day. Sumner—by now desperately anxious that Britain sought a pretext for war—admitted the perils of an arbitration scheme. Cabinet was shocked when Sumner read to them letters he had received from Cobden and Bright describing the warlike excitement in England—there were plenty of Englishmen content to unleash upon the United States "a fleet surpassing in destructive force any naval armament the world ever saw."[16] Seward's dispatch bag bulged with advice from his trusted advisers abroad—Adams, Dayton, Bigelow,

---

[14] *Ibid.*, p. 133.
[15] Basler, *Works of Lincoln*, V, pp. 62–64.
[16] This is Cobden's verdict some weeks later. Cobden to Sumner, Jan. 12, 1862, q. Cohen, *JSH*, p. 211.

Weed—to yield the prisoners. In a display of moderation (insufficiently emphasized by historians) the north's major newspapers—
even Bennett's *Herald* in an abrupt about-face—foreshadowed the
final settlement.

Seward behaved throughout as if all would be well (after seeing
Seward on December 23, Lyons sent out his normal invitations to
Christmas dinner, not a sign that he expected war!). The Secretary
of State knew, first unofficially from Mercier, then from a dispatch
sent by Thouvenel and read at the Christmas Day cabinet, that
French opinion sustained Britain. Thouvenel appealed to Franco-
American maritime tradition, expressed in treaties between the
two countries and upholding neutral immunities. Privately pro-
northern, Thouvenel urged the north to yield to the British demands. Officially the French wanted peace, but Seward was aware
of London rumors that Napoleon planned to ally himself with
England against the Union, provided he was given a "free swing
in taking Syria."[17]

After two days discussion, which Seward likened to the "Fires
of Tophet," cabinet accepted the solution offered by the Secretary
of State. Seward's compromise brought peace, saved northern face,
and won political success, even if it disconcerted purist defenders
of American sea-law. He liberated the prisoners, but justified the
capture of neutral vessels that carried enemy agents, including
envoys, travelling on hostile missions: dispatches were contraband
"and the bearers or couriers who undertake to carry them fall
under the same condemnation." Wilkes had acted legally, except
for leaving the capture unfinished; by cherished Amercian principle, as laid down by Madison in 1804, "the question shall not be
decided by the captor, but be carried before a legal tribunal, where
a regular trial may be had, and where the captor himself is liable
to damages for an abuse of his power." Seward's patriotic smokes-
creen obscured the fact that he had capitulated to a high British
view of belligerent prerogatives on almost every issue at stake
except that of adjudication. For this he earned rebukes, obliquely
from Sumner in a learned Senate speech in January, a speech
brilliantly reaffirming American doctrine, and privately by future

---

[17]James Leslie to Seward, Dec. 4., 1861, q. Blumenthal, *Franco-American Relations*,
p. 129.

Secretary of State Hamilton Fish, who thought Seward's defense "verbose and egotistical; in argument flimsy."[18] But, as public acclaim in the North indicated, Seward showed himself more realistic than some of his critics: the North's civil war interests required a strong posture on belligerent rights, at least temporarily; while the war effort and commercial stability demanded an end to uncertainty concerning a possible Atlantic war. Only too obviously, the north could ill afford to blunder into a British war, a war that would bring about what all the efforts of southern diplomacy had so far failed to encompass, a steel encirclement of the loyalist states.

* * *

The course of events during the *Trent* imbroglio raises some interesting questions. No one doubts the outrage felt by British public opinion, ominously comparable to that shown by Frenchmen over the Ems telegram in 1870; nor that Russell's ultimatum to the United States enjoyed overwhelming popular support in Britain. Whether the mood for war would have survived drawn out American temporising or a restrained call for negotiation is another matter. Peace opinion grew in Britain after the demand had been dispatched to Washington, as men realized the tragic dimensions of the crisis. Second thoughts were encouraged by pacifist free traders and their political associates (like Milner Gibson at the Board of Trade), by the Quakers and Nonconformist congregations, by "men of the 'middling classes', men of Republican proclivities, of the Bright and Cobden school, and many religious persons."[19] Arbitration grew popular as a solution. On the other hand, the Lancashire working classes seemed for war, packing into anti-Yankee meetings.[20] Of thirty-three political meetings reported in Britain to the close of December, only six favored a strong peace line or arbitration. Yet the peace lobby made a powerful impact at the official level. There is a strong sign that the crisis was basically negotiable in a letter of Russell's to Palmerston

---

[18]Fish to Sumner, Dec. 29, 1861, in Pierce, *Sumner,* IV, p. 54.

[19]U.S. Consul at London, Freeman Morse, to Seward, Dec. 18, 1861, q. Ferris p. 491. Also David Large, "Friends & the American Civil War: The Trent Affair," *Friends Hist. Soc. London Journal,* XLVIII (Autumn 1957), 163–167.

[20]Ellison, *Support for Secession,* Ch. 7.

on December 16: "I incline more and more to the opinion that if the [American] reply is a reasoning, and not a blunt offensive answer, we should send once more across the Atlantic to ask compliance . . . I do not think the country would approve an immediate declaration of war."[21]

Nor was the overall military situation as clear-cut in England's favor as Englismen liked later to make out. Despite the grandly impressive war preparations made by the Admiralty and War Office—perhaps the single most persuasive factor inducing the Americans to settle—Canada was vulnerable to American attack, and British shipping to Yankee raiders, while the impossibility of British territorial conquest of the United States was universally conceded. Even a fully garrisoned Canada could hardly hope to hold off Union forces advantaged by a central position, good internal lines of communication, plus excellent rail and canal links with the Great Lakes. (Map 2) In fact Canada was far from fully garrisoned. As it turned out, a frenetic British attempt to send extra troops by sea to Canada before winter ice blocked the St. Lawrence was partially botched: had war broken out, a large part of the expedition, which became stranded in New Brunswick, would have been in jeopardy from enemy ambush. (Map 3).[22]

In the last analysis, the British were prepared to tolerate the loss of Canada, and to rely on a massive naval offensive to win any war. They planned to retrieve Canada, and other losses, at the peace table afterwards. Vice-Admiral Milne's North American squadron, reinforced from the Mediterranean and Channel fleets and boasting eight battleships and thirteen frigates and corvettes, planned rapidly to annihilate the Union navy's blockading fleets. Enemy shipping was to be destroyed in the main sea-lanes at the outset of war, Washington and the seaboard cities harassed, perhaps even bombarded, and an unbreakable blockade imposed upon the north. Encircled by enemies, the north would presumably capitulate. This was an aggressive blueprint for war, but it did not provide an automatic guarantee of victory. The United States possessed the industrial capacity to build a modern ironclad fleet,

---

[21]Russell to Palmerston, Dec. 16, 1861, q. *EDA*, I, p. 215.

[22]The best account of Britain's military and naval plans is in Kenneth Bourne, *Britain and the Balance of Power in North America, 1815–1908* (London, 1967).

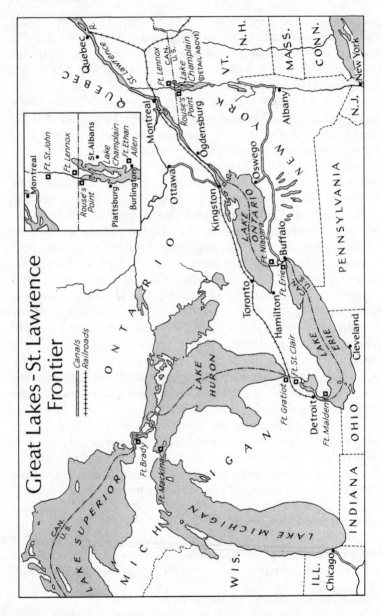

Great Lakes–St. Lawrence Frontier

Canals
Railroads

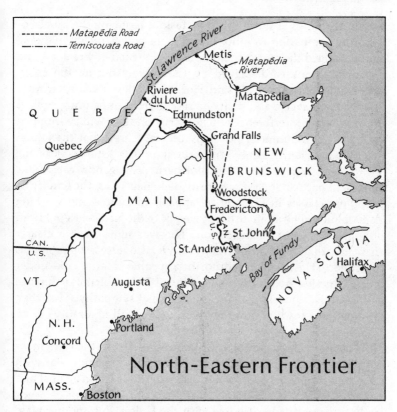

and was already building turretships—armored floating citadels mounting revolving guns—that were certain to create havoc against the type of wooden warships the British would be forced to use in the shallow waters of the American coast. Ultimately, the outcome would depend on the strength of northern morale, on the willingness or otherwise of northerners to mobilize their continental resources and latent industrial power in a bid to achieve self-sufficiency against British mastery at sea. All in all, the outcome of an Anglo-American war was something less than a foregone conclusion.

What were the repercussions of the *Trent* affair? Most obviously, the north was free to continue the Civil War. The achievement of a peaceful settlement boosted the prestige of the Lincoln administration, which now exploited public demands for new, and more smashing, blows at the south. The task of reducing the rebels, of restoring the nation to unity and a more powerful international status, seemed the more urgent in view of the harshly realistic and expedient attitudes displayed by the powers during the crisis. "Hereditary Aristocracy," said Horace Greeley, "yearns toward Hereditary Slavery, and plans its rescue from impending ruin. If one pretext for interference will not serve, another will be trumped up."[23] Charles Sumner, and many others, feared that the Union had obtained "a truce only" from foreign rivals. One result of the *Trent* crisis was to stimulate northern propaganda campaigns abroad. In particular efforts were made to neutralize the enmity of the upper classes in England by appeals to middle and working class opinion. The affair also lent weight to the Radical Republican program of Negro emancipation. The war must have a clearer character, that of an antislavery crusade, if overseas opinion was to support it. An embattled northern people in arms and under ordeal, divided politically and hounded by problems of finance and administration longed for international sympathy. That they did not get it readily, that they won only "chill neutrality" from Britain and France, was not forgiven.

It is usual to emphasize that Britain responded to the settlement with a sense of relief at narrowly escaping a damaging war with a kindred people, a relief soon translated into reaction against any policy of truckling too closely with the Confederates or of needlessly courting further trouble with the Union. Put another way, the vested peace interests of the Atlantic world had survived their severest threat, and continued to be the underlying predeterminants of civil war diplomacy. Such generalities, while partly true, mask the subtle reality of the developing situation.

The release of Mason and Slidell did, of course, generate relief. It fulfilled the requirement of peace without dishonor; it encouraged Bright and the Manchester school and all who hoped that reason would prevail in international affairs; it even convinced some people that the north, including Seward, felt conciliatory to England, that transatlantic democracy was not necessarily irresponsible. A liberal like John Stuart Mill found it impossible to think "without something like a shudder, from what we have

---

[23] *NYDT*, January 3, 1862.

escaped"—the emancipators of the slave collaborating with, and thus helping to set up in a commanding world position" a powerful republic, devoted not only to slavery, but to pro-slavery propaganda. . . ."[24]

Viewed in another light, however, the *Trent* affair augured less well for Anglo-northern relations. Offsetting the peace efforts of "the quiet and religious citizens of the middle classes," archtypal sympathizers of the United States, came the unexpected alienation from the north of proletarian opinion, particularly in Lancashire, where prosouthern and mediationist sentiment tenaciously persisted. Economic interest in a restored cotton supply, a liberal regard for oppressed nationalities, and an emerging anticapitalism seem to have motivated working class rejection of the Bright-Cobden view of the Civil War. Instead of the democratic utopia beloved of earlier English radicals, the war promoted a new image of a capitalist, racialist, and centralist United States.

Finally England's military and official elite commonly drew the moral from the *Trent* that a hard line provided the best way of dealing with the Americans. Britain's muscle-flexing produced a sense of exhilaration that obscured the real uncertainties that had existed in the military situation. The Duke of Cambridge did not regret the martial demonstration: "It will be a valuable lesson to the Americans, and to the world at large, and will prove to all what England can and will do, when the necessity for so doing arises."[25] The fact was that the British now possessed a ready-made blueprint for war with the north; and this placed them in an insuperably stronger military and diplomatic position *vis-à-vis* the United States than at any time prior to the *Trent.* A case might be put that the outcome of the affray—far from smoothing relations across the Atlantic—encouraged a more truculent British disposition toward joining in projects for mediation of the war, or recognition of the south, than would have been the case if the *Trent* had not occurred. The relief with which Americans in London received the news of peace, and the government's subsequent cold-shouldering of Mason and Slidell, soon gave way to misgivings about the

---

[24]*Frasers' Magazine,* LXII (Feb., 1862).
[25]Cambridge to Doyle, February 27, 1862, q. K. Bourne, "British Preparations for War with the North, 1861–2," *EHR,* LXXVI (Oct. 1961), 630.

future. Minister Adams (realizing that he must now "remain in this purgatory a while longer") expected the "gale" of opinion blowing in the north's favor to be as fickle as that which had previously run against them. Richard Cobden calculated that three-fourths of the Commons would gladly vote the dismemberment of the American Republic. Bright exulted that "the warmongers here are baffled for a time." But he warned Sumner, from information he had received, that Palmerston and Napoleon "do intend at an early period to recognize the independence of the South, and to repudiate or break the blockade."[26]

[26]C. F. Adams, *Diary*, February 8, 1862, q. Ferris, p. 523; Morley, *Cobden*, pp. 156ff; Bright to Sumner, January 11, 1862, *MHSP*, XLV, pp. 156ff.

CHAPTER IV

The Blockade and the Cotton Famine

THE NEW YEAR WAS DOMINATED BY PROBLEMS arising from the Union naval blockade. Blockade-running, already a flourishing industry, returned astronomic profits to its organizers, many of them British or European. Ports such as Nassau in British New Providence, St. George's in Bermuda, and Matamoros in Mexico became thriving entrepôts for the illicit trade. Cotton and other southern exports made their way to these centers, and thence to Europe, while goods destined for the Confederacy were here transshipped from large neutral vessels to flotillas of small blockade-runners. The ships best fitted for blockade-running were light-draft, speedy, with limited tonnage; at night, by hugging the rebel shoreline, they eluded the vigilance of the heavier Union cruisers, which were usually forced by coastal shallows and other hazards to anchor four or five miles offshore. Small, fast paddle and screw steamers made excellent blockade-runners, many being built especially for the trade in Mersey or Clyde shipyards.

The real effectiveness of the Union blockade is a favorite matter of dispute. The number of successful runs made through the blockade of Gulf, Carolina, Georgia, and East Florida ports during the war—and these are strictly minimum and confirmed figures—was almost 5400, a success rate of 85 percent. Steam blockaders achieved a 92 percent success rate.[1] However, the light tonnages of runners need to be remembered, and also the fact that a sub-

---

[1] Marcus W. Price, "Ships that Tested the Blockade of the Carolina Ports, 1861–5" *Am. Neptune,* VIII (1948), 196–241; "Ships that tested ... Gulf Ports, 1861–5," XI (1951), 262–290; XII (1952), 52–59, 154–161, 229–238; "Ships that tested ... Georgia and East Florida Ports," XV (1955), 97–132.

stantial proportion of successful runs occurred in the first year of the war, when Union blockaders were few and crews unfamiliar with the demanding routine of blockade duty. The cordon tightened upon the south with each year. Modern naval opinion is inclined to the broad view that the blockade achieved its major objective by scaring off a potentially massive neutral trade with the south. It did this by blocking off the major channels to the relatively few big ports such as Charleston, Wilmington, Savannah, or New Orleans. The blockade accelerated inflation in the wartime south, perhaps discouraged more rapid industrialization, and bred war fatigue. Although runners brought in essential arms and supplies, greed for profits caused many shippers to waste space on luxury items. By paying low prices for plantation cotton, speculators profiteered at the expense of the southern consumer and government, creating bitterness and defeatism.[2] Not least, the Union blockade deprived the southern navy of needed bases.

The Confederacy's now-notorious "ambassadors," Mason and Slidell, determined upon an all-out assault in London and Paris against the blockade. Such a strategy seemed well advised in early 1862: the blockade could be readily attacked as an attempt to close by proclamation over three thousand miles of southern coastline, whereas the Union navy was effectively sealing off only a few major ports. By American and French doctrine—forged against the British navy's aggressive use of blockade during the Napoleonic wars—a true blockade must be enforced by a cordon of ships placed in front of a port, or line of coast, and strong enough to prevent ships entering or leaving. The Paris Declaration of 1856 (Article 4) defined a binding blockade as one maintained by a force sufficient "really" to prevent access to an enemy port. Britain, however, had long resisted narrow or technical definitions of blockade, and asserted the belligerent's right to blockade an entire coast. Mason's attempt to budge the British on this point proved to have disastrous repercussions for his whole mission.

Because it suited naval interests, and because Anglo-American trade was less seriously bruised by an ineffective blockade, the

---

[2]John B. Heffernan, "The Blockade of the Southern Confederacy," *Smithsonian J. Hist.* II, No. 4 (1967–8), 38. See also Map 5.

British navy displayed noticeable forbearance concerning the enforcement of Lincoln's blockade proclamation of April 1861.[3] Examples of ineffective blockade were met at first by the practice of British warships merely representing the facts to the commander of the blockading squadron. After November 1861, even this was abandoned. Russell's crown law office in June 1861 advised avoiding discussions "upon abstract principles of International Law" with the Union, which appeared "upon the whole to have acted liberally in regard to this blockade." The *Trent* affair served to underline the importance of a naval blockade as England's most formidable offensive weapon.

At the same time that the southern lobby mobilized for a parliamentary denunciation of the blockade, Russell resurrected the language of the Anglo-Russian Convention of 1801 in a dispatch to Lyons. In it, he justified a blockade which created only "an evident danger" for ships entering or leaving an invested port. Such a doctrine alarmed neutrals and southerners as a resurrection of paper blockades. But, when the ministry made a parliamentary defense of its stance in March, it won a comfortable victory. W. G. Gregory, the prime assailant against the blockade, appeared in a less than patriotic light when he borrowed ammunition from the French jurist d'Hautefeuille, who accused England of selfishly conniving at an illegal blockade to justify future arrogant pretensions. (Gregory struck a more persuasive note with his phrase "that secession was a right, that separation is a fact, and that reconstruction is an impossibility.") The Solicitor-General, Roundell Palmer, riposted that England rightly resisted "new fangled notions and interpretations of international law which might make it impossible for us effectively at some future day to institute any blockade, and so destroy our naval authority—that great arm of our independence and safety." Blockades, he said, had never been entirely airtight, and probably never would be, especially in view of improvements in warfare and the use of steam power. According to the government's law officers, the blockade was

---

[3]For details, J. P. Baxter, "Papers Relating to Belligerent and Neutral Rights, 1861–5" *AHR*, XXXIV (1928), 77–91; M. R. Pitt, *Great Britain and Belligerent Maritime Rights . . . 1856 to . . . 1909* (Unpub. Ph.D. thesis, Univ. of London, 1964), 33ff.

effective at major ports; they were not willing to maintain that an effective blockade must cut off access to small coasters using shallow inner channels to evade capture.[4]

Two rather dubious assumptions of the day told against the South in the debate: that interruption to the world's raw cotton supply proved the success of the blockade; and that Lancashire's unemployed cotton operatives remained stoically silent out of regard for international peace or northern democracy. Dixie's cotton output had indeed declined, but primarily because of an embargo imposed by southern growers on the export of raw staple— a piece of King Cotton blackmail. No friend of the South dared admit this embarrassing fact. As to Lancashire opinion, it varied according to region, material interest, and political alignment, with resentment at the blockade probably outweighing stoicism or apathy.[5]

Mason miscalculated by forcing an issue that involved sensitive British interests. The March debate in parliament compelled the government to make a premature public stand in recognition of the blockade, one from which retreat was difficult, and that severely limited the south's room for maneuver. Newly arrived in Paris, Slidell had no alternative but to encourage unilateral French action on the blockade. In his first interviews with Napoleon III he encountered an emperor extravagantly nervous of acting alone, or of upsetting the English. Slidell counter-attacked by playing upon the divergent maritime interests of France and England—he thereby risked stirring suspicion between the allies, rendering less likely the prospect of joint intervention, and playing into Seward's hands. Slidell outlined plausibly Britain's perfidious interest in legalizing "paper" blockades, which would probably be used in the future against France. He added that Britain could ride out the effects of a cotton famine more readily than France, while Britain's merchants enriched themselves from blockade-running. If Britain would not act against the Union navy, France must, thereby striking a blow for neutral rights, preserving her future defense interests, and getting cotton for aggrieved workers.

Unilateral action had abstract appeal for Napoleon, but balance

[4] *Hansard*, 3rd Ser., Vol. 165, Commons, pp. 1158–1231; Lords, pp. 1238–1243.
[5] Ellison, *Support for Secession*, Ch. 8.

of power considerations underlined the danger of neglecting French security in Europe for overseas adventures. Napoleon was already enmeshed in Mexico, where the French army's advance on Mexico City drove a rift between the British, French, and Spanish (see Chapter 8). The second empire could hardly afford the additional risk and expense of war with the north; in such a conflict England and other countries would only too likely watch complacently while France drew their chestnuts out of the fire. In April the "Lindsay affair" seemed to confirm the unreliability of the Palmerston administration. A millionaire shipowner, free trade M.P. for Sunderland, and southern zealot, William S. Lindsay, talked privately with the emperor on April 11, 13 and 18; he learned that Napoleon favored joint recognition of the South by Britain and France. The emperor hinted at an Anglo-French fleet movement to open New Orleans. Lindsay broached the last possibility to Lord Cowley, the British minister to France, but Cowley firmly discouraged the idea. Napoleon then made a characteristically unorthodox stroke behind the backs of his advisers: he sent Lindsay to London to inform Russell and Palmerston unofficially of his views, and also asked him quietly to sound out the Conservative Opposition leaders, Derby and Disraeli. Fiasco followed. Napoleon's ambassador in London, Count Flahault, threatened resignation because he had been by-passed. Russell also favored orthodox diplomacy, and icily snubbed Lindsay. We know now that Lord Cowley undermined the unfortunate Lindsay. Cowley passed on to Russell his suspicion that Lindsay planned to make political capital with the Opposition out of his visit, "and that you may hear of it in Parliament." Crestfallen, Lindsay reported failure to Napoleon, repeating Disraeli's guess that Russell and Seward had a secret deal not to challenge the blockade.

*   *   *

If one factor sustained Union diplomacy in the first six months of 1862, it was northern success in the field. Under Ulysses S. Grant's vigorous leadership, the Union's western campaign flourished. With the fall of Forts Henry and Donelsen in February, Grant established a stranglehold over northern Tennessee. The battle of Shiloh foiled a regrouping of rebel forces in southern Tennessee, despite early Federal disorder and bloody casualties on both sides. On the Mississippi, General Pope pushed south from Columbus with naval support; while at the end of May Confederate General Beauregard evacuated Corinth. On the Virginia front, General George McClellan's massive Peninsular campaign got ponderously under way, threatening Richmond from Chesapeake Bay and seeming to promise an early end to the war.

March 8 demonstrated the Union's expanding naval power when the spectacular, if indecisive, *Monitor-Merrimac* duel was fought in Hampton Roads. Although mutual withdrawal occurred after four hours of point-blank broadsides between the two turret-ships, resembling "iron-shelled turtles," the north clearly possessed the capacity to multiply its stock of *Monitors,* and conventional ironclads, whereas mammoth obstacles beset Confederate naval chief Mallory's determination to create a rebel ironclad navy. Britain's naval experts showed less worry than the British public, or the French navy, over the American monitors: they were useless at sea, being easily capsized; while Britain enjoyed a marked world lead in armored warships under construction, had a brilliant pioneer of turreted guns in Captain Cowper Cole, and a valuable innovation in Whitworth's new rifled guns capable of piercing armor. Nevertheless, John Bigelow in Paris felt that the performance of Ericsson's *Monitor* "had done more to reestablish us as a national power in Europe and inspire respect for our military resources than anything that has occurred since the rebellion."[6]

In March Thouvenel instructed a reluctant Mercier to canvass mediation prospects in Washington. An early peace, achieved through French good offices, would have been vastly pleasing to Thouvenel, whose whole American policy turned on the need to localize troubles likely to engulf France, while diminishing the economic effects of the Civil War on the French people. A stalemate in America looked probable to European observers. Despite Union victories, the south appeared ultimately irreducible. Mercier confirmed this impression for himself, when in mid-April he made an unofficial, and as it turned out, diplomatically unwise, trip to Richmond, now the rebel capital. Mercier met Judah P. Benjamin, the Confederacy's new Secretary of State. "We have

---

[6]Bigelow to Seward, April 4, 1862, q. Case and Spencer, p. 267.

counted too much on Europe and the power of commercial interests," Benjamin regretted. But he underlined the South's will to
survive: "the North must exterminate us or agree to separation."
If the South's coastal cities fell to Union amphibian attack, the
southern people intended to continue guerilla warfare in the back
country, after burning their cotton and tobacco.[7] Thouvenel repri-
manded Mercier for accepting Seward's pass to Richmond.
Thouvenel knew (as did Lyons, who tried to dissuade Mercier
from the visit) that Mercier's independent move would be interpreted as sign of a rift in the *entente cordiale:* London and Paris had
agreed to act in concert on America, and London was quick to
suspect that Napoleon was hatching sinister schemes. In May
news arrived in Europe of Farragut's capture of New Orleans from
the sea, and the city's occupation by Union troops under the
soon-to-be notorious General B. F. ("Beast") Butler. The Confederate camp plunged into deep gloom. Slidell, still predicting a
military stalemate, began to advance the idea of a six months'
armistice. It would be supervised by the powers, include the raising of the blockade and resumption of overseas trade, and permit
plebiscites in the border states to determine their future.

Seward's maturing stature as a Secretary of State constituted
another factor helping the North in early 1862. Seward's diplomacy displayed a fundamental cogency. It was designed to prolong
the season of Atlantic harmony that followed the *Trent* settlement; and, by exploiting Union military success, to soften Europe's nerve for intervention.

Seward first succeeded in containing a difficult situation concerning Canada. Northern-Canadian relations struck a new low during, and after, the *Trent* scare, which served to unify Canada's
diverse peoples against the Yankees, while infuriating patriotic
northerners against "these . . . 'our Canadian brethren,' these
suckling Britons to whom, like fools, we have opened our ports."[8]
Coming under heavy fire in the North was the Canadian-American reciprocity trade treaty, symbol of happier days (negotiated in
1854, it allowed free trade in farm products across the border).

---

[7]Mercier to Thouvenel, April 28, 1862, q. Case and Spencer, pp. 279–281.
[8]*Buffalo Express,* q. Robin Winks, *Canada and the United States: the Civil War Years*
(Baltimore, 1960), p. 100; generally Chs. 6, 7.

Seward in 1855 steered reciprocity through the Senate, and he still regarded it as essential to American interests: unimpeded trade between the Union and its neighbors would soften animosities caused by the Civil War, and be the best instrument for achieving a peaceful expansion of American power in the hemisphere. When the British expressed anxiety that the treaty should run its full ten years, Seward gave a reassuring answer. Canada remained a target for all sorts of northern resentments. Owen Lovejoy, the Illinois abolitionist, declared in the House of Representatives that Americans would aid Irish rebels after the war, inspire the French Canadians to revolt, and stir up Chartist insurrection in England. Canadians were commonly accused of betraying democratic and antislavery principles, and of making their country a refuge for disaffection and a potential base for Confederate guerillas. But Seward's was a calming influence, and for more than a year Canadian-Union relations had a chance to cool.

In a bid to attract sympathy from world, and especially British, antislavery opinion, Seward won Senate approval (April 24) for a mutual-search treaty with Britain, designed to suppress the oceanic slavetrade. Agreement was reached to search one another's ships for slaves, with mixed courts to be set up at strategic points around the globe to adjudicate cases. By providing for a peacetime right of search under strictly prescribed conditions, the treaty resolved a problem that had bedevilled Anglo-American relations for half a century: how to permit the Royal Navy to destroy the slave trade on the high seas while preserving immunity for American neutral rights.[9] Lincoln had shown his determination to enforce the Union's existing laws by hanging a slave trader who broke an 1820 law providing the death penalty for transporting slaves to the United States. The departure of proslavery groups from Congress made possible the Lyons-Seward Treaty of 1862. Lincoln and Seward skillfully managed the negotiations to avoid any impression of submissiveness to the British. Lord Russell sent out the draft proposal, but Lincoln preferred that the United States

---

[9]See R. W. Van Alstyne, "The British Right of Search and the African Slave Trade," *JMH*, II (1930), 37–47; A. Taylor Milne, "The Lyons-Seward Treaty of 1862" *AHR*, XXXVIII (October, 1932), 511–525; Conway W. Henderson, "The Anglo-American Treaty of 1862 in Civil War Diplomacy" *CWH*, XV, No. 4 (December, 1969), 308–319.

should appear as originator of the treaty. Lyons and Seward collaborated to give the world just this impression, while Lyons pretended that Washington had imposed upon him an unwelcome ten year limitation. The treaty was then rushed through the Senate with minimum publicity during an executive session. Sumner and Seward exulted, Seward exclaiming: "If I have done nothing else worthy of self-congratulation, I deem this treaty worthy to have lived for." The cordial reception given the treaty in London, Paris and elsewhere possibly hastened the President's cautious progress toward the goal of Negro emancipation as a Union war aim.

Were issues such as Negro freedom capable of affecting the diplomacy of the powers? This is a difficult question, like so many other Civil War issues. In our own cynical age, it is no longer fashionable to believe that moral outrage against slavery significantly qualified the calculations of power politics. John Bigelow, writing in a different climate, thirty years after the war, believed that slavery "fatally handicapped" the rebels, was their "shirt of Nessus . . . Their success in war meant the perpetuation of slavery —that and nothing else. This in due time became apparent to the people of Europe."[10] Even James Spence's popular pro-southern tract *American Union* (1861) rejected slavery as a "gross anachronism . . . the brute force of dark ages obtruding into the midst of the nineteenth century." (And southerners put creed before calculation when they dismissed Spence in 1864 for persisting in such heresy.) Moral outrage against slavery certainly affected public sentiment in Britain, and cannot be lightly dismissed in an age when public opinion exerted unprecedented sway over English foreign policy.

On the other hand, many Englishmen believed the war to be about empire not slavery. Antislavery feeling was commonly combined with anti-Yankee, antipopulist, and racialist views. There existed widespread recognition of the deepseated complexities of the Negro problem in America, and scepticism that force could resolve them. Racial prejudice cut across the ranks of both Yankee and rebel sympathizers. Thus the novelist Thackeray opposed bondage, but felt repelled by "these strange people with retreating

---

[10]John Bigelow, "The Confederate Diplomatists and their Shirt of Nessus," *Century,* XLII (May, 1891) 113.

foreheads, with great obtruding lips and jaws;" in *The Virginians* (1857) he extolled southern culture. Edward Dicey, also a white racialist, supported the North in a widely read travel account, while contending that the Negro's very weakness required that he be granted full civil rights. Laissez-faire optimists forecast that the liberated slave, participating in a free market system, must attain higher civilization. Against this, cynics discerned that racial prejudice and economic discrimination nullified black progress in the "liberated" North. The Liberian diplomat and black nationalist, Edward Wilmot Blyden, complained to Gladstone in 1862: "Both sections of the country are negro-hating and negro-crushing— intending and doing justice to 5 millions of oppressed people among them only as they are driven to it by European sentiment."[11]

Finally, British labor suspected the axis between antislavery, free trade radicalism, and capitalism. Sermons against slavery by Bright, Cobden, and their ilk seemed miserable affectation to labor leaders, showing no compassion for the wages-slavery that enchained millions in Britain. American and British capitalists condemned the southern system primarily because it fettered the free movement of the individual as a unit within the economy. Their own industrial exploitation they justified as resting upon the free play of market forces. Although workingmen's radicalism had traditionally supported transatlantic democracy, the Civil War posed disturbing issues, particularly for the older guard of anticapitalists, regretting the passing of preindustrial corporate society, as well as for new-style socialists. The American conflict seemed a struggle between two economic systems: the archaic ruralism of the south, and the new capitalism of the North. Was not the war fought to tighten the grip of northern business over the south? Why should labor abet such a goal? Was not such a conflict an irrelevancy for international labor? The labor press asked such questions more commonly in the early war years than the myth of solidarity with northern democracy would suggest. By

---

[11]Blyden to Gladstone, June 16, 1862, B. M. AddMss., 44396, q. W. D. Jones, "Blyden, Gladstone and the Civil War," *J. Negro Hist.,* XLIX (Jan. 1964), 57–58; G. N. Ray, Thackeray: *The Age of Wisdom* (London, 1958), 216–7; E. Dicey, *Six Months in the Federal States* (London, 1863), I, 69–70.

no means all followed Karl Marx, at this time a struggling journalist in London; Marx sided with the North, urging it to make a revolutionary onslaught on the slave system, a preliminary battle for the eventual emancipation of the American proletariat.[12]

* * *

In April 1862 Baron Rothschild, although a friend of the North, warned Henry Sanford, the American minister to Brussels: "I will admit to you that European intervention may not secure a bale of cotton, but here is a whole Continent in convulsion from this cause. When your patient is desperately sick, you try desperate remedies, even to blood-letting." "We are nearly out of cotton," Thouvenel told Sanford in conversation at the *Quai d'Orsay*, "and cotton we *must have. . . .*"[13] Seward's response to Europe's looming cotton crisis has not always received the attention it deserves. He held out to the European nations the vision of getting easy cotton with the compliments of the Union, and that lure exerted an insidious sway upon European imaginations: weakening the case of the ardent blockade-busters for action, distracting the Machiavellian (like Napoleon), pleasing the peace-at-any-price school. Both Russell and Thouvenel welcomed Seward's plan of opening some ports in the blockaded South to foreign ships, Russell because it diminished opposition to his "soft" blockade policy, Thouvenel because it gave him an alternative to propose to his emperor—Napoleon was becoming obsessed with the threat of a popular revolt over cotton distress, and increasingly intent on a rash interventionist stroke.

Seward wanted a *quid pro quo* for his "open ports" offer: Britain and France should withdraw belligerent rights from the South, on grounds that they had been wrongly conceded, prolonged the war and aggravated the cotton famine. According to this oddly superficial theory, the rebellion would collapse if the powers withdrew the moral support that the recognition of belligerency conferred.

---

[12]K. Marx and F. Engels, *The Civil War in the United States* (Citadel Press, N.Y., 3rd ed., 1961); files of *Reynolds' Newspaper, Bee-Hive*; Royden Harrison, *Before the Socialists* (London, 1965), Ch. 2. Harrison claims that the newer labor aristocracy, and younger Trade Union generation collaborating with middle class radicalism for better living standards, were more pro-Federal.

[13]Sanford to Seward, April 10, 1862, q. Case and Spencer, 290.

Seward never worried overmuch about consistency of argument. He was right in sensing that a European about-face on the issue would be a propaganda coup of some magnitude for the North. But he was forced to retreat from his bargaining position when his agents abroad, including Thurlow Weed, represented the extreme unlikelihood of any reversal of policy by London or Paris. Given the swelling French clamor for cotton, Seward conceded "that we may open three or four ports safely, this with restrictions, and thus pass through this last foreign peril without the South getting much aid or France (I fear) getting much cotton."[14] The cynicism was typical.

After Farragut's capture of New Orleans, Union authorities proclaimed Beaufort, Fort Royal, and New Orleans open to all trade except contraband of war. The move hardly guaranteed cotton on southern wharves. "All this year's crop is still on the plantations where it is hard to get. Any planter who tried to sell would be exposed to the retaliation of his compatriots." So the Confederate Secretary of State informed Mercier on his visit to Richmond. But the Union gesture of opening ports indicated goodwill to Europe, and especially to depressed workingmen (a democratic point worth accentuating.) Also, the rebels got the blame if cotton failed to materialize. As it turned out, the North managed to sell some cotton overseas, but cotton exports from opened ports proved disappointing. This was partly due to the embargo and cotton burning in the South, and partly to United States customs regulations preventing payment for cotton in gold and silver. If allowed his way, Seward would have permitted foreigners to buy cotton from southerners and ship it out from New Orleans, even if they paid in specie.[15] Meanwhile he had obtained a short breathing space and, by his bluster on belligerent rights, at least distracted the attention of European statesmen from the larger issue of southern sovereignty.

Talk of cotton shortages raises the whole question of the celebrated "cotton famine." The nature of the so-called "famine,"

---

[14]Seward to Chase, April 25, 1862, q. Case and Spencer, 292.

[15]Van Deusen, *Seward,* p. 321. During the war, Lincoln permitted the licensed export of cotton from occupied territory, largely in order to reduce the foreign peril. See T. H. O'Connor, "Lincoln and the Cotton Trade," *CWH,* VII (1961), 20–35.

particularly in Britain, was very misunderstood at the time, and has been since. Only now are its true dimensions becoming clear.

In the first place, King Cotton diplomacy commonly overlooked certain facts about Britain's cotton economy. The cotton textile industry was a resilient industry, always one of the first to bounce back after cyclic depressions. The big mill owners, with relatively low overhead costs and ample opportunities for stockpiling, readily sat out hard times by retrenching their armies of operatives. Crises, moreover, caused sharp price fluctuations and thus speculative opportunities for those with wit and reserves. Nor was cotton still the lynchpin in the British economy. Heavy industries and transport had supplanted cotton as the leading industrial sector as early as the 1840's. Comparatively self-contained, cotton had limited links with other producing sectors, so that the "famine" did not generalize itself to bring down the economy. On the contrary, the war brought a windfall to other industries, to noncotton textiles, armaments, shipbuilding, and the merchant marine, while dislocation and readjustments were minimized and localized.

In the second place, Lancashire knew that cotton's abiding dilemma was not shortage of raw fibre but glut, both in supply and markets. This had happened often in cotton's history. The industry, compulsively self-improving and setting astronomic output targets, habitually ploughing back profits, now paid the price of an overproduction crisis. This crisis cannot be dismissed as a superficial and short-term phenomenon, a problem driven from the scene by the American-inspired famine. A mass of evidence suggests that the overproduction crisis was deep-seated and prolonged. It is possible to go further. Economic historians are now testing the hypothesis that the fundamental cause of the cotton upheaval of 1861–1865 was this condition of over-extension, with the Civil War making an essentially contributory (even a distorting) psychological impact.[16]

The timing of secession was palpably astray in one respect, for English factories and warehouses were stockpiled high with cotton bales in 1861: the result of a variety of factors causing optimism,

---

[16]See Eugene A. Brady, "A Reconsideration of the Lancashire 'Cotton Famine'" *Agric. H.* XXXVII, No. 4 (October, 1963), 156–162. W. O. Henderson, *Lancashire Cotton Famine, 1861–5* (Manchester, 1934) gives a more traditional account.

including confidence in the seemingly limitless expansion in world markets, joy at the Cobden-Chevalier treaty (promising a lively French market), all helped by a series of bumper crops in Dixie. The world's markets were gorged with cotton in all its forms. Everyone, observed a contemporary historian, "was looking out for buyers . . . they forced their wares upon apathetic speculators and unwilling manufacturers."[17] 1861 closed with the specter of surpluses, not scarcity, still haunting the cotton world of Lancashire. There was a sensitive indicator to this. Speculators proved reluctant to gamble on an American shortage pushing up prices for stockpiled raw cotton and finished goods.

King Cotton theory was a washout in the first year of the war, a phony threat to those in the know. Lancashire expected a quick finish to the war; and, in any case, showed deep-seated confidence that supply always matched demand. There was no problem of long-term supply. Cotton would grow prolifically in warm temperate and tropical regions. But, as the *National Review* soberly calculated, to secure an adequate supply from new sources "would be a work of time, of arrangement, of vast capital laid out with a view to future returns. We have to meet an immediate, not a prospective, deficiency. . . . What we have to do to meet the actual emergency is, not to set about growing cotton elsewhere, but to procure as large a supply as possible from quarters *where it is already* grown. We shall lack cotton in 1862, and most likely only then; and it is idle to tell us whence and how we may procure it by 1864 and 1865."[18] England needed a normal yearly requirement of around 2.3 million bales. To meet that demand cotton experts calculated that Indian (mainly "Surat") cotton—inconvenient because of its short staple but usable—could be made to supply about 1 million bales, and other sources (Egypt, Brazil, West Indies) perhaps half a million bales. As it was expected that higher prices for products would offset falling production, and given previously saturated markets, this would prove a reasonably satisfactory compromise. Prices for "Middling Orleans" cotton rose

---

[17]R. A. Arnold, *History of the Cotton Famine* (London, 1864), 44. Also John Watts, *Facts of the Cotton Famine* (London, 1866). Such writers were well aware of the over-production aspect.

[18]*National Review*, XIII (October, 1861), 452, 456.

only sluggishly, from seven pence per pound in November 1860 to nine and a half pence by October 1861. More cotton was actually reexported from Britain in 1861 than in 1860. Over 2.2 million bales landed at British ports in 1861—less than the record 2.6 million bales of 1860 but close enough to the normal yearly average. Although 1.6 million bales came from the boom American crop of 1860, India supplied almost a third of the 1861 cotton imports.

So much attention became riveted upon India as an alternative source of cotton that the French suspected a plot on the part of British imperialists to create one more world monopoly, the reason perhaps for their acquiescence in the blockade. Lancashire strove in numerous ways, short of spending much money, to encourage cotton culture in India, a diversification advocated in the past without great success. The Indian government appropriated almost 100,000 rupees by late 1861 to improve roads from the cotton hinterland in the Gujarat and Deccan to the coastal ports. Gold medals and cash prizes were offered to successful growers. Beyond this the Secretary of State for India, Sir Charles Wood, a devoted free trader, would not go. He objected to government assuming the role of capitalist, cultivator, or promoter, and feared disrupting settled Indian customs and agrarian system so soon after the Mutiny. In the outcome it was high prices rather than any program that sent Indian production soaring. Bombay, the chief outlet, boomed, and remained the world's greatest cotton-export center until the 1870's. By 1862 India was supplying over one million bales. By the war's end its annual average output amounted to 900 million pounds, a rise of 50 percent on prewar levels. India made no small contribution towards foiling southern strategy.[19]

1862 proved to be the year of crisis. By autumn the mills worked short-time, many closed down, and cotton prices spiralled to twenty pence per pound. Over 330,000 were unemployed in the industry by November, leaving only 200,000 in full employment. A massive relief campaign began, a significant factor in alleviating

---

[19]P. Harnetty, "The Imperialism of Free Trade: Lancashire, India and the Cotton Supply Question, 1861–5" *J. Brit. Stud.*, VI, No. 5 (Nov. 1966), 70–96; Frenise A. Logan, "India: Britain's Substitute for American Cotton, 1861–5," *JSH*, XXIV, No. 4 (November, 1958), 472–480.

distress and calming emotion. The distress was almost universally attributed to the disruption of supplies caused by the Civil War. Newspaper editors, cabinet ministers, backbenchers, radical orators, even economists took this view, although the latter pointed to contributory factors. From Lancashire's cotton interests and members of parliament came only a curious reticence. Richard Cobden warned Sumner in July: "I feel quite convinced that unless cotton comes in considerable quantity before the end of the year the governments of Europe will be knocking at your door."[20] Cobden's fears were well grounded. In the attempts at British intervention explored in the next chapter, a highly significant part was played by the belief, hardly questioned, that England badly needed American cotton.

Recent research now raises the fascinating possibility that such a climate of crisis rested upon an economic misapprehension. Eugene A. Brady, after calculating the actual stocks of cotton held in mills and at ports in the United Kingdom during the "famine" years, claims that there never occurred a serious physical deprivation of raw cotton. True, the volume of raw cotton imported dropped markedly in 1862 (524 million pounds compared with 1257 million pounds in 1861). This impressed contemporaries more than the fact that ample stockpiling in earlier years was providing an effective cushion against real scarcity. In fact cotton stocks in 1862 were at virtually the same level as in 1858 (1862: 183.2 million pounds; 1858: 189.9 million pounds.) The lowest ebb in reserves came in 1863 (137.7 million pounds), by which time unemployment was easing, alternative supplies yielding more materials, and the value of exports almost back to normal due to higher prices. The main effect of the Civil War, Brady says, was to induce *expectations* of a future input shortage. "These expectations resulted in a greatly increased price for raw cotton as a result of a speculative bidding up of the price of fairly ample stocks of cotton housed in factories and in warehouses of the United Kingdom, which made cotton manufacturing operations relatively unprofitable."[21] Strengthening this interpretation is the fact that every year between 1862 and 1866 Britain, far from striving to

[20]Cobden to Sumner, July 11, 1862, *AHR,* II, No. 2 (January, 1897), 307.
[21]Brady, p. 157.

conserve its supply, increased its reexports of raw cotton to countries such as France. The evidence suggests that overproduction and overfed world markets were still the fundamental problems for the industry. High prices induced by the war merely offered a further incentive, perhaps a good excuse, to impose voluntary checks upon production until markets should improve. This meant short time or unemployment for the cotton operative.

CHAPTER V

The Mediation Crisis

THE CONFEDERACY'S ABLEST SECRETARY OF STATE, JUDAH P. BENJA-
MIN, took office on March 19,1862, a timely promotion made by
his friend President Davis, just before a Congressional investigat-
ing committee censured Benjamin's performance as Secretary of
War. Benjamin had become a target for those sniping at Davis'
handling of the war, and a scapegoat for southern unpreparedness
and lack of resources—a better target because of his Jewish origins,
his tactlessness in dealing with proud southerners, his lack of
military training, and a certain sense of cynical realism which did
little to win him popular support. But his cynical realism served
him well as foreign minister. Benjamin, the man, has eluded his
biographers, as he eluded his contemporaries. Suave, controlled,
complex, he brought to the office legal skill, knowledge of Europe
and European languages, a close liaison with Davis, and a necessary understanding of *realpolitik.* Less than a month after taking
over the miniature State Department, housed in the Richmond
Customs House along the corridor from the president's harassed
staff, Benjamin proposed a "cotton bribe" that might snare a cove-
tous Napoleon. The Confederacy proposed a treaty conceding to
France the right to send its products free of duty into the south
for a defined period, in the expectation that Napoleon would
abandon "the policy hitherto pursued." Benjamin offered to make
cotton available to French ships "at certain designated points."
100,000 bales, he guessed, would cost the south $4.5 million, but
would represent to France a grant of $12.5 million at the current
price of 25 cents per pound in Europe. "Such a sum would main-

tain afloat a considerable fleet for a length of time quite sufficient to open the Atlantic and Gulf ports to the commerce of France."[1] On April 18 the Confederate Senate authorized the President to offer Britain, France, and Spain special trade privileges and other inducements to break the blockade. But for the time being Benjamin was making the offer exclusive to France, hoping to entice her from her intimate embrace with a non-interventionist England.

As it turned out, Benjamin failed to bring to bear his undoubted skills upon a rapidly evolving European situation in mid-1862 because of communication difficulties. The Union's blockading squadrons disastrously interrupted the flow of intelligence, dispatches and instructions between Richmond and its agents during the vital years 1861 through 1863. The mere half-dozen members of Benjamin's department were forced to obtain overseas news from northern newspapers and out-of-date European sources. Southern dispatches were often lost, or captured; they were published in the Union press with embarassing regularity. Before Benjamin began using fast blockade-runners based on Nassau or Bermuda from mid-1863, delays of six months were commonplace between mailing and receipt of documents.

Mason and Slidell did their best under these frustrating conditions, feeling keenly that their unofficial position in Europe was "painful and almost humiliating."[2] They were heartened by news that McClellan's offensive against Richmond, planned to demoralize the enemy and decimate the Army of North Virginia—now commanded by the redoubtable Robert E. Lee—had been repulsed in the swamps of the Chickahominy and James Rivers. Armed with Benjamin's "cotton bribe," Slidell interviewed the emperor at Vichy on July 15. Napoleon could not fail to be tempted by what the south offerred: cotton, to quelch domestic complaints, plus the prospect of forestalling the British in making the Confederacy an economic satellite of France. Slidell also pledged southern aid in destroying the Juárez regime in Mexico, which he alleged was being propped up by the Yankees; France and the Confederacy shared a common interest in setting up in Mexico "a respect-

[1]Benjamin to Slidell, April 12, 1862, q. Robert D. Meade, *Judah P. Benjamin: Confederate Statesman* (N.Y. 1943), p. 253.

[2]Slidell to Mason, June 21, 1862, q. *EDA,* I, 307.

able, responsible, and stable government." But the emperor proved cautious. Slidell spoke in glib terms of decisive French action against the blockade: it would be easily accomplished, bring an early peace, highlight England's "torturous, selfish, and time-serving policy" on the blockade, and be followed by widespread recognition of the south. But Mercier's reports warned that France could not rely on the United States backing down in any confrontation with the powers. "At the rumor alone of intervention", Seward had warned Mercier, "all the factions will reunite against you." Napoleon feared war if he attacked the blockade, or if he recognized the rebels; while mediation "would, if offered, be refused and probably in insulting terms by the North."[3]

Soon after the interview at Vichy Napoleon sent a coded telegram to Thouvenel, who was in London for an International Exhibition. It read: "Ask the English government if they don't think the time has come to recognize the South." The telegram might have changed history, had it not arrived after Thouvenel's departure for Paris. "I should have hesitated a great deal to use [it]," Thouvenel confessed to Flahault, ". . . I could not conceive how we should be in more of a hurry than England or that we should risk to take on the sole burden of a job from which she would obtain the benefit and draw down upon us all the resentment which Americans now feel toward her." Seward had maintained strong pressure on London. A note of June 20 declared intervention, or mediation favoring the south, entirely unacceptable to the United States. If undertaken, such measures would force the Union to foment a retaliatory "servile war," a slave uprising. The British and French foreign offices fended off Confederate demands for recognition in mid-July. But it was becoming clear that the fluctuating fortunes of war might soon cast all things into the melting pot.

*   *   *

The failure of McClellan's Peninsular campaign, and Lee's brilliant counteroffensives after the relief of Richmond, transformed the military situation, and seemed convincing evidence of the south's capacity to survive. The awesome and bloody grappling of the two great armies in campaigns such as the "Seven Days" (June

---

[3]Slidell to Benjamin, July 25, 1862; see Case and Spencer, 300–305.

25–July 1) caused humanitarian outcry in Britain, and appeals for peace. The Victorian mind experienced enormous difficulty in accepting that such a terrible war could be persisted in, or that modern states were capable of the unprecedented mobilization of resources that it needed. The northern people, surely, must either sue for peace, or go bankrupt. There ensued the most intense public discussion of the question of foreign intervention to be witnessed during the war. Although the Liberal government officially maintained its "hands off" policy, there appeared to be maximum public receptivity to the need for intervention of some sort. General Butler's draconic regime in captured New Orleans provided poor advertisement for the Union; his instruction that women who insulted an officer or the flag should be treated like women of the streets outraged Victorian consciences, and resulted in a most undiplomatic squabble between Palmerston and Adams. The Yankee camp in London became despondent as the tide ran against them in Virginia, and then in the European capitals.

The great debate over intervention highlighted the problems that were likely to plague any international move. As Seward had plainly shown, the north implacably opposed an armistice that should presage any diminution of the Union; any mediation plan coming out of Europe would thus need to be backed by a covert threat of force. Even Richmond seemed cool to mediation, the more ardent secessionists preferring to win independence on the field, and being wary that a reconstructionist settlement might be imposed by outsiders on the south. What was the value of a ceasefire that neither side would accept? Slidell at least kept open the option of mediation: he urged Napoleon to make an armistice initiative. This would throw the responsibility of the war's continuance on the Yankees, and their refusal to talk peace would open the road to recognition and armed intervention, either by France or the powers in combination. The north (Slidell said) must then back down, for northern policy was based on bluff and bluster. But the prospect of a real war with the United States warmed few hearts in England, or even in imperial France (more dedicated in reality to peace than to the foreign adventurism which historians have so lovingly made characteristic of the regime.) Nobody in England countenanced the sacrifice of national interests in the abstract pursuit of peace in a distant continent, and not even to get cotton for Lancashire (if that was ever practicable.) People wanted an American peace at no price. The question was whether such a bargain was on offer.

Mediation, on closer look, bristled with difficulties. What should be the basis of settlement? Were the Negroes to be freed as the price of southern independence? Was a truce to be temporary, or permanent? What would be the boundaries separating Union and Confederacy? Presumably the military situation would dictate the lines of separation, although some canvassed the use of plebiscites (popularized by Cavour during Italian unification). Walter Bagehot, no lover of the south or slavery, advised the north to settle for the *uti posidetis* before the rebels should "reconquer New Orleans, drive the Federals out of Tennessee and Missouri, obtain a secession vote in Kentucky, again defeat McClellan and again menace Washington." Many English liberals shared Bagehot's fear that the growing savagery of the Civil War threatened to extinguish the civil liberties of "the freest republic in the world." He suggested that the classic preconditions for mediation now fully existed: the north's war aim, to restore the Union, was unattainable; the war was degenerating into a barbaric war of extermination, causing untold human and economic ruin; neutrals were being injured beyond the bounds of endurance; and the military situation provided the guidelines for a peace settlement.[4]

On July 18, the Commons debated a mediation motion. That it was sponsored by the same William Lindsay, Napoleon's unofficial emissary, who had estranged Russell in April, did not help its chances of success. Lindsay bragged to Russell that a fortnight would see a majority of M.P.'s defy the whip on a motion for southern recognition, and hinted at a cabinet crisis over America. It was not an astute judgment. The opposition saw no political advantage to be won on the Civil War, which divided both sides of the house. Disraeli advised against alienating "the Manchester party" (Cobden's supporters, whom the Conservatives were trying to woo on other issues), and the Tory leadership decided to hew to a line of strict neutrality.[5] Palmerston successfully asked the house to leave a delicate matter in the hands of the executive.

---

[4] *Economist,* August 30, 1862.
[5] W. D. Jones, "British Conservatives and the Civil War," *AHR,* LVIII, 532–3.

Nevertheless the debate was an important one. It seems to have convinced Russell that "the great majority are in favor of the South," and his conversion to an interventionist stance swiftly followed.[6] The pro-southerners, Lindsay, Vane Tempest, Seymour Fitzgerald, Whiteside, and Gregory, justified separation of north and south on grounds of self-determination, humanitarianism, and English self-interest. Separation would even, they said, advance the Negro cause: in this respect, Lincoln's slowness to accept black emancipation as a Union war aim paid dividends to his enemies, who pictured slavery being retained in any reconstruction of the Union, but gently passing away in an independent South. The southern brief was helped along by growing pressure for relief of the cotton "famine." The Farnall report, work of the special commissioner for the distressed areas, revealed 80,000 operatives unemployed and 370,000 averaging half-time, and claimed that cotton stocks had fallen to under 200,000 bales. Speakers in the house, with the interesting exception of the members for Lancashire, harped ominously on the famine. Taylor, from Leicester, believed however, that workingmen saw that intervention would "produce a stain on the antislavery flag of England." He added: "Never was so tremendous an issue so easily, so lightly . . . raised." What was the point of an "armed truce" that would last only until the south felt strong enough to strike again, or the north strong enough to overwhelm the seceders? W. E. Forster's speech made a neat illustration of Manchester doctrine: intervention meant war, and the dubious benefits of war were outmatched by its economic and social costs. "We could keep the working population of Lancashire in luxury for less than the price it would cost us to interfere." Forster argued that America was being wracked by a revolution, "an entire change in the social system," provoked over the place of slavery in society. It would be immoral for the powers expediently to intervene in such a struggle without accepting any responsibility for the social outcome of their acts.

When Palmerston spoke, he displayed once more the restraint that had been a major factor in chastening the ardor of Parliament on America. Were not the two sides engaged in conflict staggering to the imagination? "The Thirty Years' War in Germany was a

---

[6]Russell to Lyons, July 19, 1862, *PRO* 30/22, 96; q. *ibid.*, 529.

joke to it in point of extent and magnitude . . . is that the moment when it can be thought that a successful offer of mediation could be made to the two parties?" The south, Palmerston stated flatly, had not yet "firmly and permanently" established its independence. He conceded "the vast importance to this country of a speedy termination of the war", but agreed with Forster that intervention would only produce "greater evils, greater sufferings" for the English workers.[7]

Despite his seventy-eight years, Palmerston rode at the height of his carefully nurtured popularity, still consummately skilled in the arts of parliamentary management and—despite rivals like Gladstone—still dominant within the ministry. His private letters show that his parliamentary performance masked his growing receptivity to the idea of an armistice initiative. Like Russell he did not fail to notice the Commons' sympathy for the rebel cause. The Civil War had been a considerable bug-bear to him. The dislocation of Atlantic trade had made commercial and shipping interests politically irritable, and cut into government revenues. The war created irreconcilable demands for ministerial economy—an obsession with Gladstone at the Exchequer—and an expanded defense program. Palmerston stoutly resisted retrenchments that would erode England's defense capabilities. In private the prime minister exhibited extreme irritation with the north during the post-*Trent* months. British ships were being hauled into New York as prizes by the Union navy "without rhyme or reason"; Britain would not submit to "the scandal and inconvenience of having Federal and Confederate squadrons watching and fighting each other" off the English coast; convoys might need to be supplied for merchantmen passing through their home waters, British ports closed to American warships, and offending Yankee captains "dealt with in a very summary manner."[8] On one occasion the prime minister confided to Russell his feeling that England would gain by the separation of north and south, one of the rare expressions of this class to be found in the private papers of government members. As his biographer cautions, such expressions reveal at worst "the jingo, not the interventionist", and stand out in sharp

---

[7] *Hansard,* 3rd Ser., CLXVIII (July 18, 1862), 522–6, 572.
[8] Extracts from Palmerston's letters early 1862; q. Bell, *Palmerston,* p. 314.

contrast "to the very cool and correct official pronouncements which were issuing simultaneously from the Foreign Office and Admiralty."[9]

As the north's military and political disarray deepened in the aftermath of the Peninsular disaster, Palmerston warmed to the idea of mediation. On July 29 Gladstone revealed to his wife that Palmerston "has come exactly to my mind about some early representations of a friendly kind to America, if we can get France *and* Russia to join."[10] By early August discreet plans had been initiated for an armistice proposal. Palmerston wrote to the Queen on August 6, just prior to Parliament's adjournment, suggesting that October would apparently be the proper time. Russell, about to accompany the bereaved Queen on a trip to the Continent, suggested a cabinet on the matter when he returned before October. He agreed that an armistice should be the first step, "but we must be prepared to answer the question on what basis are we to negotiate."[11] An answer was never satisfactorily devised.

* * *

The Union disaster at Second Bull Run in the last days of August discredited Lincoln's new general on the Virginia front, John Pope, brought about the reinstatement of the demoted McClellan, and pushed southern morale to dizzy heights. Lee invaded Maryland, threatening to isolate Washington and inflict devastating blows within Pennsylvania. Stonewall Jackson's daring exploits in support of Lee excited admiration abroad.[12] Russell, and others, believed the war was about to end. Palmerston thought the Federals "got a very complete smashing . . . even Washington or Baltimore may fall into the hands of the Confederates." By September 14, Palmerston declared himself willing to consider a Franco-British approach to the warring parties, recommending an "arrangement upon the basis of separation." Russell, still abroad, spoke of mediation "with a view to the recognition of the independence of the

---

[9]Bell, *Palmerston,* p. 315.

[10]Morley, *Gladstone* (London, 1904), II, 75.

[11]Palmerston to Queen Victoria, August 6, 1862, q. Bell, p. 327; Russell to Palmerston, August 6, 1862, q. *EDA,* II, 32.

[12]M. Charles P. Cullop, "English Reaction to Stonewall Jackson's Death", *West Virginia Hist.* XXIX (1967), 1–5.

Confederates. I agree further that, in case of failure, we ought ourselves to recognize the Southern States as an independent State."[13] As Cabinet approval was deemed necessary for such a step, a meeting was planned for October 23 or 30.

Unexpectedly, the first signs of hesitation came from France, which Russell assumed to be eagerly awaiting the call. By a stroke of luck for the north, the allies moved awkwardly out of step in the next crucial months, with Napoleon failing to exploit the only occasion during the war when the British neared voluntary involvement. Thouvenel became a source of difficulty for Russell. When sounded on the idea of an "armistice without mediation," offered by a safe number of European countries, Thouvenel hedged. He was increasingly at loggerheads with Napoleon over America, Italy and Austria, and expected to be sacked in a coming cabinet shuffle. Convinced that the French people had tired of war and adventurism, Thouvenel detected little enthusiasm for the cause of southern recognition, and advised Russell to wait for the results of the mid-term Congressional elections in America. Nor was Thouvenel optimistic, as Russell strangely seemed to be, that Russia would join the mediators. The French had themselves sounded the Russians in July on possible Anglo-French-Russian cooperation on America, and been unceremoniously rebuffed. Prince Gorchakov, the Tsar's foreign minister, made no bones of the fact that Russia favored the north and reunion. Russell discounted Thouvenel's misgivings. Thouvenel's star was waning, and Russell, no doubt confident of winning over the emperor, went ahead without formal French assurances. Privately, Thouvenel nourished little hope that the north could avoid imminent intervention by outside powers. "The undertaking of conquering the South is almost superhuman," he admitted to Dayton, nor was a democracy like the United States fitted to force millions of hostile people into subjection. Thouvenel toyed with a compromise settlement that envisaged a weak confederation of north and south, united merely for defense and foreign policy, thus providing at least token counterweight to the British in the hemisphere.

When Russell returned to England on September 22, he lost no

---

[13]Russell to Palmerston, and vice versa, Sept. 14, 1862, Russell to Palmerston Sept. 17, 1862, q. *EDA*, II, 38.

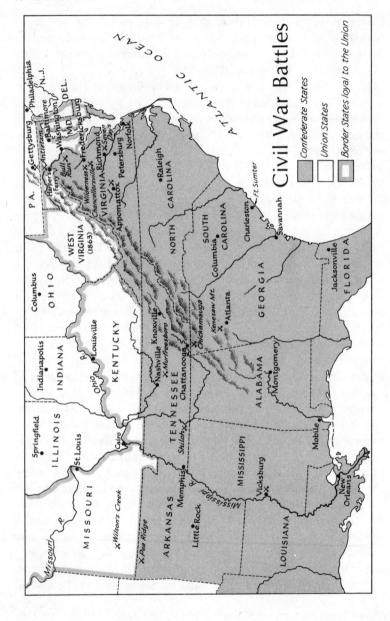

Civil War Battles

Confederate States

Union States

Border States loyal to the Union

time in thrashing out mediation possibilities with Palmerston, who by now also wanted Russia added to the mediators. Gladstone, an obvious ally in the cabinet, they kept informed, Russell describing the latest proposal to him on September 26 in the formula: "Mediation on the basis of separation and recognition accompanied by a declaration of neutrality." Gladstone apparently took this briefing too much to heart. Palmerston's version of the plan included cessation of the blockade. But Palmerston was never blind to crude realities. Throughout he accepted that the issue might well turn on the outcome of McClellan's attempt to stem Lee's offensive at South Mountain and Sharpsburg: "If the Federals sustain a great defeat, they may be at once ready for mediation, and the iron should be struck while it is hot. If, on the other hand, they should have the best of it, we may wait awhile and see what may follow...."

At the battle of Antietam, neither side inflicted a crushing victory, but the strategic advantage accrued to McClellan's army. Although he allowed Lee's battered battalions to retreat intact, "Little Mac" had stopped their apparently resistless advance into Pennsylvania. The battle of Antietam is often described as a critical turning point in the diplomatic history of the war. But it is by no means certain that a southern victory at Antietam would have produced British intervention, for events were to show a surprisingly virulent opposition in cabinet to any departure from strict neutrality. On the other hand, Palmerston, Russell, and Gladstone constituted a formidable phalanx when united on foreign affairs. The significance of the setback to southern arms that took place at Antietam was twofold: it eroded the unity of the triumverate, by making Palmerston lukewarm; and it seriously weakened the legal basis for rapid recognition of the south, a key part of Russell's original project. The plans actually considered by cabinet were thus milder than those canvassed before the battle. Antietam also evoked Lincoln's preliminary proclamation of Negro emancipation, which complicated, if it did not at first seriously divide, cabinet and public opinion.

Opposition to Russell's first mediation plan came from Lord Granville—a senior Whig-Liberal statesman—before Britain realized the full significance of Lee's enforced retreat across the Potomac after the gory battles of Antietam Creek. An ex-foreign minister, Granville expressed a "long rigmarole" of doubts concerning a "decidedly premature" move on arbitration or recognition, and even stronger doubts concerning the effect upon European stability of international intervention in America. An Anglo-American war, which seemed decidedly on the cards, would be hard to localize and could throw Europe into the melting pot. Such a war, "whether the French went with us or not," would remove English constraints from Napoleon III, who might gasconade more freely in Italy and elsewhere.[14] Granville's doubts, plus the uncertainty of the military situation, set Palmerston back-pedalling. The whole matter, he complained querelously to Russell, "is full of difficulty, and can only be cleared up by some more detailed events between the contending armies." By sustaining northern morale Antietam increased the risk of the Yankees declaring war against a potential mediator. Neither Palmerston, nor the military and Colonial Office experts, welcomed a warlike situation as winter closed in on Canada: they remembered too well the winter mobilization and trauma of the previous November, the time of the *Trent* crisis. Better, in Palmerston's view, to conduct any argument with the north in the spring of 1863 "when communication with Canada was open, and when our naval force could more easily operate upon the American coast." The prime minister had not yet entirely backed out of an immediate move: he thought that Russell's scheme might be salvaged if Britain acted in tight conjunction with other powers, a "European Confederation," or if "an absolute offer of mediation" could be watered down into "a friendly suggestion" that the time for an inevitable separation had arrived. He was even prepared to consider what he thought a very pro-northern arrangement, an armistice "not accompanied by a cessation of blockades."[15]

Russell kept tinkering with mediation plans. Their rationale is at times baffling. For one thing he never came to grips with the question of Russian participation in any intervention. By October 1, through Baron de Brunow, Russian ambassador in London,

---

[14]Granville to Russell, Sept. 27, 1862; Granville to Stanley, October 1, 1862; q. Lord Edmond Fitzmaurice, *Life of Granville, George Leveson Gower, 2nd Earl Granville* (London, 1905) I, 442–444.

[15]Palmerston to Russell, October 2, 1862, q. *EDA*, II, 43–44. For the Russian overture below, and Seward's note to Adams, August 2, 1862, *ibid.*, II, 45–46.

Russell had invited the Tsar, Alexander II, to join with England and France in offering "good services" for peace. Russian participation might pacify the north as a sign of the good intentions of the interveners. Indeed Russell seems to have regarded Russian cooperation as essential, if the Union were ever to accept mediation. Yet no one with diplomatic knowledge seriously believed that Russia would join in a patently antinorthern move. Russia's power interests demanded a strong United States as a counterweight to Britain navally; Russia was self-sufficient in cotton, and enjoyed a good image in the Union. Russell's note to the Tzar would obviously need to contain arguments highly compelling to the Russian foreign office. Instead it begged the outstanding questions. What would happen if the north proved obstinate and rejected overtures from the powers? Britain, said Russell, would recognize the Confederacy "as it seemed likely that this could be done without giving the United States a just ground of quarrel." Who could believe this? Seward had made long-standing public threats that recognition would be regarded by the north as a *casus belli*. Moreover, it is virtually certain that Russell knew unofficially the terms of a dispatch received by Adams on August 16 from Washington declaring American hostility to any form of mediation. If Britain, alone or jointly with other powers, approached Adams with any proposal "to dictate, or to mediate, or to advise, or even to solicit or persuade, you will answer that you are forbidden to debate, to hear, or in any way receive, entertain or transmit, any communication of the kind." The dispatch ordered Adams to suspend his functions immediately if Britain acknowledged southern independence. Russell was being transparently less than candid with the Russians. Perhaps he relied on northern defeatism to neutralize Seward's threats or even to overthrow the Lincoln government. Such chances, we must remember, seemed not at all far-fetched in October 1862, despite Antietam.

Gladstone rudely broke the secrecy in which Russell and Palmerston had been working when, on October 7, in one of the more inspired "leaks" of the age, he publicly proclaimed at Newcastle his faith in the imminence of southern independence. It seemed a preliminary announcement of cabinet's determination to recognize the south. In fact Gladstone acted without authority, and without knowing that Palmerston's hesitations on America had been thoroughly revived by Antietam. Gladstone had been touring Tyneside, was out of touch with London and perhaps carried away by the adulation of the vast crowds that turned out to hear the rising statesman of Liberalism. They heard him say that "Jefferson Davis and other leaders of the South have made an army; they are making, it appears, a navy; and they have made what is more than either, they have made a nation [loud cheers]." To Gladstone, the statement was one of fact, not a sign of southern partisanship. He sympathised with the American experiment in democracy, and often claimed that American unity better suited British national interests than division of the continent: a residual cluster of northern states would pose danger to Canadian security, while a cluster of slave states would covet a Latin American empire. Gladstone disliked the slave philosophy of the south and the cynical methods of secession. But he was in good company with liberals like Bagehot and Lord Acton in opposing any attempt to maintain the Union by force. Gladstone's commitment to the principle of local self-determination had been illustrated in his fight for Italian independence. Southerners, like rebellious Hungarians, or Italians, or Poles, enjoyed a right to self-government. Union nationalism, as espoused so mystically by Lincoln, carried little appeal for Gladstone, who viewed nationality as a matter of cultural, intellectual, and economic affinities. In the long run, communities based on irreconcileable differences of civilization—as north and south were divided by slavery—must move apart. The Union, Gladstone conceded, was probably too big to last, despite its sophisticated federal system.

All the ingredients of the Newcastle speech can be found earlier in Gladstone's thought. But, as the carnage mounted in Virginia, as arbitrary arrests and "Mr. Lincoln's lawless proclamations" multiplied, Gladstone deplored the war in more intense terms, as "an immense mischief, not merely to democratic but to all liberal and popular principles whatever." He perceived the monolithic tendencies of the wartime democracy, and feared that the rebellion would be suppressed only by denial of the Republic's foundation ideals.

Behind Gladstone's advocacy of southern recognition, and mediation, lay the belief, by now very common in Britain, that the

Union had reached the end of its tether. Even John Elliot Cairnes' pro-northern *Slave Power* called for a "Mississippi Compromise": independence should be granted to that tract of land east of the Mississippi and south of the border states, with Louisiana "reserved for the North and for freedom." Cairnes' verdict weighed heavily with Gladstone; as did also John Stuart Mill's judgment of southern impregnability, and Mill's appeal to preserve as free soil in any settlement the regions west of the Mississippi. Privately, Gladstone feared riot in Lancashire, and wanted mediation *before* trouble erupted, for if that happened the world would delight in accusing Britain of intervening out of stark self-interest. He called the north to drink the bitter cup, and come to the peace table.[16]

Gladstone's speech tripped off a high level controversy within the government. Palmerston and Russell only mildly reproved the Chancellor of the Exchequer: although Gladstone's statement threatened to compromise British impartiality, and poached on foreign affairs, Palmerston ran a lax ship on matters of cabinet collectivity and ministerial independence. But the speech caused a stir on the stock market (indicating the strength of interests wanting the war to continue for speculative reasons); and it alerted the pro-northerners and "do-nothings" among the ministers. The Secretary of War, Cornewall Lewis, emerged as most eager to show that Gladstone's was not the voice of cabinet. In a speech at Hereford on October 14 Lewis insisted that, until the north showed itself incapable of continuing the contest, rebel independence could be granted only in defiance of the historic criteria of international law. When Russell sent a circular to ministers on mediation, Lewis sent a countermemorandum (October 17), and more memos followed. Adams wrote prophetically in his diary: "We are now passing through the very crisis of our fate."

Russell's memorandum proposed joint pressure by Britain, France, Russia, Prussia, and Austria, to induce both parties "to agree to a suspension of arms for the purpose of weighing calmly the advantages of peace against the contingent gain of further bloodshed and the protraction of so calamitous a war." His case

---

[16]See: C. Collyer, "Gladstone and the American Civil War" *Proc. Leeds' Philosophical Soc.* VI (May, 1951), 583–594; R. L. Reid, ed., "Gladstone's 'Insincere Neutrality' during the American Civil War" *CWH,* XV, No. 4 (December, 1969), 293–307.

rested upon the assumption of military stalemate, the alienation of border states from the north, and the death of Unionism in the south. Even if defeated, the south could be held only by military subjugation and civil despotism. Ideally, Russell wanted the prizes of peace—a reopened cotton trade and lucrative southern markets —without losing northern goodwill and trade, or being sucked into a war that would threaten Britain's vulnerable shipping trade, and the loss of Canada. Not wishing to alarm his colleagues, he quietly dropped his previous threat to recognize the south if the north spurned Europe's "most friendly and conciliatory" offer.

Cornewall Lewis' counter-memo was tough-minded, and cut sharply through Russell's bland optimism to ask some awkward questions. Lewis was Gladstone's chief rival for the future Liberal leadership, but political motives do not explain their disagreement on mediation. Lewis, whose mind Bagehot once described as "complication-proof," wanted British aims clearly spelt out, and the repercussions of intervention carefully weighed. What Pandora's box might the powers not open by interference? What did Britain intend on slavery, the border states, and the territories? Was she in a position to act honest broker in such perplexing matters? Would the embattled sections listen to offers of mediation? The north appeared to be unyielding in prosecution of the war, and would surely resent as one-sided an armistice that proposed to lift its naval stranglehold over the rebels. Had Russell faced up squarely to the chance of an open break with Washington, to Canadian vulnerability, to the liklihood of an expanded defence budget? Would the British people support a war with the United States?

Lewis dwelt uncomfortably on England's legal obligations. Historic British recognition policy, he held, forbade acknowledgment of sovereignty while a *bona fide* struggle for supremacy still took place between an imperial power and insurrectionary subjects. Antietam showed that the Union had not abandoned its drive to quell rebellion. Recognition of the insurgents in such circumstances would be rightly resented by the north as a breach of neutrality and friendship. Lewis was strongly influenced by the antirecognition arguments of his brilliant young relative and barrister, William Vernon Harcourt, and the two men worked closely in harness against the "interventionists" during October and November. In a range of Civil War controversies Harcourt established a formidable reputation as an international lawyer, and also as a pamphleteer, writing under the pseudonym "Historicus." His perennial theme became the peril of intervention, and the need to defer to solemn precedents and usages between nations. The justice and equity of British practice, he pleaded, were immeasurably more important than considerations of expediency or partisanship. Britain's duty was to offer not only political but "moral" neutrality. For his part, "the principles of one party and the aims of the other seem to me alike so indefensible as to leave to the impartial spectator little room for sympathy with either."[17] Harcourt held up as models for British emulation George Washington and the great American statesmen of the era of the French revolutionary wars. They had stood out nobly against the excited passions of their people to resist intervention against the mother country.

Emancipation of the slaves bulked large in the battle of the memoranda. On September 22, Lincoln issued his preliminary edict, declaring free, as from January 1, 1863, all slaves in areas still in rebellion. According to historical tradition, Lincoln's Emancipation Proclamation marked a watershed in the international history of the Civil War by mobilizing new British support for the north from the autumn of 1862. Research has diminished the popularity of such an interpretation. Although mid-Victorians condemned slavery on moral, religious, liberal, and economic grounds, the new Darwinist biology strengthened dominant ideas of Negro racial inferiority. Britain's experience in her West Indian colonies seemed to show the ruinous social and economic effects of immediate and unplanned emancipation of the slaves. Britain's Irish experience also indicated the difficulties of imposing social change on a recalcitrant people by imperial force. Ellison's study reveals apathy and opposition to emancipation from working-class groups in Lancashire, and the persistence there of pro-southern sympathy. Such evidence deals a blow to the old view that emancipation nerved the English masses to withstand the famine, and to resist intervention in America. Joseph Hernon argues with persuasion that hindsight into the final triumph of the Unionist and

---

[17] *Letters by 'Historicus' on Some Questions of International Law, reprinted from the Times* (London, 1863), pp ix–xiii.

antislavery causes in 1865 led historians to oversimplify wartime British opinion, caused them to exaggerate the strength of support for Unionism and its antislavery program.[18] The proclamation, he says, did not effect a great change in British public opinion.

The mixed reception accorded the preliminary proclamation in Britain bears out some of these criticisms, although we need to know much more about proletarian and nonconformist opinion outside Lancashire. However, much evidence still stands to the effect that the northern image improved, especially in the long run, after Lincoln adopted a war aim more intelligible to European opinion. The repercussions of the proclamation must not be analysed out of existence. It did not cause an immediate and wholesale conversion to the Union cause, or against intervention. But it did add a new dimension to the dialectics on mediation that cannot be ignored.

For Lord John Russell, for the activists, it now became necessary to repudiate the idea that Lincoln's edict changed anything, that he had converted the war into a moral crusade. The critics could point to Lincoln's long agonizing over the decision to emancipate; his oft-stated claim that the north fought to preserve the Union, not for Negro freedom; his frank admission that emancipation was essentially a practical war measure. Russell's cabinet circular made much of the cynicism of a proclamation that freed no slaves in states that remained loyal to the Union: "The right of slavery is made the reward of loyalty; the emancipation is not granted to claims of humanity but inflicted as punishment on their owners." Russell prophesied slave uprisings, declaring that plunder and incendiarism would follow in the wake of the "liberating" Union troops. Gladstone agreed. He had said, quite early in the war, that he had "no faith in the propagation of free institutions at the point of the sword." Slavery, he pointed out, had sheltered historically beneath the power of the whole Union. In future slavery would be more exposed to the force of world opinion if the south bore its responsibility alone.

For the anti-interventionists, such arguments were largely beside the point. Lincoln's edict might be expedient, a military rather

---

[18]Mary Ellison, *Support for Secession: Lancashire and the American Civil War* (Chicago, London, 1972), Ch. 3; J. M. Hernon Jr., "British Sympathies in the American Civil War: a Reconsideration" *JSH*, XXXIII (1967), 357–9.

than a moral act, but it signalled the north's renewed martial vigor and augured ill for the prospects of any armistice. Again, was the distant hope of slavery's natural death in an independent south worth the instant establishment of a stark slave state through blatant British act and sponsorship? Could England become slavery's virtual guarantor? "To my mind," wrote "Historicus," "in the one word 'slavery' is comprehended a perpetual bar to the notion of English mediation as between the North and the South; a bar to amicable mediation, because it would be futile; to forcible intervention, because it would be immoral . . ."[19]

The Lewis-Harcourt approach turned the scales. Legally scrupulous, mirroring traditional middle-of-the-way Whiggery, their ideas chimed in with the sober pacifist desires of the "intelligent middling classes." Their misgivings about American entanglements crossed party lines. Palmerston took care to sound Lord Derby on mediation a week before the projected cabinet. The Opposition leader's reluctance probably sealed the fate of Russell's design. Derby opposed war and gestures that would only goad the north without procuring cotton. Derby, Disraeli and the ranking Conservative officers adhered to this "hands off" policy for the duration of the war. They tried to rein in the impulsive southern sympathizers on the backbench, and resisted the clamors of the warhawk Tory press. The "Tory Democracy" program—looking ahead to the widening of franchises—aimed not to alienate Manchester radicalism by a partisan stand against the northern democracy. Hence, perhaps, the opaqueness of Derby's speeches on the war. All that one Tory could make out from them "is compressed in the following summary: (1) Gloomy prophecies. (2) Impossibility of foreseeing any termination to the war & ergo to the Distress. (3) An oracular silence as to the merits of the two sides."[20]

Faced with cabinet rifts, Tory opposition, commercial uncertainty, and the retreat of Lee's mauled army to Virginia, the pragmatic Palmerston reverted to his "original view of the matter." Nor did he appear unduly worried that his old rival Russell, and

---

[19] *Letters by 'Historicus', op. cit.,* p. 49 (*Times*, November 17, 1862). Extracts from the cabinet memos are to be found in E. W. Ellsworth, "Anglo-American Affairs in October of 1862," *Lincoln Herald,* LXVI, No. 2., (1964), pp. 89–96.

[20] Lennox to Disraeli, September 23, 1862, q. W. D. Jones, "British Conservatives and the Civil War" *AHR,* LVIII, p. 533.

the troublesome Gladstone, might lose face within the cabinet. On October 22, Palmerston told Russell he was "much inclined to agree with Lewis." Asking for an armistice would court "injury to our position," and be futile as each section would stick to its war aims, and become pledged more firmly to them. "We must continue," he said, "merely to be lookers-on till the war shall have taken a more decided turn." Russell, displeased, and recognizing that "no good could come of a Cabinet," postponed the October 23 meeting. On that day, Palmerston remained at his Broadlands home; but an informal meeting of ministers listened to Russell defend his armistice idea as consistent with neutrality. However, Russell and Gladstone found themselves outnumbered by followers of the Lewis position. That afternoon Russell assured Minister Adams that the British government did not, at present, incline to change its position on neutrality. Russell added, however, that no promises could be made for the future.

The British government had drawn back from the brink, and the decision—or indecision—now appears of major Civil War significance. It appeared less so at the time. Should the Confederates again begin sweeping all before them, mediation must surely be revived. Palmerston and most of the ministry regarded the matter as closed, at least temporarily, but Gladstone and Russell proved embarrassingly reluctant to accept any deferment. Russell, piqued by Lewis's sarcasms, replied to them in a postcabinet memo that defended mediation by no less than five powers. Gladstone, in yet another memo (October 24), urged action by England, France, and Russia. The concept of using international sanctions, of applying international moral force, to preserve world peace became Gladstone's controlling ideal, later developed in his Concert of Europe philosophy. Curiously in this Gladstone agreed with the arbitrationist theory of the Manchester School, who yet conspicuously opposed mediation in the case of their favorite American democracy. Cobden's scathing denunciations of war, made during the Crimean conflict, now rebounded upon him. Gladstone wanted peace by moral force, mediation in the name of humanity, while Cobden seemed willing to accept peace dictated by Union bayonets. The fatal flaw in Gladstone's philosophy, from Cobden's standpoint, lay in his failure to discriminate between the Concert ideal and what would be the reality—gunboat diplomacy by the powers, spawned out of interest and threatening general conflagration in the western world. Ironically, people with generous and peaceful intentions have been prolific breeders of impetuous programs in international affairs.

While the British debated mediation, France, indeed all Europe, was distracted by upheaval in Italy. The Italian question lay at the heart of Napoleon's European diplomacy, and was entwined with hemispheric affairs. (Chapter 8 fits Napoleon's Mexican intrigues into the mosaic of his Austrian-Italian strategies.) The emperor's pro-Italian policy always threatened to alienate his Catholic and conservative supporters, who feared the evacuation of French troops from Rome where they protected the Papal States against the Italian nationalists. Garibaldi precipitated a crisis by marching to "liberate" Rome in August 1862. The Italian government at Turin first covertly encouraged Garibaldi, but then repudiated him, and Italian troops dispersed his volunteers at Aspromonte (August 27.) Italy plunged into political confusion, verging on civil war in the south. Obliged to appease the clerical and pro-Austrian groups who had gained strength at court, Napoleon dismissed the pro-Italian and liberal Thouvenel from the *Quai d'Orsay.* The experienced conservative diplomat, pro-Austrian Edouard Drouyn de Lhuys took Thouvenel's place. Thouvenel had obstructed Napoleon's recklessness on America not simply from personal, but from national, considerations. His successor, Drouyn de Lhuys, found himself subject to the same national pressures. He also turned out to be an advocate of strict neutrality, almost an isolationist, on America. Algeria had convinced Drouyn that France wasted her energies in colonialist adventures, when her destiny would be fulfilled or lost in the European heartland. France's abiding peril was of diplomatic isolation in Europe, hence Drouyn's support for British and Austrian alliances. Hence also his fear of estranging France's friends by acting alone, or overambitiously, in the new world. Suspicion of Napoleon's world-ranging designs already rose intolerably high over the acquisition of Nice and Savoy, French penetration of Syria, the occupation of Rome, and Mexico. Although Drouyn aligned himself politically with Empress Eugénie and the clerical party, he proved unsympathetic to the program of French involvement in Mexico that they sponsored.

How then do we explain the American mediation proposals which issued from the *Quai d'Orsay* in late 1862 and early 1863? Drouyn cannot be considered a weak minister, and he had broken with Napoleon in the past over foreign policy: we may assume that Drouyn agreed with the need to make at least a gesture for peace in America. Like most European statesmen Drouyn wanted an end to the uncertainty of the war. Even the Russians warned their northern friends of European impatience for a settlement. Drouyn and Napoleon felt driven by domestic factors to try something— especially by the need to appease emotions of outrage over unem- ployment caused by the cotton famine. The evidence suggests that Drouyn tolerated peace moves that took no serious risk of war with the United States. In the outcome France chanced little by suggesting mediation in conjunction with a safe number of other big powers, or by offering harmless suggestions for direct negoti- ations between north and south.

The Confederacy was desperately unlucky in the timing of events in October. Luck, and European turmoil, caused Britain and France to move out of step. Not until the very end of October did Napoleon respond to the British initiatives of September. By that time the abortive British cabinet meeting of October 23 had taken place, the lines of battle had been drawn within the ministry. Inertia favored the status quo. Napoleon made his own armistice proposal in notes sent to London and St. Petersburg on October 30. The emperor suggested a joint offer by the three maritime powers for a six-months truce in America on land and sea. The French wished to end the "prodigious shedding of blood" before the emancipation edict touched off servile war; they also wished to end the cotton famine that fostered a "most painful situation" for Europe's great centers of labor. Drouyn drafted the notes, and they impress as characteristically prolix. But the omissions are interesting. The notices said nothing about recognition of the rebels—and this despite the fact that in interview with Slidell at St. Cloud, shortly before, Napoleon talked of a northern refusal on mediation affording good reason for recognition, "and perhaps for more active intervention."[21] The French were studiously vague on the role to be taken by the mediating powers: they would be

---

[21]See Case and Spencer, Chapter 10; Owsley, pp. 328–336, 353–359.

nonpartisan, they would smooth the way for negotiations "which might hopefully follow" between the belligerents; they would intervene "only to the extent allowed by both parties." Finally the plan seemed super-optimistic in hoping that the north would accept the opening of southern ports. Privately, Drouyn doubted that the Russians would cooperate; and even Slidell poured cold water on a scheme that permitted France to be outnumbered by a pro-northern Russia and too-circumspect England.

The British rejected the overture, a move often interpreted as the death stroke to southern hopes of foreign intervention in the Civil War. Drouyn's note precipitated much the same division of forces within cabinet as had arisen in October. But the context had subtly changed. By thrusting himself into the foreground Napoleon roused British suspicions of his deeper designs, and stirred a chauvinistic reluctance to be led from Paris. Moreover, the news from America showed that the Democrats were doing exceptionally well in the mid-term Congressional elections, with a possibility of winning New York. The signs seemed clear of a swelling tide of disgust with Republican mismanagement of the war, with their policy of Negro emancipation, their abridgment of civil liberties and their plans for widespread conscription. Centrifugal forces were tearing apart the north. But whereas the French proposed foreign action to accelerate those disintegrating forces, and hasten a north-south accomodation, many Englishmen feared intervention would have the opposite effect. "It would be, indeed, a fearful reflection for us at a future day," warned the *Times,* "that we had by an untimely meddling defeated the efforts of the American Constitutionalists, and forced the nation once more under the power of a faction [the Republicans] which must have fallen without our aid."

Napoleon's six-month truce plan offerred embarassment for Palmerston, renewed challenge for the noninterventionists, and hope resurrected for Russell and Gladstone. Russell, however, fumbled his opportunity. The surviving records bespeak a sense of bafflement in those exposed to the Foreign Secretary's arguments, and deservedly so. Russell expected north and south to rebuff any approach from the powers; but on the use of an abortive overture he threw no light, assuming (against much evidence) that intervention would strengthen the hands of northern Peace

Democrats. He spoke vaguely of making good offices "such as would be creditable to us in Europe." This may have reflected, as Lewis guessed, a fear of displeasing France; or, perhaps, a yearning, like Napoleon's, to be seen to be doing something about the cotton famine. But Russell's vagueness raised suspicions that he wished to speed up recognition of the south (an event he predicted for next spring), or that he sponsored a program of forcible intervention. For the puzzle of slavery, which perplexed Palmerston, Russell had his solution. Negotiations would result either in restoration of the Union, when all slaves should be emancipated with compensation to owners, or in separation, when "we must be silent on the trend of slavery, as we are with regard to Spain and Brazil."

On November 7 Cornewall Lewis circulated to cabinet a twenty-five page memorandum which bore unmistakeable marks of Harcourt's forensic eloquence. In it he re-presented the objections to an intervention which would "abet southern iniquity," prove utterly unable to discover an acceptable moral foundation for solving the problems of slavery and boundaries, and which only puerile optimism expected to be short, simple or peaceable. Harcourt put much the same case in influential letters to the *Times* on November 7 and 17, later printed as tracts.[22]

The French suggestion of a suspension of arms at sea for six months constituted the real stumbling block in the plan, as far as Palmerston, most ministers, and diplomats like Lord Cowley were concerned. The *Times* presumably peddled Palmerston's opinion when it doubted that the Federal government would submit to a one-sided arrangement: "Such an armistice would undoubtedly be very convenient to the South, very convenient to England, and very convenient to France . . . But what would the North get by it? To her it would be a request to allow us to tie up her right arm."[23] The chance of the western powers "going into this matter as a European league" on such a dubious mandate seemed remote, and the chance of their preserving unity in such an adventure even

---

[22]"Historicus", "The International Doctrine of Recongnition", *Times*, November 7, 1862; "Neutrality or Intervention?". *Times*, November 17, 1862. Printed in *Letters by Historicus on some Questions of International Law* (London, 1863).

[23]*Times*, November 12, 1862.

remoter. As Lewis quipped in his memo: "A single intervening Power may possibly contrive to satisfy both the adverse parties; but five intervening Powers have first to satisfy one another."[24] European countries had, after all, fallen out among themselves in almost every instance of joint intervention since Navarino in 1827. "Historicus" forecast that dissentient sections of the mediating powers should end by ranging themselves in hostile camps side by side with the original belligerents, the outcome endangering the peace of Europe. Intervention, he concluded, was like revolution: ". . . its essence is illegality, and its justification is its success. Of all things, at once the most unjustifiable and the most impolitic is an unsuccessful Intervention."[25]

During the deliberations it became known that Russia had refused to act jointly with Britain and France. The Russians would accept a North-South rapprochement; and had in fact secretly instructed their minister at Washington, Stoeckl, that he might act in concert with the other powers if Washington were to become genuinely conciliationist. But they opposed a premature move which would discredit them with their northern friends and prejudice future peace overtures. Russell was prepared to risk acting without Russia, but he found few followers among his colleagues.

At cabinet meetings on November 11 and 12 prudence prevailed, and the French were politely informed that overtures would be best postponed until better prospects existed of their being accepted by the contending parties. Palmerston (according to Gladstone) "gave to Russell's proposal a feeble and half-hearted support," while Russell "rather turned tail" after ministers had picked his plan to pieces.[26] According to Lewis: "Everybody present threw a stone at it of greater or less size, except Gladstone, who supported it, and the Chancellor [Westbury] and Cardwell, who expressed no opinion"[27] Russell admitted, under questioning from Lewis, that there was no chance of Washington accepting the proposal, and this clinched the matter for the majority. Confeder-

---

[24]November 7 memo, q. *EDA,* II, 62.

[25]"Neutrality or Intervention?" *Times,* November 17, 1862.

[26]Gladstone to his wife, November 12, 13, 1862; q. Morley, *Gladstone* (London, 1904), II, p. 85.

[27]Lewis to Clarendon, November 13 (?), 1862; q. Maxwell, *Clarendon,* II, p. 268. Westbury belatedly came out in favor of Russell's plan.

ate independence was inevitable. Why risk war to speed the process? The *Moniteur* considered the British response not a refusal but an adjournment, and Gladstone shared the sentiment. (The Orleanist *Débats* declared it impossible "to descend lower in the depths of what may be called deliberate Machiavelism. . . .") Like Slidell, Gladstone hoped the French would act alone: "It will be clear that we concur with them, that the war should cease."[28]

Across the channel, Drouyn and Napoleon splashed their peace plan in the press. They gave the impression of acting with indecent haste to make maximum political capital out of the affair. But there occurred an unwanted effect which they did not foresee. Northern animus shifted from the British—whose mediation deliberations had been decently shrouded in secrecy—to the French. Drouyn published his October 30 note on November 13 (before he had even received an official reply from London,) and followed by publishing the British and Russian rejections on November 16. The Emperor's wooing of opinion largely succeeded. He gained credit for attempting to procure cotton, while being able to shift the blame for continuing unemployment on Britain and Russia. (Britain, forced into counter publication, blamed Russia, northern obstinacy, and the danger of Atlantic war.) But Dayton exploded indignantly, and Franco-American relations began a downward slide. Dayton learned of the French armistice plan, humiliatingly and after equivocation from Drouyn, only one day before it appeared in the *Moniteur.* He suspected a cynical plot to feather the French nest in Mexico or to silence enemies of the regime at home, and reacted with a display of patriotic temper which impressed Drouyn.[29] The American minister aptly blended a sense of aggrieved national innocence with a salutary reminder of his country's historical mission and power. It was unfeasible to ask the north to forsake its war aims, to disband armies and navies raised

---

[28]Morley, *Gladstone,* II, p. 85. I have taken the *Moniteur* and *Débats* quotes from NYH, December 5, 1862.

[29]Dayton to Seward, November 12, 1862, q. Case and Spencer, pp. 368–369. American suspicions had been raised when, on October 28, Admiral Reynaud commanding the Antilles and America station arrived at New Orleans on the frigate *La Guerriere.* The French-speaking and secessionist residents hailed the visit with delight. It coincided with the mediation note and was held in England to show French determination to intervene.

at immense national cost, just when victory was about to materialize. Europe should put up with cotton shortages. Such hardships were the common lot of every war. Spreading a large map on Drouyn's desk, he indicated the huge slave populations still held in bondage in the south. Was it worthy of the world's great nations to prevent their emancipation, now at last made possible by exercize of the presidential war power? Jabbing at Louisiana, Florida, and Texas, Dayton exclaimed that the people of the *whole* United States had either paid large sums or fought wars for those territories. The north would never "yield them up without a death struggle; France, I am sure would not!"

Slidell and his colleagues had ridden the crest of hope in early November but they were not too downcast by the British and Russian rejections. Susceptible to conspiracist theories, Slidell speculated that the British had deliberately enticed the emperor into a commitment, then snubbed him with premeditated malice. (Russell's clumsy handling of events had at least permitted such an hypothesis.) If it was true, Napoleon would go on out of pique. "If on the contrary he did not expect the acceptance of his proposition, judging from his character and antecedents, he will not be disposed to leave his work unfinished and will act alone."[30] But Louis Napoleon was not Napoleon I, and he was not willing to persist in a strong interventionist move without the security of allies. France still made available its good offices, would indeed soon offer them unilaterally, but Seward could safely ignore such anodyne interference. For his part Drouyn showed no disappointment that Britain and Russia determined to "maintain a role of absolute abstention," and he informed Mercier that France was resuming its previously passive attitude.[31]

---

[30]Slidell to Benjamin, November 29, 1862, q. Owsley, p. 358.
[31]Drouyn de Lhuys to Mercier, November 13, 1862, q. Case and Spencer, p. 369.

CHAPTER VI

Maintaining Morale

WHAT IMPACT DID THE EUROPEAN EVENTS we have recounted make within the Union? Most Americans never suspected just how close the British had come in October to meddling in American affairs. On November 3, the *New York Herald* dismissed intervention as a "dead cock in the pit." A week later even the *Richmond Examiner* appeared to concede defeat abroad, saying of Cornewall Lewis's isolationist speech at Hereford that "it extinguishes the light and closes the last prospect of European intervention in the active stages of the war: for it is England that controls the action of Europe on this question." Both sides deplored the faithlessness of their so-called friends abroad, and declared that only by mobilizing their own resources would victory be assured.

Despite the strains of war, and a growing bitterness against Britain and France, northern opinion exhibited persistent confidence in the nation's chance of avoiding foreign intervention. A number of factors underlay such confidence. Not least was faith in the capacity of Lincoln and Seward to "contain" potentially explosive problems arising out of maritime conflicts with England, or out of French aggression in Mexico. Again, Americans expected rivalry between the major powers, together with an unstable balance of power in Europe itself, to force caution upon America's envious onlookers. As Horace Greeley put it: "The greater the danger of collision among themselves, the less European Governments will feel an inclination to meddle in transatlantic strife."[1] The eastern newspapers—many of them employing well-informed European correspondents—reported near civil-war in Italy, a looming Aus-

---

[1] *NYDT,* December 12, 1862.

tro-Prussian clash, imminent insurrection in Poland against Russian tutelage, France and Russia angry at the prospect of a British candidate on the Greek throne and the eclipse of their influence in the eastern Mediterranean. The great powers seemed too vulnerable to interfere singly in the Civil War, and too distrustful of each other to combine. W. C. Bryant said contemptuously of the trans-channel powers that "neither will move without the other in an effort to end this quarrel of ours, and neither can afford to interfere. With France, as with England, it is a question of pounds, shillings and pence; and the game of forcible intervention is too costly to play at."[2]

When Bryant spoke thus of "pounds, shillings, and pence" he echoed a widespread northern conviction that the system of international economics itself, like the balance of power system, acted as a restraint upon Europe's warlike tendencies. With some irony, eastern financial and commercial interests ignored the standing reproof of their own national crisis—where war broke out although it undid the work of generations of economic consolidation—to proclaim the superior power of economics over emotion in the international arena. The "bonds which should keep the peace" were the integrating linkages that bound the British, and to lesser extent, the French economies to the North American. In the case of Britain, cited extensively in northern newspaper comment, dependence upon the United States, still Britain's most valued customer, continued to be marked: the United States took a range of manufactured goods including fine fabrics, steel, metalware, arms, liquor, and pottery, and absorbed a significant segment of British investment. Why should England risk an Anglo-American war, which must place this trade in jeopardy, by direct disruption in the short run, by economic retaliation and alienation in the longer run? War against the Union would not guarantee cotton, while its likely consequence should be to plunge into distress millions more of English workingmen, raising the specter of social anarchy. England, merely by allowing the Civil War to take its course, would in any case reap the gains of neutral profiteering and benefit from the weakening of American commercial rivalry.

---

[2] *NYEP,* November 7, 1862.

Specifically reinforcing this economic argument was the King Corn (as opposed to King Cotton) theory: the view that British dependence upon American wheat and foodstuffs constituted a powerful factor guaranteeing British neutrality. King Corn marshalled a veritable army of followers in the north; nor were their views as ridiculous or ill-balanced as historical fashion suggests. Needing to feed an expanding population, Britain had become by the late 1850's the center of a large-scale international wheat market, within which the major competitors for dominance were the United States and Russia, with Prussia and France of slightly lesser significance. American prairie wheat proved its superior competitiveness during the Civil War years. Whereas the United States furnished, on average, almost 25 percent of the U.K.'s wheat, flour, and maize imports across the 1850's, that figure rose to 44.7 percent in 1861 (22 million hundredweight), 45.3 percent in 1862 (27 million hundredweight), 37.3 percent in 1863 (15.8 million hundredweight.) In 1861 the U.S. furnished 5.4 million quarters of grain and flour imports into Britain, Russia 1.9 million, Prussia 1.5 million, France 0.4 million. The remarkable northern export performance was helped by poor harvests in Britain (causing reliance on foreign corn to rise to almost 50 percent in 1860-63), crop failures in France, bigger acreages and increased mechanization on the prairies, and the release of surpluses for export caused by the disappearance of the southern market.

The revisionist historian Louis Schmidt popularised the King Corn theory in an influential article of 1918. However, later critics, including the business historian Eli Ginzberg writing in 1936, undermined Schmidt's thesis. Their case rested on the premise that American predominance was a matter of price, not necessity; they claimed that, in the event of northern corn being withheld from Britain, grain prices would skyrocket generally, attracting sufficient supplies from alternative sources to offset American losses. Reaction to Schmidt has, one suspects, gone too far. Russia and Prussia—the main alternative suppliers because of crop failures in France—would have needed to multiply their grain exports to Britain by a factor between two and three if they were to fill the gaping hole caused by interruption to the American corn trade. Such spectacular expansion seems unlikely, particularly in view of Russia's political troubles in the Polish grainlands from 1862.

Again, should England be forced to rely on its own grain, at a time of poor harvests, supplemented only by high-priced imports from Europe, the threat of dear bread would become politically crucial. The curves of dear bread and popular disturbance ran in remarkable parallel in eighteenth and nineteenth-century Britain; and dear wheat contributed to the unpopularity of the Crimean War. Northerners, keen watchers of the trade statistics, argued that an Anglo-American war must, at the very least, produce considerable short-term dislocation to the English corn trade in the period before market readjustments took place. On the whole the King Corn argument was not pressed to extremes. English anxiety over corn was seen as only one of a mosaic of economic, social, and strategic factors making an Atlantic war politically unlikely.[3]

A final, clinching factor swayed northern opinion and seemed to make war on America unfeasible for Europe's oligarchies: the presumed attachment of Europe's common people and bourgeois liberals to the democratic United States. Had not America been the missionary center for the world's infant democratic movements ever since the Revolution? Did not despotic Europe's downtrodden subjects flock in their millions to America's hospitable shores, to her free, enlightened, civilized form of government? Had not America's enemies, in revenge, openly encouraged the diabolical scheme of secession? "Bitter comments, vile misrepresentations, scandalous lies, have been circulated throughout the whole of the European continent, with the purpose of impressing upon the people, the masses, the governed, that republics were unfeasible,

---

[3]The subject is dealt with more fully in *North, South and Powers*, pp. 268–272. See L. B. Schmidt, "The Influence of Wheat and Cotton on Anglo-American Relations during the Civil War" *Iowa J. Hist. and Politics*, XVI (July, 1918), 400–439, which is criticised by E. Ginzberg, "The Economics of British Neutrality during the American Civil War," *Agric. H.*, X (October, 1936), 147–156. Also R. H. Jones, "Long Live the King?" *Agric. H.*, XXXVII, No. 4 (October, 1963), 167–168. Schmidt's critics question whether the wheat-peace argument strongly influenced English opinion, although Cobden and other anti-interventionists used it extensively. The King Corn idea is perhaps most effectively attacked by diplomatic historians such as E. D. Adams, who deny its impact at the official decision-making level. In this respect it is worth noting that at least one cabinet minister, Milner-Gibson, president of the Board of Trade, argued nonintervention on grounds of American wheat and foodstuffs. (Speech at Ashton, January, 1863, NYT, February 9, 1863.)

... that freedom was but a name." But the people were not convinced, "the masses judge our present struggle correctly."[4] Any attempt by their rulers to provoke war with the Union would provoke social crisis and class warfare.

Americans found unbearable the thought that overseas populaces and genuine progressives might desert the chosen people. Where the people of Europe appeared lukewarm, they must be still in chains, their opinions manipulated or suppressed by the governing classes. Hence the eagerness, not without pathos, with which the northern press seized upon the slightest evidence of Federal sympathies among those outside the centers of European power and prestige. By vigorous mythologizing, such signs were turned into significant peace and Unionist movements. Pro-northerners such as Cobden and Bright, John Stuart Mill, John Elliott Cairnes, and W. E. Forster in Britain, Count de Gasparin and Edouard Laboulaye in France, assumed the stature of hero figures in the Union, while their writings on the war were widely reprinted and dispersed. Again, the setting-up of an American relief fund for Lancashire's distressed cotton workers made a homely and unofficial gesture of brotherhood from the American to the British people. The American International Relief Committee launched a highly successful appeal in December, 1862, while the owners of the vessel *George Griswold* offered free carriage for a cargo of grain and food to go to Liverpool.[5] Stuffed with pork, flour, and wheat, loaded free by New York stevedores and skippered without pay, it sailed on January 9, 1863, America's answer to the *Alabama.*

Viewed from a wider historical perspective, the great European debate on the issues of the Civil War and the question of intervention excited a profound psychological influence in the United States. The nearest parallel in recent history may be found in the hostile reaction outside America to the Vietnam war of the 1960's. From foreign nations an avalanche of words preached the Civil War's futility and the impregnability of the South. The damage to northern morale, coming at a time of military reversals following

---

[4] *NYH,* October 20, 1862.
[5] D. Maynard, "Civil War 'Care': Mission of the George Griswold," *N. Eng. Q.,* XXXIV (September 1961), 291–309.

the Seven Days carnage, has never been adequately assessed. A fund of bitterness built up against the powers, and left a potent legacy. Cynically, Americans came to accept that the Anglo-French-American world would remain at peace only if the stark considerations of power politics, economic and political interest recommended peace. Reliance could no longer be placed on tradition, sentiment, cultural affinities, or "the crimson thread of kinship."

* * *

The building of Confederate vessels of war in Britain precipitated enormous resentment in the north over England's "pseudoneutrality." The escape of the raider *Alabama* from British jurisdiction in July 1862 started a ruckus which was not to end until the Geneva arbitration of 1872. The facts of the *Alabama* case are now well-known.[6] Working against considerable odds—poor communications with Richmond, money shortages, no official representation in London—the south's chief naval agent in Europe, James D. Bulloch, skillfully brought to fruition the first stage of Mallory's ambitious naval program for the Confederacy. Deprived of dockyard facilities at home, the south would commission the building abroad of a small but superior fleet of swift propeller-driven cruisers. Heavily armed for their size, fast enough to elude capture by more ponderous Union warships, the raiders would frighten Yankee shipping from the high seas, weakening enemy morale. The cost of imports to the north would soar, as American trade was driven to neutral flags. Backed by the south's fiscal agents, the Liverpool firm Fraser-Trenholm, Bulloch in mid-1861 arranged the construction in Merseyside docks of two gunboats, to become the *Florida* and *Alabama*. The *Florida*, 191 feet, screw-propelled, three-masted, sailed out of Liverpool without armaments on March 22, 1862. The British government refused to act, holding that the building of an unarmed ship did not violate existing

---

[6]The following account is indebted to Frank J. Merli, *Great Britain and the Confederate Navy* (Indiana University Press, 1970); Douglas H. Maynard, "Plotting the Escape of the *Alabama*," JSH, XX, No. 2 (May, 1954), pp. 197–209, and "Union Efforts to Prevent the Escape of the *Alabama*," MVHR, XLI (June, 1954), pp. 41–60; Rupert C. Jarvis, "The *Alabama* and the Law," *Historic Soc. Lancs. and Cheshire Trans.*, III (1959), pp. 181–198.

neutrality laws. Nor had Adams' agents and spies, under the energetic control of Consul Dudley in Liverpool, been able to unearth usable evidence of Confederate ownership of the ship. The *Florida* steamed to Nassau in the Bahamas where her armament was completed. British inaction was a triumph, at this stage, for a more traditional legal interpretation of the Foreign Enlistment Act of 1819 (soon to be associated with the "strict construction" of the statute).[7] The act forebade the "equipping, furnishing, fitting out, or arming" in British territory of any vessel with the intent that such vessel should be used to commit hostilities against any state with which Britain was at peace. Lawyers who harked back to the original intention of the act claimed that it had not meant to prohibit the right of neutrals supplying contraband in the form of ships to belligerents. The veto on arming, equipping etc., was designed to prevent armed vessels waging war immediately they had cleared port, thus transforming neutral territory into a base of military operations. On this view it was unexceptionable to build unarmed ships (akin to ordinary contraband), and it was open to a belligerent buying such a ship to fit it for war outside British jurisdiction. Bulloch acted on such legal advice. No comparable case had, however, been brought under the act, and more stringent views of neutral obligations existed—not least among Foreign Office advisers apprehensive about Britain's naval interests in a future war. When Adams redoubled his efforts to prevent the escape of Bulloch's second, more powerful, cruiser—Number 290 in John Laird and Company's Birkenhead shipyards, 220 feet, capable of over twelve knots from twin engines—Russell found himself in a perplexing situation.

After construction delays, the 290 was launched on May 15, 1862, given engine trials on June 12, and seemed likely to clear Liverpool in mid-July. Adams on June 23 asked Russell to stop the projected expedition; he offered circumstantial evidence, obtained by Dudley's spies, indicating that the 290 was constructed as a vessel of war and was being built for the South. The Crown Law Officers advised an investigation to test the truth of the allegations, and favored the vessel's detention if the charges were corroborated. At the same time the Board of Customs advised against

---

[7]The legal tangle is discussed more fully below, Chapter 7.

unwarranted detention, claiming that customs surveillance of the 290 had failed to uncover evidence to justify a prosecution. There is little doubt, given the weakness of the American evidence and the verdict in the *Alexandra* case a year later, that a test case against Lairds would have failed. Russell accepted the customs view: the onus of proving violation of the act was put upon American agents. On July 21 Dudley submitted sworn depositions to the collector of customs at Liverpool and demanded the 290's arrest. (One affidavit alleged that an attempt had been made to enlist a seaman in the Confederate service aboard the 290. Had this charge been sustained, the ship could have been detained only so long as the fine of £50 per recruitment remained unpaid!) The collector requested an urgent ruling from the Board of Customs "as the ship appears to be ready for sea." Two days later the northerners learned that the Board had rejected their request for seizure. Pressure upon the Foreign Office seemed more likely to succeed. From Robert P. Collier, Q.C. and Judge Advocate of the Admiralty, Adams obtained an acrid opinion against the immobility of the customs, and sent it to Russell's department with the most recent documentation of "contraventions" of the act. Collier warned that the *Alabama*'s escape would give the Federal government serious grounds for remonstrance. Treasury, in charge of customs, had already suggested the wisdom of a legal opinion from the Crown Law Officers. On July 23 Russell ordered an urgent decision by the officers. So far, as Douglas Maynard comments, the speed at which the American documents had been processed set an enviable record for any bureaucracy. A Union success was blocked by two things: the Board of Customs stubbornly adhered to its original stand; while the Queen's Advocate, Sir John Harding, was incapacitated by mental illness from dealing with the documents which had been delivered to his care. The papers were not retrieved from Harding's desk until July 28. Meeting hurriedly that evening, the Solicitor-General and Attorney-General recommended immediate seizure of the ship. They advised against a "narrow construction" of the act which would "give impunity to open and flagrant violations of its provisions." The *Alabama*, however, fled to sea the next morning, ostensibly on trials, leaving without armaments, "not as much as a signal gun or musket." Official procrastination, later criticized at the Geneva arbitration, prevented the Treasury telegram ordering seizure from reaching the Liverpool collector until July 31, or other officials who might yet have detained the *Alabama* on the British or Irish coast until it was too late. Eluding Union naval pursuit, the *Alabama* made its way to the Azores, where it was armed according to Bulloch's carefully matured plans. Under Captain Raphael Semmes, it began a two year career of havoc to Union commerce.

The escape, and news of the building of sister raiders to the *Alabama* in shipyards at Liverpool and Birkenhead, stirred a hornet's nest in America. Seaboard interests grew progressively alarmed at the damage inflicted upon northern shipping by the "privateers." Such perils attracted high insurance rates to American vessels and goods, and caused a flight of trade to neutral flags. To the northern mind, the activities of Lairds, Thompsons and other British shipbuilders exceeded the legitimate commercial proceedings of neutrals. Although Americans had been notoriously ardent in the cause of neutral profiteering in other people's wars, they viewed in a new dimension the stakes at issue in the present controversy. Britain (and later France) seemed verging dangerously near to war by remote control, intervention without the drawbacks of actual war. This view, despite its exaggerations, embraced a more modern concept of neutrality which made allowance for developing war technology, impossible under the antiquated terms of England's Foreign Enlistment Act. From all sides remedies were urged upon the government: intensify the Union navy's striking power, equip special raider-hunters, tighten the blockade (one effect would be to stop the exodus of cotton bales used by Bulloch to pay for his cruisers), use strong diplomacy in London. Seward, who had threatened to issue letters of marque to American privateers in mid-1862, sympathized with moves to have an enabling bill on the matter introduced in Congress. British shipping would be the obvious target. To this threat of reprisal, which made due impact in England (even in Liverpool, where maritime interests were starting to chafe at the damage caused by raiders to neutral property on belligerent ships), was added a clamor for reparations against the British for war losses caused by the *Alabama* and her cohorts. The clamor intensified with each sinking, and hardly ceased for a decade. Reparations might not be a practical proposition in 1862; but as Bennett said darkly they could be filed away, "to be brought to light and urged with the whole power of the nation as soon as we have put down the rebels and restored the republic to all its former greatness." Who should be surprised then if, in retaliation for England's villainous treachery "in our time of tribulation," Canada was seized and held "until full and satisfactory retribution be made . . . ?"[8]

*   *   *

In the dying weeks of 1862 Seward barely survived a cabinet crisis precipitated by a Radical Republican caucus, including followers of Treasurer Salmon Chase. Dissatisfied with the prosecution of the war, and with Seward's conservatism on the issue of Negro emancipation, the radical caucus attacked Seward's ascendancy over Lincoln. Charles Sumner was one of the critics. Although still chairman of the Senate Foreign Relations Committee, Sumner now openly disparaged Seward's diplomacy. Seward's approach appeared to Sumner to be unprincipled, while his policies neglected to exploit world antislavery opinion. During the cabinet crisis Sumner did little to dispel rumors that he would be Seward's successor in the near future.

Seward celebrated his reprieve by spurning a French attempt at unilateral mediation, made early in the new year. The French proposed that north and south sit down and negotiate an end to the war. The negotiations might take place during hostilities, thus overcoming northern objections that an armistice would be used by Davis and Lee to reorganize their forces. It was a surprisingly mild proposal to come from the supposedly aggressive Napoleon III. The Emperor wanted to avoid embroilment with the Yankees when the January uprising in Warsaw promised to create a European upheaval; at the same time it was domestically wise for him to pose as a peacemaker. French unemployment caused by the Civil War was not in fact massive—at the height of the economic crisis, in late 1862 and early 1863, it amounted to little more than 220,000, localized in Lille, Roubaix, Tourcoing, Rouen, Bordeaux, Aix and Besancon. But the opposition press magnified the distress, making it politically significant. Napoleon once again performed the trick of publicly splashing an official dispatch before it reached

---

[8]*NYH,* October 19, 1862.

the recipients, making maximum propaganda for his good intentions.

Whether Napoleon or Drouyn expected any real effect from their mediation move is a moot point. Slidell opposed the whole idea as impractical, but King Leopold of Belgium and important southern sympathizers within the official elite wanted action. The north seemed trapped in a military quagmire, outgeneralled by Lee, demoralized by defeats such as Fredericksburg, politically divided over the conduct of the war, the need for conscription, arbitrary arrests, and Negro emancipation. Greenbacks depreciated, high prices for gold and railroad stocks on the New York market were interpreted abroad as symptoms of failing union credit, the result of a deluge of paper money issuing from the Treasury. Minister Mercier believed that France might exploit Copperhead peace sentiment, and catalyse a northern reaction against the war. Mercier interpreted as a "definitive" change in public opinion the swing to the Democrats in the mid-term elections—they won New York and Pennsylvania, and moved within challenging distance of the Republicans in Congress. However, Mercier's advice that Napoleon should try a "conciliatory act" before the new, less warlike, Congress met, badly misguaged American sensibilities. Even the Copperhead press opposed foreign meddling. Mercier underestimated one vital fact: conflict in the north over the war took place within a closed system; and the fiercest of political disagreements were nevertheless over ways and means of achieving essentially American ecopolitical aims, or "destiny." French, or any outside, intrusion risked almost certain rejection because it flowed from alien, and probably competitive values.

Congress showed no inclination to censure Seward when he gave a polite but unyielding negative to the French note. Direct "conversations" between commissioners of north and south could obviously precede a truce at any ripe time—indeed Congress provided a natural forum for the reconvening of the whole country's representatives and discussions on a national peace. French interposition appeared superfluous, and only likely to aggravate the forebodings of Americans concerning French designs in Mexico: "They do not like to see His Majesty's hand always in their business," Dayton observed, accurately enough. Seward used the chance to play from strength, because of Napoleon's European embarrassments and signs of a widening rift in the Anglo-French accord. Mercier did his cause no help by indiscreet attempts to drum up political and press support for mediation; his intrigues with Horace Greeley and the adventurer William Cornell Jewett had nettled Seward before the arrival of the French note.[9] Seward reiterated the Union's determination not to treat with armed insurrection in order to diminish national authority. His reply offered no hope to Paris: the war was winnable, and was being won; political contention within the north was a sign, not of defeatism, but of democratic health; nobody was in favor of "foreign intervention, of mediation, or arbitration, or of compromise with the relinquishment of one acre of national domain, or the surrender of even one constitutional franchise."

Amidst the frustrations of the war, northerners relieved their aggressive emotions by venting them against the overseas powers. They longed for the time when "with treason crushed at home, we may be free from this half-patronizing, half impudent tone of European Powers toward us, and may again, as of old, go on in our own course of development. . . ." Many an editorial labored the theme that American expansion, interrupted by the war, would resume at its close, and American power would then stretch to its natural limits in the hemisphere. "Those who take advantage of our present troubles to intrude will some day reap the whirlwind they are surely sowing," warned the *New York Herald.*[10] The war merely drove underground the idea of American imperial mission, or diverted it into new channels. The expansionist idea was a muted idea among those who believed that the national wrong of slavery must be expunged before the energies of the American people could attain truly unfettered expansion. But to regard this stance as characteristic of the northern majority would be rash. Many of the opponents of abolitionism at heart condemned the sectional war as a basically unnecessary interruption to America's

---

[9]Mercier became associated with an unofficial mediation scheme independently sponsored by Greeley, and Jewett, who became almost a professional "peace monger" in the latter war years. The intricacies of the episode, which bore no direct relation to the official French move of January 9, are unravelled in Warren F. Spencer, "The Jewett-Greeley Affair: a Private Scheme for French Mediation in the American Civil War," *New York History,* V, No. 51 (1970), pp. 238–267.

[10]See *NYH* November 30, December 3, 26, 1862.

destined fate. Seward had been sympathetic to this view; and the whole idea of the "foreign war panacea," whether in his hands or others, predicated a return to a style of national politics based on a unanimity of purpose and direction. Such energies and ideals now became diverted into the campaign to subdue the rebellion. When that task should be completed, no new foundation need be laid for the erection of a postwar empire.

CHAPTER VII

Neutrality on Trial: The War at Sea

THE INTERNATIONAL FATE OF THE CONFEDERACY was by no means an irretrievably lost cause in 1863. Richmond's shipbuilding operations in Britain promised both to create a southern navy and to trip off an Anglo-northern war; while the Union navy raised almost unbearable tension between London and Washington by its vigorous repression of blockade-running. Nevertheless, Confederate diplomatic success ultimately depended upon two factors. The first was transformation of the war itself, either by decisive southern field victories or by growth of a massive peace movement in the north. The second requirement was maintenance of a stable power equilibrium in Europe, necessary to provide a secure base of operations for any interventionist project. 1863 fulfilled neither condition. In the first regard, Lee's magnificent triumph at Chancellorsville in May was more than counterbalanced in July by the strategically decisive Union victories at Vicksburg in the west and Gettysburg in the east. Nor did the Copperhead peace movement assume the giant proportions needed to convince Europe of the imminent collapse of the Union war effort. Instead the northern army grew massively, even under blundering generals, while the gallantry of rebel arms and the skill of rebel commanders threatened only to prolong an awesome conflict.

In the second regard, often forgotten, Europe erupted spectacularly into crisis over Poland, and then Schleswig-Holstein. The Poles proclaimed their long-awaited insurrection against Russian misrule in Warsaw in the new year of 1863, after Russian attempts to conscript troublesome radicals. The European ramifications of the Polish situation were serious enough, threatening general war and destruction of the existing power balance. A policy of nonentanglement in America seemed the elementary course for Britain and France to pursue if they were to have free hands for European action. Even within a purely European theater, the western powers found it exceedingly difficult to concert their policies in the face of mutual distrust and diverging interests. But the global dimensions of the upheavals of 1863 provided an added background to European diplomacy, and brought the American hemisphere again into consideration. In March, Russell warned Lyons that Poland could lead to "great consequences," such as a Russo-American agreement or a new balance of power in the world at large.[1] Bungling European policy might bring together the beleagured collossi of east and west, allowing them to achieve the primacy on the world stage to which their resources entitled them. This might take place during the war, or after it. Prophecies that Russia and the United States would become world super-powers, dividing the globe into two great spheres of influence, are commonly found in the early and mid- nineteenth century. Alexis de Tocqueville had made such a prediction in his renowned *Democracy in America;* so had Perry McDonough Collins in his *Voyage Down the Amoor* (1860), which compared the Russian drive to the Pacific across Siberia with American continental expansion. James Gordon Bennett's *New York Herald* put the speculation in crude power and race terms in November 1862 (a time when northerners were grateful to Russia for rejecting Napoleon's armistice overture). It is, in many respects, a remarkable statement:

In the Eastern hemisphere the destiny of Russia is to absorb all the minor states around her, and she is every day making rapid progress in that policy. She will soon be, if she is not already, the great Power of Europe and Asia. In the Western World the United States is destined to play the same part. One of these governments is an absolute despotism; the other is a representative democracy. But both are suited for the regions and the races where they prevail. Both are philosophical, and will fulfil their destiny without coming into collision or competition with the other. Not so the milk and water governments that stand between them. . . .[2]

---

[1]Russell to Lyons March 7, 1863, q. J. Kutolowski "The Effect of the Polish Insurrection of 1863 on American Civil War Diplomacy," *Historian,* XXVII, No. 4 (1965), 565.

[2]*NYH,* November 27, 1862. For the views of Collins, Matthew F. Maury, Seward and others on American destiny, and the role of rival powers for world supremacy, see Charles Vevier, "American Continentalism: An Idea of Expansion, 1845–1910," *AHR,* LXV, No. 2 (January, 1960), 328–329.

For Charles Francis Adams in London, the Polish complication offered a welcome respite for the north. It allowed a "favorable interlude" for the growth of northern military power "needed to protect us from the possibility of European intervention."[3] The British cabinet had become passive on America, Russell admitting to Lyons, on February 14, "I see no use in talking of good offices" until north and south were heartily sick of tearing each other apart. Rising support in England for Lincoln's Emancipation Proclamation possibly played some part in cooling off the mediationist fevers of the previous year; but Polish preoccupations assumed more importance. In particular Napoleon's European machinations raised trepidation in England, achieving Seward's aim of rifting apart London and Paris, the north's insurance policy.

Warsaw erupted just as Napoleon awaited Washington's reaction to his offer of unilateral mediation. The riots cooled any ardor he may have had for persisting in a course of action that proved to be repugnant to the Lincoln government. Against France's best interests the emperor meddled in the Polish question. He risked losing Russian friendship, creating a self-defeating instability in Europe, quarrelling with Britain, and limiting his autonomy of action in North America and Mexico. But he hoped to conciliate French liberals and Catholics, united, for once, in sympathy for the Poles; and to make territorial gains for France out of any revision of boundaries emerging from events. When Bismarck offered to help Russia by quelling disorder on Poland's German frontier, Napoleon saw an opportunity to redraw France's Rhenish border at Prussian expense. He proposed an Anglo-French remonstrance against Prussia. Suspicious of Napoleonic ambitions, Britain refused. However, in March Britain agreed to concert with France and Austria in remonstrating with Russia over its policy of coercion in Poland. By covert threat of intervention, the western powers hoped to convert the Russian Tsar, Alexander II, back to a program of constitutional reform in Poland. At the same time, Napoleon's partners intended to restrain him from any impulsive moves leading to a European war. The reluctance of Britain and Austria to act effectively with France ultimately destroyed Napo-

---

[3] Adams to Seward, February 26, 1863, q. Kutolowski, p. 563; also Russell to Lyons, February 14, 1863, q. *EDA,* II, 155.

leon's attempts to promote an international settlement in Poland. Napoleon harvested from events the enmity of his Russian ally, the estrangement of the British, and the disenchantment of French opinion. While the Poles won only fair words from the west, and were duly crushed by the Tsar's army, the real beneficiaries turned out to be the Prussians and the Yankees.

Richmond might reasonably have expected to benefit from world sympathy for the Polish insurrectionary movement, which had parallels with the south's national struggle. Instead, another lesson became clear: that popular sympathy for small suppressed nations (like the Poles, Danes, and Confederates) was a minor factor in international politics; the powers would interfere in such affairs only if overwhelming considerations of national interest led them to do so. Britain, unequipped militarily to intervene effectively on the European mainland, emerged with diminished prestige from the Polish, and then the Danish, crises of 1863, clinging to the policy of nonintervention. The Second Empire, formerly so formidable, now betrayed increasing signs of ineptness, unpredictability, and a slide into diplomatic isolation. These were discouraging portents for Jefferson Davis and Benjamin.

In the south itself anger mounted against European powers which offered the Confederacy no skerrick of official recognition, whose neutrality in practice favored the north, and which recognized the obnoxious blockade. Benjamin regarded the British posture on the blockade—in particular Russell's "evident danger" thesis[4]—as a contravention of the 1856 Declaration of Paris (to which the south was now a signator), and favoring belligerent over neutral rights. In 1862 he requested an explanation from Britain, but was ignored by Whitehall, behavior he thought "discourteous and even unfriendly." Mason's protests on the subject got the same cold reception from Russell, who refused to grant the Virginian an interview. Only one thing prevented Benjamin withdrawing the London mission, he told Mason in October, 1862: rebel confidence that a distinction must be drawn between the ministry and the British people. (Northern officials often made the same distinction.) President Davis' new year message to the Confederate Congress berated Europe for accepting a paper blockade, which Davis

---

[4]See above, Chapter 4.

compared unfavorably with the Berlin and Milan decrees and orders-in-council of the Napoleonic wars. Jefferson Davis had a legalistic cast of mind (as anyone who reads his *Rise and Fall of the Confederate Government,* 1881, will agree); and his indignation at Britain's defiance of the strict terms of the Paris treaty of 1856 was genuine. In a starchy note to Russell on January 3, 1863, Mason hinted at a stormy withdrawal from his post. Russell wrote Mason a soothing reply: he knew that an open breach ought to be avoided if Britain wanted an open door into a finally independent Confederacy. But Mason won little except civility, for Russell stubbornly refused to waver from the stand taken by the ministry since February 1862. British passivity on the blockade, steadily improving in efficiency, ensured French passivity. Napoleon was not willing to give direct aid to either the Poles or the Confederates without the British. Together they might impose peaceful change; alone Napoleon dared take no risks.

Confederate hopes in England thus became pinned on a changed situation: on the pressure of the cotton famine, a breakthrough by Lee and his army, or a change of government at Westminster. Cotton unemployment, however, eased during 1863 and was cushioned by a massive relief program; alternative sources of cotton supply, especially Indian, yielded more tonnage; and the value of British cotton exports reverted almost to normal due to higher prices. A success by Lee seemed distinctly on the cards in early 1863: Union generals such as Hooker inspired little respect abroad, and the rout of Hooker's army by Lee at Chancellorsville in May fulfilled the predictions commonly being made during the winter and spring. On the other hand, the apparent unbeatability of the rebels also encouraged a "do nothing" outlook. Why interfere when rebel vigor would soon, and of itself, ensure a peace settlement?

Mason's hopes for a Tory takeover in Parliament underestimated the strength of Palmerston's political resources. The ministry maintained itself in office in 1863, although Poland and Schleswig-Holstein made it a difficult year. In any case, the instincts of the Conservative leadership were for a bipartisan agreement on the continuation of neutrality, and a policy of restraint on America. Lord Derby prescribed the party line in February: " . . . regretting as I do to differ from any of my friends, I confess I cannot bring myself to the conclusion that the time has arrived at which it is either wise, politic, or even legitimate, to recognize the South."[5]

Such cautious sentiments prevailed even in the House of Lords, where southern support rode high. On March 23 Lord Campbell spoke persuasively, urging the aptness of the season for recognition of the rebels. He made play of the fact that the capitalists of London, Frankfurt, Paris, and Amsterdam seemed in no doubt of southern viability. Only four days earlier a loan floated by the south through the French banking house of Erlanger had been offered on the London and continental money markets. In two days it was oversubscribed three times in London, and by the time of the debate the bonds had rocketed from Erlanger's guaranteed price of 77 to over 90. The members of the House of Lords could not know that within weeks the speculative bubble would burst: cotton bonds fell below par and Confederate "bulling" became necessary to sustain the market and southern political credit.[6]

Although Campbell's motion failed, he raised some unsettling prospects. Should England fail to secure southern friendship while it was still available, it could end the war friendless in the North American continent. The present policy of not giving umbrage to the United States provided poor security for Canada in the event of northern victory in the Civil War: "As if aggressive Powers had ever been restrained, by wanting pretexts, from the wars they were inclined to." The north might attack Canada in the drunkenness of pride, if victorious, and in the bitterness of failure, if defeated. A policy of drift courted the creation of separated powers in North America, both irrevocably hostile to England. "We may be forced, now to guard Canada from one, now the West Indies from the other." England should choose the lesser evil, an alliance now between Britain and the Confederates. Canada would then be safer from the aggressive Yankee state, which "will then have to contemplate the chance of an attack upon his rear as well

---

[5]See W. D. Jones, "British Conservatives and the Civil War," AHR, LVIII, 534–535.

[6]The hope of gaining political leverage for the south within Bonapartist circles also underlay the Erlanger project. Although the Erlanger loan did not go as planned, and has had a bad press from historians, it elicited vitally needed funds for use in Europe in 1863–4 in the face of great difficulties. See J. F. Gentry, "A Confederate Success in Europe: The Erlanger Loan," JSH, XXXVI, No. 2 (May, 1970), 157–188.

as the bombardment of his cities and destruction of his commerce." Campbell asked which was the rosier prospect: Britain installed as paramount influence in the new Confederacy? Or the reappearance of an expansive United States? Having crushed the south, "a power more rapacious, more unprincipled, more arrogant, more selfish and encroaching, would arise than has ever yet ... multiplied the fears, and compromised the general tranquility of Europe."[7]

It was the acute problem of being a neutral in the midst of the north-south naval war that seemed most likely to drag a reluctant England into the Civil War morass. Friction between Britain and the United States arose over two major issues: Confederate efforts to purchase a modern naval striking force from British shipbuilders; and the Union navy's interference with neutral shipping, arising out of its efforts to police the blockade. Ignoring the complexities of the legal issues at stake, patriotic opinion on both sides of the Atlantic became highly inflamed, and there was in 1863 much loose talk of an Anglo-American war.

In the British parliament on March 27 Lord Palmerston defended his government against the charge that it acted unneutrally in permitting the escape of the *Alabama.* The *Alabama,* he said, could not be seized because it sailed from England unarmed and received arms, equipment, and crew in a foreign port. This view dovetailed with the legal advice on which Bulloch, the architect of the south's shipbuilding program, acted: namely, that it was legal to arm and equip a ship within British ports, provided it was not intended for use against a state at peace with Britain; that it was legal to build a ship ("unequipped" for war) within Her Majesty's dominions, the intent of building being irrelevant; that it was legal to arm and equip such a ship outside British jurisdiction. We know now that the ministry sought political safety by taking refuge in a narrowly legalistic view of the Foreign Enlistment Act, against the advice of its Foreign Office lawyers and the instincts of the Admiralty. The law officers had urged detention of the *Alabama* in 1862, on grounds that it was constructed as a vessel of war. Although it carried no arms within British waters, the lawyers believed that evidence on its structure could be used to establish that the ship

---

[7] *Hansard,* 3rd ser. v. 169, Lords (March 23, 1863), pp. 1714–1734.

had been "equipped, furnished, fitted out, or armed" within the meaning of the act. Although they had no real proof of Confederate ownership, they intended to call witnesses who would make it "reasonably clear" that the 290 was about to cruise for the south. Now having failed to detain the 290 in time, the ministry declared municipal law inadequate to justify seizure.

The government's political strategy may have included a desire not to appear to be buckling under to pressure by pro-northerners. In the winter and spring of 1863 a remarkable spate of public meetings took place throughout Britain, sponsored by Union and Emancipation Societies and radical friends of the United States. The most striking of these mass meetings, held on March 26, at St. James' Hall, London, made a show of reconciliation between the middle-class Cobdenite radicals and London trade unions. E. S. Beesly, the Positivist intellectual, emphasized the need for class solidarity between British and northern labor; all reformers should recognize as one the causes of Northern Democracy, Emancipation, and Franchise Reform in England.[8] The meetings called for an end to slanted neutrality, or any more *Alabamas.*

The shadow of future "violations" of British neutrality on a mammoth scale lay across the whole dialogue. British shipyards were secretly building a number of vessels destined for the south. They included two warships with iron piercers designed for blockade-breaking—the famous "Laird rams" begun in Lairds yard at Birkenhead in July 1862, scheduled for delivery in March and April 1863, and costing the Confederacy almost £94,000 each. There was also a 3000 ton armored frigate (larger than the rams) building at the Clyde yards of James and George Thompson, contracted for in May 1862 but not launched until February 1864. (This was the "Number 61" built for Lieutenant James H. North, costing £180,000 and later sold to the Danes as the *Danmark.*) Thompsons were also building, for Lieutenant George T. Sinclair of the Confederate navy, a raider modeled on the *Alabama,* but more powerful; part wood, part iron, combination sail and steam, eight-inch guns. Contracted for in October 1862 at a price of over

---

[8]Royden Harrison, *Before the Socialists* (London, 1965), 64–77. Adams felt there was a swing of working and middle class opinion toward the Union from late 1862; he sent to Seward numerous letters and petitions, and resolutions of pro-Federal meetings. Federal funds undoubtedly greased some of these operations, but rebel attempts to compete fell very flat. *Foreign Relations,* 1863, Vol. 1.

£46,000, this vessel (secretly the *Texas*, christened the *Canton*, later *Pampero*) ran behind schedule in April 1863, and fears of seizure led Sinclair to investigate the possibility of transferring the ship to technical French ownership.[9]

British customs officials received orders to report all suspicious naval construction. More assiduous were the efforts of northern agents and hired detectives employed by Union consular officials, by far the most skillful and indefatigable being the Liverpool consul Thomas H. Dudley.[10] Dudley disagreed violently with British insistence that the burden of proof lay upon the prosecution in the case of unneutral shipbuilding. He urged publicly that charges made by responsible American officials should elicit an investigation by the British authorities, who alone had access to shipyards, contracts, and papers. In a hostile Liverpool community, Dudley amassed staggering evidence of southern activity; affidavits were taken from shipyard workers, sailors, turncoat southerners, anybody who could testify to the warlike equipment of vessels, or their Confederate connections. Adams funnelled the information to Russell, and pressed for British action. The Bostonian businessman, John Murray Forbes, on a secret mission to England in early 1863, considered Dudley's work vital: it would, he thought, be worth £50,000 to stop the Laird rams, for, if they sailed, war might result, and this would "cost 2000 millions."[11] On his return Forbes successfully recommended to Lincoln and

[9]See D. H. Maynard, "The Confederacy's Super *'Alabama'*," CWH, V (1959), 82; Frank J. Merli, *Great Britain and the Confederate Navy* (Indiana U.P., 1970); W. D. Jones, *The Confederate Rams at Birkenhead* (Tuscaloosa, 1961).

[10]Brainerd Dyer, "Thomas H. Dudley" CWH, I, No. 4 (Dec. 1955), 401–413; and Thomas H. Dudley "Three Critical Periods in our Relations with England during the Late War: Personal Recollections. . . ." *Penn. Mag. Hist. & Biog.*, XVII (1893), 34–54.

[11]Dyer, "Dudley," p. 407. The Forbes-Aspinwall mission was sent to Britain to purchase ships to prevent them from coming into the possession of Confederate agents. An open move along such lines would have placed north and south on the same footing. Seward heard rumors that the British government would have rejoiced to see the north enter the market for ironclads, thus getting London "off the hook" on the question of damages over the *Alabama's* depredations. See: D. H. Maynard, "The Forbes-Aspinwall Mission," MVHR, XLV, No. 1 (June, 1958), pp. 67–89. Unable to purchase raiders in the British market, Forbes and Aspinwall poured money into the northern espionage system in England, and strove for the cause of Atlantic peace by making valuable contacts with parliamentary leaders and influential business interests.

Seward that Dudley's grant of £2000 per year for espionage service be greatly increased.

Bulloch's naval program was threatened with complete disruption when on April 5 British customs seized at Liverpool the 120 ton *Alexandra,* a newly built wooden screw steamer, secretly destined for Confederate service. The seizure—the beginning of many —represented a retreat from the British government's parliamentary stand over the *Alabama,* and a victory for the more flexible interpretation of the Foreign Act embraced by the Foreign Office. Despite its earlier protestations, the ministry now acted on what looked suspiciously like "suspicion of intent" to cruise on belligerent service instead of proof; and it had a case not markedly stronger than that which existed against the *Alabama.* Why the change of heart? It is possible to contend that, nervous at the *Alabama* damages bill being remorselessly calculated across the Atlantic, and concerned to forestall a diplomatic confrontation with the United States, the government preferred to sanction a harsher stand against southern shipbuilding by court decision, rather than to make a politically risky appeal for a tightening of the statute.[12] Clearly, Russell and other ministers were anxious to resolve a worrisome issue, and to abate the nuisance of raider building. American pressure was important—but not decisive—in hardening this resolve. Yankee threats created backlash, and would have been more impressive had Union military fortunes been more glowing. Gladstone believed that, precisely because their cause was lost, "the Americans of the North seem to have a strong claim of honor upon us for the vigilant execution of the law."[13]

Britain's long-term naval interests favored stricter controls over raider-building. This factor may have been decisive. The Admiralty disliked and feared the *Alabama* precedent, an example likely to rebound against the Royal Navy in future wars. England's predominance in seapower might be upset unless neutral nations— and especially the United States—were restrained by international rules from supplying lethal modern raiders to Britain's foes. Such

---

[12]See Merli, Chapter 8.
[13]Gladstone to Russell, April 27, 1863, PRO 30/22–33; q. Jones, p. 56. For the Geneva Arbitration sequel, see Jarvis, pp. 194–198.

danger rose proportionately for Britain as swift improvements took place in naval technology: England's massive lead in conventional warships would be rendered worthless if rivals without great maritime resources could simply buy their way across the "battleship gap" of the future, purchasing vessels with formidable armor and fire-power. In the short run, such naval logic led the British to squash Confederate operations. In the long run, it led even further. After a Royal Commission, the British Parliament in 1870 passed legislation designed to prohibit even the building of ships for use by belligerent powers. Then, during the famous Washington Treaty negotiations of 1871, Britain agreed to arbitrate the *Alabama* reparation claims on the basis of a completely new code of rules—containing severe sanctions against commerce-raiding—instead of by reference to the 1819 law that applied during the alleged violations. Inevitably, this cost the United Kingdom the case, and over $15 million dollars in damages, awarded in the Geneva Arbitration of 1872. As the price of conciliating the United States, and protecting British naval interests, it was a bargain.

The seizure of the *Alexandra* precipitated a celebrated trial in London's Court of Exchequer. Its outcome kept wide open the shipbuilding controversy. Public opposition was spirited to the crown's prosecution of the ship under the 1819 act. The opposition sprang from a variety of motives, from conviction that the south was getting a raw deal, from *laissez faire* approval of free trade in ships, greed for neutral profits, and resentment at high-handed government action that seemed to warp the law "to suit the temper of a foreign minister." The sanctimoniousness of the Yankees on the issue was, to say the least, indecorous when northern agents were recruiting for the Union army in Ireland, and when the north was massively importing arms and strategic stores from Britain. Why, men asked, were ships exempt from the grisly trade of war? Britain's neutrality regulations concerning prizes and access to neutral ports already in practice favored the north. But when the south tried to redress the naval imbalance that lay at the root of such a situation, Britain threatened to slam the door on neutral trade in ships. The United States, moreover, appeared inconsistent. American law in the past, for example during the Crimean War, permitted the sale of ships, which might arm in the manner of the

Alabama, regardless of destination. The north itself in July 1861 applied to Lairds to build a completely armed ship for the Union. Nor would the Lincoln government change its laws on the subject in tandem with Britain.

Sir Hugh Cairns, a brilliant courtroom performer, appeared as defense counsel, while the crown's case was led by the Solicitor-General, Roundell Palmer, in unfamiliar trial role. Minister Adams and the prosecution collaborated closely, and a northern observer, William M. Evarts, was permitted to scrutinize the preparation of the case. The crown alleged that the *Alexandra's* warlike structure provided sufficient proof of its hostile character and intent. With three-inch teak bulwarks, facilities for a crew of two hundred, hatchways and hammock racks suitable to a small class man-of-war, the steamer was clearly convertible to a raider. The defense claimed it was built as a yacht, but also held that it was "perfectly competent for any person to build a ship easily convertible into a ship-of-war, and sell that ship to any belligerent power." The object of the act of 1819, according to Cairns, was very circumscribed; arming and equipping within port was proscribed simply "to prevent the ports of this country from becoming arsenals, out of which expeditions might issue." Even had the crown been able to establish that the ship was armed according to the act, it had no clear proof that the vessel was being built for the CSA. In a dramatic move, the crown produced the ex-paymaster of the *Alabama,* who had pawned information to Adams and Dudley. But he was unable to show much beyond a connection between Bulloch and the firm of Frazer, Trenholm and Co., well-known financiers to the south and allegedly "mixed up with" the building of the *Alexandra.* A strong presumption existed that Confederates implicated in the escape of the *Alabama* were supervising the *Alexandra's* construction. But as the *Alabama* case had never been adjudicated, and as legal ownership of the *Alexandra* was indisputably vested in a British firm, the prosecution's case lapsed badly.

The presiding judge, the octogenarian Tory Sir Frederick Pollock, declared that ships constituted a legitimate part of that trade in munitions expressly permitted neutrals by American jurists. The object of the act was not to protect belligerents, but to maintain peace within Her Majesty's dominions. (In the first judicial pronouncement to be made on the *Alabama,* his lordship stated his opinion that, if the *Alabama* had cleared from Liverpool without arms, and was armed outside British jurisdiction, then the act was not violated.) Provided builders avoided immediate equippage in British waters, they might legally fulfill a contract to build a ship, "leaving those who bought it to make what use they thought fit of it." The ship's structure, it followed, was irrelevant. In 1911 Brooks Adams, son of Charles Francis, portrayed Pollock as a sinister figure, and interpreted his charge to the jury as part and parcel of the British aristocracy's conspiracy against northern democracy.[14] The prosaic reality was that Pollock's rulings merely declared the legal orthodoxy of the time. The jury's verdict for the defendants met with wild court-room applause. Adams forecast the decimation of northern commerce by hosts of British-built raiders. But the case became snarled in legal complications as the crown attempted to appeal to the Exchequer Chamber over the objections of the judge. The case continued unresolved until early 1864, when the *Alexandra* was finally released.

Meanwhile, the naval war had produced an accumulating series of incidents involving Union interference with the British flag at sea. London and Liverpool flourished as bases from which British shippers, in close collaboration with southern purchasing agents and merchants, traded contraband for cotton. Supplies useful to the Confederacy were off-loaded from merchantmen at neutral ports off the American coast—chiefly British Nassau in the Bahamas and St. George's in Bermuda, Danish St. Thomas, and Spanish Havana—whence blockade-runners attempted the perilous last leg of the voyage to rebel territory. Neutral Matamoros, in Mexico near the mouth of the Rio Grande, became a thriving center of munitions trade with Brownsville, just across the river in Texas. Vessels sailed from Europe to Matamoros, confident that they were legally immune from Union harassment. The passage of goods to Confederate territory was then completed by a safe land transit from Mexico. (Map 5).

The Union navy struck at the indirect trade with the south by

---

[14]Brooks Adams, "The Seizure of the Laird Rams," MHSP, XLV (December, 1911), 270–287. For the trial proceedings, Westminster June 22, 1863, see *U.S. House Executive Documents,* 38 Congress, 1st session, *CDS,* CDS, 1180 (1863), "Seizure of the Ship Alexandra."

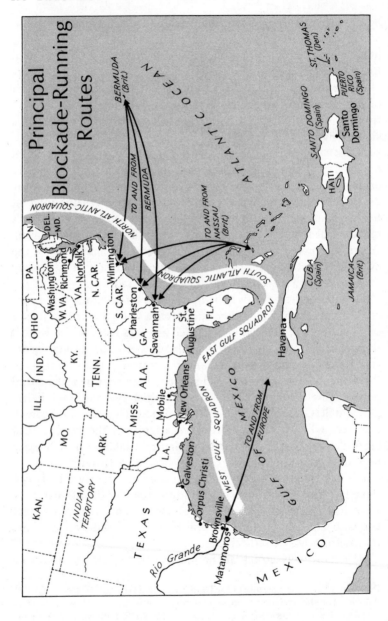

Principal Blockade-Running Routes

harassing the big merchant ships on their primary cruise to neutral ports. To make matters more galling for the British, the north justified such action by British precedents, and entrusted the task of sealing off sealanes to that same Charles Wilkes who had violated the *Trent*. Wilkes obtained charge of the American West Indian station in the summer of 1862. Now a rear-admiral, Wilkes had his warships hover off—virtually blockading—Nassau and St. George's and intercepting suspicious vessels. In a similar way the British navy had lain off New York and Boston during the Napoleonic wars, and seized vessels entering and leaving, but without claiming the practice as a right. Secretary of Navy Welles now emulated that example, winking at the practice, but apologizing, when obliged, for blatant departures from modern usage. British shippers yelped that arbitrary seizure was being made of vessels whose names appeared on Union blacklists, lists drawn up by Adams and his consuls naming ships suspected of trading with the south. The close surveillance of British colonial harbors, and their use by Union ships as bases of operations and coaling stations, created numerous incidents and encroachments on neutral rights, and turned the colonists into philo-Confederates. Welles had ordered his squadron not to "chase, fire upon, board, or seize" vessels within the three-mile limit marking off neutral territorial waters; but reckless officers sometimes observed the command in the breach. A heated quarrel arose between Spain and the United States when the U.S.S. *Montgomery* pursued the *Blanche* (which had been running the blockade from Texas to Havana under British ensign) into Cuban waters and took possession of her.[15] Although the steamer was beached by her captain on the Spanish shore, she was boarded by an armed crew of Americans who allegedly insulted a protesting Spanish official and destroyed the ship by fire. An American disavowal of the act averted a serious breach between Madrid and Washington. The *Montgomery's* captain was dismissed from the navy on Lincoln's insistence, and Consul Shufeldt was replaced at Havana, but neither Britain nor

---

[15]Bernath, p. 100 and following. The incident occurred on October 7, 1862. The *Blanche* was actually an American warship taken by the rebels and illegally transferred to British ownership, a fact which weakened seriously the British claim for damages.

Spain received compensation for damages. On another occasion (May 30, 1863) a Union cruiser landed shells upon Eleuthera Island in the Bahamas in an attempt to disable a Confederate steamer it had forced ashore there. A Union navy court ruled that the guns had been fired from international waters, but this hardly satisfied the English press: "If at Eleuthera, why not at the Isle of Wight, in Southampton Water?" enquired one editor.[16]

The noisiest *fracas* built up in the spring of 1863 over the *Peterhoff* case. On February 25 a Union cruiser captured the screw-propelled British-owned *Peterhoff* five miles off St. Thomas in the Caribbean on suspicion of carrying contraband, despite being headed towards the neutral port of Matamoros in Mexico. A war scare ensued "second only to that which resulted from the *Trent* affair."[17] The stock market shook, marine insurance rates spiralled, and merchantmen demanded convoy escort in the West Indies. Public hysteria declined when details of the ship's cargo became public, but the gut anger over Yankee arrogance at sea persisted. A generation of Englishmen bred on free trade ideas found itself out of accord with the "belligerent pretensions" practiced by England itself against the seagoing commerce of other nations in an earlier era. With exquisite irony, Washington now employed those claims against British neutral trade with the Confederacy. Opinion at large appeared less ready than the governors at Whitehall to grasp the consoling fact that the Americans were surrendering historic doctrine on neutral rights, and that Britain stood well placed to take shrewd advantage of the change.

The *Peterhoff* case illustrated the medley of forces at work. It also showed how motives of enlightened self-interest recommended governmental restraint on both sides of the Atlantic. In order to stop trade threatening the Union's entire war effort—the neutral trade to the West Indies and Mexico—Lincoln's navy was forced to capture merchantmen according to the doctrine of continuous voyage (or ultimate destination). It was a doctrine entrenched in decisions of British prize courts, directed classically against Ameri-

---

[16] *Army & Navy Gazette,* July 6, 1863; q. Bernath, p. 114.

[17] Bernath, *Squall Across the Atlantic,* p. 67; generally Chapter 8. Also F. L. Owsley "America & the Freedom of the Seas, 1861–5" in A. Craven ed., *Essays in Honor of William E. Dodd* ... (Chicago, 1935), pp. 203 ff.

can neutral trade in past wars; and had been fiercely disputed by American jurists and opinion. It had matured as a device to counter the ingenuity of American traders during Britain's war with Napoleon. British orders-in-council of the 1790's restricted a booming American trade between the French West Indies and metropolitan France. Merchants tried circumvention by landing cargoes from the French colonies in the United States, paying duty upon them, and re-exporting them as American goods. British courts ruled (as in the 1805 *Essex* case) that such voyages were not "broken" (i.e., constituting a bona fide importation into America) but were "continuous": the intent of the transaction being to complete an illicit trade to an ultimate destination in a belligerent port. The essential principle developed that voyages between neutral ports must be *bona fide:* expedients designed to conceal a cargo's ultimately hostile destination were illegal. Thus for a ship to touch at a neutral port (usually its ostensible destination) before running into a blockaded port (its real destination) did not exempt the ship from seizure and condemnation by a prize court. Nor did the device of transmitting cargo to hostile places via a succession of voyages in separate vessels. During the Civil War British ships such as the *Bermuda, Stephen Hart,* and *Springbok* were seized under this rule, which clearly forbade the trans-shipment of goods from big ships to blockade-runners at Nassau and nearby ports. That such ports were adjacent to the southern coast, and could themselves hardly pose as genuine markets for munitions, was strong incentive for closely scrutinizing neutral trading in the area. Inevitably, neutral sensibilities were offended by strict application of the doctrine. Naval captains, and later prize courts, had to decide upon difficult questions: of intent to run a blockade, true destination, ownership of cargo, and whether cargo could be classed under a variety of types of contraband. As ships' papers were commonly destroyed on capture, or were falsified, and because ingenious methods were used to conceal irregularities, American courts admitted circumstantial evidence to sustain captures. English merchants claimed that the north was deliberately driving British trade away from the Caribbean—probably with a motive of supplanting Britain's position in the islands' economy—and was exploiting the delays of prize litigation as a war measure.

The *Peterhoff* capture introduced an extension of the theory of continuous voyage. That vessel carried a cargo of artillery harnesses, army boots and blankets, quinine and chloroform—subsequently classed by an American court as contraband when intended for Confederate use. The ship was to anchor in neutral waters off the mouth of the Rio Grande, and lighter its cargo up river to Matamoros. The United States government contended that an ultimate destination for the cargo could be established in Brownsville, in belligerent Texas. The New York district court accepted, in July 1863, that a voyage became illicit if completed by *overland* route to a hostile destination. The cargo and ship were thus forfeit. (This precedent was cited by Britain in World War I to justify closing off wartime trade with Germany through ports in Holland and Scandinavia.) The court was outdoing even British doctrine. An 1801 ruling of the British court of Admiralty recognized the legality of neutral trade to or from the blockaded country by inland transportation. After the Civil War, the American Supreme Court, presided over by Salmon Chase, held that carriage of the *Peterhoff's* cargo inland from Matamoros to Brownsville did not render the ship itself liable for violation of blockade.[18] Treaty arrangements between Mexico and the United States guaranteed free navigation on the Rio Grande. Although Union cruisers had tried a *de facto* blockade of the mouth of the river, and harassed trade with Matamoros in a variety of ways, Matamoros was legally unblockaded. Chase held that overland transit to Texas did not breach any blockade, and he released the ship. The cargo, however, he condemned according to continuous voyage, as destined for rebel use.

As in the shipbuilding controversy, considerations of future naval interests strongly influenced the Admiralty and Foreign Office. The British government made representations on behalf of the *Peterhoff's* owners—as it consistently supported merchant interests believed to be *bona fide* victims of Union aggression—but accepted the district court decision with equanimity. Admiral Milne's North American squadron continued to respect orders not to interfere with Union seizures of British ships, except in territorial waters. For his part Secretary Welles renewed his general order that

---

[18]Details of a complex case in Bernath, Chapters 4 & 5.

officers conform to international usages in search and seizure. Despite British pressure, Seward generally followed the policy of referring cases such as the *Peterhoff* to the prize courts, foreswearing government interference in questions of claims and compensation. The restoration of British mail captured on the *Peterhoff* constituted a significant exception to this practice. Welles and Seward quarrelled over the matter. Welles (and also Sumner) wanted sealed packages of letters which had been taken from the ship's mailbag opened, as they might contain evidence against the *Peterhoff,* and opposed any knuckling-under to London. Seward ordered the mail kept inviolate in line with an agreement he had made with Britain in 1862, a pact to which Welles was not a party.[19] Seward urged release of the mails to reduce the war risk with England, and to safeguard America's future requirements as a neutral. In a celebrated arbitration between his ministers, Lincoln ordered the mails forwarded and forbade future belligerent interference with neutral mails.

A parliamentary debate on the prize cases took place at Westminister as Lincoln settled this affair. Adams, for once imprudent, had pulled a hornet's nest upon his head by granting a note of immunity to northern merchants wanting to ship arms to Matamoros to aid the Juáristas. He fulminated therein upon "the multitude of fradulent and dishonest enterprises" being financed by Englishmen to Mexico. This leaked to the press. Adams was excoriated in Parliament for setting up to license foreign trade. The *Quai d'Orsay* protested at Adams' concurrence in an intervention project in Mexico, a violation of American neutrality. Whitehall added its support. Seward offered regrets to the French, and disclaimed to Lyons any wish to interfere with lawful British trade. His apology, the release of the *Peterhoff* mails, and the transfer of the abrasive Wilkes from the West Indies station, did much to abate exasperation abroad.

The Confederacy's last formal attempt to win the British Commons to official recognition of its legal rights and its revolutionary success—the Roebuck intervention—has been described as a fiasco and an anticlimax. And so it proved. But at the outset it

---

[19]Van Deusen, *Seward,* p. 351.

seemed to promise much, and with reason. J. A. Roebuck's intrigues with Napoleon III were founded upon the Emperor's very real readiness to join England in a peace move which would elicit cotton, and secure his flank in Mexico. If that could be achieved before north and south splintered themselves entirely into fragments, thus depriving him of possible future counterweights against England, so much the better. The United States regarded the whole affair—drenched in publicity—as perhaps the most menacing of the war, and threatened a break with France over it. Nor could the British government regard lightly the political perils of seeming once again to demonstrate spinelessness towards the Yankees. Public anger over the *Alexandra* and *Peterhoff* cases placed the ministry on the defensive.

When Roebuck gave notice of a motion on recognition in May, Palmerston's minions sought to kill the idea and put out rumors that Louis Napoleon no longer favored joint intervention. Such at least was the story going the London rounds. In order to scotch it Roebuck and Lindsay journeyed to obtain reassurance from Napoleon himself at Fontainebleau on June 22. They left the interview convinced they had obtained what they wanted, that is, an affirmation of French willingness to move in conjunction with England on recognition, and authorization from Napoleon to deny any contrary rumor in parliament. They understood that the French ambassador in London, Baron Gros, was instructed to straighten the record and to sound out the Palmerston government on a joint move. Duplication of official and amateur diplomacy led to endless complications. Napoleon's first inclination (expressed to Slidell) was to make a direct and formal proposition of joint intervention to the British. This would have been the simplest and most effective strategy. Napoleon's cabinet, however, feared another rebuff from London, an unendurable wound to French pride. The legacy of Anglo-French distrust engendered by Mexico and Poland was now having its effect. Russell was thought capable of betraying the French by passing on a direct proposition to Washington. The United States might retaliate with a punitive stroke in Mexico and Napoleon would be dragged unwillingly into a war of England's deliberate making.

Napoleon indiscreetly conveyed these fears to Roebuck and Lindsay, charging that England had previously leaked an interven-

tion proposal of his to Seward.[20] With incredible artlessness Roebuck repeated the charge in the Commons. Napoleon was
chagrined at betrayal of a confidence, and the Commons erupted
in chauvinistic dudgeon against the French. Members of the house
thought it odious enough that Roebuck should present himself as
Napoleon's "courier" to parliament. But his credit collapsed entirely when, contrary to his confident assertion, it appeared that
no French communication on joint intervention had been sent to
London. Russell, then Layard and Grey, denied having received
any written or verbal indication from Napoleon showing a wish
to join England in intervention. Moreover, they added, Baron Gros
had made a point of calling on Russell, stating that he had no
orders on the subject. There seemed two possibilities to the thun-
derstruck southern lobby: they had been double-crossed by Napoleon (on intelligence from Paris they soon rejected this) or by the
British government.

Roebuck, it turns out, was the victim of his own impetuousity,
contingency, and a touch of Foreign Office casuistry.[21] Napoleon
had in fact acted. He told Drouyn that he wanted Palmerston
unofficially informed "that I am resolved on recognizing the independence of the Southern Provinces." This was strong, if unofficial, and exceeded the French cabinet's position: ministers were
against making an initiative, insisting that France should only
follow a British lead. However Drouyn, approving the cabinet's
caution, watered down Gros' orders to: "See Lord Palmerston and
in the course of conversation give him to understand that the
Emperor has no objection to recognize the independence of the
South." Gros, understandably, read no sense of urgency into this
injunction. Unable to see Palmerston, who was ill, Gros did not
interview Russell until June 30—the day of the debate on Roebuck's motion—and then on the subject of Poland. As Gros ex-

---

[20]This at least was the Lindsay-Roebuck version of the interview. If Napoleon
referred to the only formal proposal acknowledged by the British, the armistice
plan of October 30, 1862, his complaint has no force; the plan was openly printed
in the *Moniteur* before the British had even formally replied, and it was conveyed
to Seward by Mercier, not Lyons.

[21]Much ink has been spilled on the mystery of the Roebuck affair, and it is still
not completely solved. For a detailed study, Owsley, Chapter 13. Case and Spencer
add valuable material from the French archives.

plained to his superior: " . . . it is very likely that I incidentally said to him that having no official communication to make to him on this subject of the recognition of the Southern States, I was personally persuaded that the Emperor was disposed to recognize them." Gros was angry at the gloss placed on this exchange by Russell in parliament. If it was exceedingly informal, Gros' approach was "very likely" not quite nonexistent, and certainly not a direct rebuttal of Roebuck's claim. Moreover Russell already had intelligence from his minister Cowley indicating that Gros had received orders remarkably similar to those described by Roebuck. As Owsley observed, the French should have known "the old British custom of denying the existence of all unofficial, informal communications to or from the British Foreign Office. A thing did not exist unless it went on record. . . ."[22]

Inevitably, Roebuck's motion flopped. He did his cause no help by an almost paranoid attack on the ministry and a racially "mongrelised" northern democracy. The American Colossus he described as the "great bully of the world": "I am determined to do all I can to prevent the reconstruction of the Union, and I hope that the balance of power on the American continent will, in future, prevent any one State from tyrannizing over the world as the Republic did." England should intervene and "London will be the Imperial city of the world." Roebuck's hysteria awoke little response in parliament. The pro-southern Lord Montagu reluctantly compiled a long list of objections to recognizing the south. Recognition and neutrality were in practice incompatible while a contest still raged for supremacy between the factions. Why should England respond to what was really a cry for alliance against the north? War against kinsmen would be unpopular, mean heavy taxes, and loss of English lives; and would be difficult to wage at a distance of three thousand miles with English shipping vulnerable to American privateers and Canada an easy prey. War would also cut off a major supplier of grain. Recognition, without war, would earn undying northern resentment, and not gain a bale of cotton. In any case, after Chancellorsville, the rebels appeared poised for victory, and arms would decide—as foreign intervention never could—the points at issue between north and south.

[22]Owsley, p. 462.

By now Gladstone too had come to reject England's capacity for impartial intervention: "The very facts of our enormous interests in the American Continent, make us, as it were, a party in the struggle. . . ." So was France disqualified, even more decidedly because of its engagement in Mexico. The overriding theme of the June debate is a fatalistic acceptance of the fact that the war had acquired such a destructive momentum that outsiders—whether motivated by humane outrage at its pointlessness and waste of life, or by realpolitik—were powerless to end it.[23] If the south prevailed it must be by way of manly self-reliance and historical inevitability. If England was the key, and England would not move, this spelt the end of Confederate diplomacy.

Slidell, long prophesying England's unreliability, showed no surprise at Roebuck's failure. Slidell's project now was to free France from the English embrace, and push it into a continental league pursuing concerted policies on America. Considering that Napoleon had failed to create a similar league to act on the closer problem of Poland, the plan suffered obvious difficulties. A Franco-Spanish axis seemed a possibility. The Serrano government, which had been building up the Spanish navy, saw advantages in confirming southern independence. An entente between Spain and the infant CSA would provide protection for Spain's slave colonies in the Caribbean. But Madrid hesitated to act without powerful European friends; otherwise it risked the loss of luscious Cuba to a resurrected United States. Slidell's efforts to cajole Spain into intervening with Napoleon, but without England, were interrupted by the fall of Serrano's regime. Napoleon must have doubted whether the combined naval resources of Spain and France would be enough to deter the north from war. There was no certainty that even the deterrent of the British navy provided sufficient insurance for an allied intervention. Most of all, Napoleon had no intention of getting entangled in an American war, putting his Mexican venture in deadly jeopardy, while England sat on the sidelines. That would be playing Palmerston's game. Better to allow events their head in America, keep nominal friendship with both sides, while hoping for southern success. In the latter circumstance Maximilian's kingdom might yet be kept intact.

[23]*Hansard,* 3rd ser., v. 171 (June 30, 1863), pp. 1771–1842.

The Roebuck fiasco brought about just what Napoleon had been at pains to avoid, publicity to his interventionist desires and a first class row with the United States; and all without gaining any American commitment from England. Seward demanded an explanation of Napoleon's reported resolve to recognize the south: any demonstration of activity "prejudicial to the unity of the American people, will be necessarily regarded as unfriendly." Seward's protest left Washington urgently, only days after the great Union victories at Vicksburg and Gettysburg, and reflected his alarm that Napoleon might act impulsively before he heard the news from the battlefields. Drouyn and Dayton managed to restore an atmosphere of Franco-American cordiality, after Drouyn took refuge in the evasion that no official communications had passed between London and Paris on the matter of recognition. Drouyn made soothing assurance of his country's benevolent intentions, and its renunciation of unilateral intervention in America.

The prospect of a European war over Poland captured all attention in June and July. On June 17 France, Britain, and Austria remonstrated yet again with the Tsar, demanding a truce and a European congress to settle the crisis on the basis of amnesty, reforms, and Polish independence. This was almost exactly the type of international precedent the Confederacy welcomed, and the Union abhorred. But in practice the expectation of war in Europe unwhetted appetites for more distant complications. As John Bright remarked to the House of Commons on June 30, if Napoleon "is to engage at the same moment in dismembering the great Eastern Empire and the great Western Republic, he has more ambition than Louis XIV. . . ." Russia remained intransigent, and Napoleon soon showed himself to be no Louis XIV. His suggestion of a punitive stroke by the allies against Russia in the Baltic elicited from the British only an offer of neutrality. The project of western intervention on behalf of the oppressed Poles ultimately foundered on the shoals of divergent national interests, despite almost undiluted public support for their cause. Polish exiles mounted an effective propaganda campaign in Britain. But, as an historian of the movement explains: "When the realities of possible war and moral protest converged, virtually every group, class, and interest (except the Radicals and some Catholics) reappraised the Polish issue on a self-interested, nationalistic, and materialistic basis."[24] Fear was strong, especially, that France would reap the spoils, "and tear asunder the European order." Considering that the Civil War was a more divisive issue in Europe, the moral for America was obvious.

Events once more aroused the lurking fear that the Russian and American giants might join hands. In April, Napoleon, perhaps for appearances, invited the north to join in the allied note of protest to St. Petersburg. The United States had only one possible reason for accepting: to negotiate a deal by which northern support for Poland would be traded for French guarantees not to recognize the south. Otherwise, the case was overwhelming against rebuffing Russia, America's major friend in Europe; and against endangering traditional American attachment to the principle of nonintervention, at a time when its erosion might prove fatal.[25] Seward brushed aside the offer, professing to believe that the problems of the gallant Poles would be solved through the enlightenment of Tsar Alexander II.

In September 1863 a sensation was created in New York when a "fleet" of six Russian warships straggled into harbor, a move widely interpreted on the seaboard as an overt show of Russian friendship to the Union in its time of crisis. "We were seized with a Russian mania," the *Herald* reflected afterwards, "We indulged in banquets, speeches, we even went so far as to compare Alexander with Lincoln."[26] There was loose talk of an impending defensive alliance between free America and Tsarist Russia: Lincoln had freed the slave in America, Alexander had freed the serf in Russia; both shared common enemies, the treacherous powers of Western Europe; both would become superpowers who were capable of dividing the world between them. In the welter of rhetoric, traditional American sympathy for the Polish cause was repressed,

---

[24]J. F. Kutolowski, "Mid-Victorian Public Opinion, Polish Propaganda, and the Uprising of 1863," *J. British Studies*, VIII, No. 2 (May, 1969), p. 110.
[25]H. E. Blinn, "Seward and the Polish Rebellion of 1863," *AHR*, XLV (July, 1940), 828–833.
[26]*NYH*, November 12, 1863.

although Charles Sumner and others of the Polish "lobby" reminded their countrymen of "Tartar tyranny" in Poland.[27] Sumner delivered a long analysis on American foreign policy at Cooper Institute on September 10 (just before the Russians arrived). In it he noted that western intervention in Poland was as yet unarmed, and at least on the side of liberal institutions: " . . . we have but one friend—Switzerland—in Europe." Sumner, and a number of prominent eastern newspapers, suspected the real purpose of the Russian naval maneuver. It was, as Sumner guessed in a letter to Bright, to keep the ships from being "sealed up at Cronstadt," should the Polish crisis erupt into a European war.[28] Rear-Admiral Lisovskii, commanding the Russian Baltic fleet (a not very seaworthy three frigates, three clippers and two corvettes), had been instructed in July to proceed to New York. In case of war between Russia, England and France, Lisovskii was to destroy allied commerce and attack weakly defended enemy possessions.[29] In obedience to similar strategic needs, Rear-Admiral Popov brought his small Pacific squadron into San Francisco harbor in October. There it was in a handy position to harass the Pacific trade routes. To its admirals St. Petersburg was silent on aiding the north, on an alliance or naval cooperation with the United States. The ships stayed in American waters for seven months, during which time a portion of the press began to regret the popular hysteria whipped up on behalf of the Russians. But the affair, with its hints of a secret Russo-American alliance, aided Seward's diplomacy, and passed into American folklore.

---

[27]See Joseph W. Wieczerzak, *A Polish Chapter in Civil War America* (New York, 1967), especially Chapter 7. For writings on the "fleet" myth, see pp. 177–178. See also Albert A. Woldman, *Lincoln and the Russians* (New York, 1952). "Copperhead" and anti-war papers tended to be more pro-Polish, as did American ethnic papers for their own politico-religious reasons: e.g. *Chicago Times, Columbus Crisis, Boston Courier, New York Express, Irish American, New York Staats-Zeitung,* and *Echo z Polski.*

[28]Sumner to Bright, October 6, 1863, q. Wieczerzak, p. 155.

[29]F. A. Golder, "The Russian Fleet and the Civil War," *AHR,* XX, No. 4 (July, 1915), pp. 803–804.

CHAPTER VIII

The Laird Rams and Mexico

ALTHOUGH EUROPE SEEMED ON THE BRINK OF WAR, the world's newspaper headlines in early July concerned the Union victories at Gettysburg and Vicksburg. The battles at Cemetery Ridge, where Lee lost vital casualties in frontal assault on Meade's entrenched soldiers, and the successful siege of Vicksburg, which gave control of the Mississippi to Grant's army of the west, made the Union predominant in both eastern and western theaters, and proved of huge strategic significance. The war, nevertheless, seemed unlikely to end quickly. Gettysburg spelt the end of Lee's desperate last throw to achieve a peace settlement by an offensive feat of arms. But by good generalship and enemy indecision he managed to keep intact the remnants of the Army of Virginia in its retreat across the Potomac. Meade's inability to interfere with Lee's escape was proof of the terrible price in lives that the Federals paid at Gettysburg. Military deadlock loomed. Politically, prospects of a quick peace disappeared with the failure of reunionist projects. Political squabbling and resistance to the draft within the north handicapped any rapid storming of the south. Seward was known to be privately opposed to the Negro emancipation proclamation, and reputed to be sponsoring negotiations with Confederate Vice-President, Alexander H. Stephens, offering repeal of emancipation as a preliminary step to reunification of the sections. The Radical Republicans strongly opposed any such capitulation, and rumor had Lincoln's cabinet divided, Chase and Seward at loggerheads, and the Republican party split between its moderate and abolitionist wings.

Disunity within the north was publicized to the world with the New York draft riots in July. The riots themselves had complex motivation: class anger at conscription laws that gave easy exemption to the rich, war-weariness, anti-abolitionism by the New York Irish poor who feared the creation of cheap pools of free black labor. The insurrection turned into a ghetto pogrom by the Irish against the Negroes, and was put down forcibly by police in pitched battles. Press reports magnified the casualties into tens of hundreds, and even ardent Unionists abroad were sickened by the slaughter. However, the atrocities of the rioters—Negro lynchings, destruction of a hospital for black children, anarchistic attacks on property—weakened sympathy for the uprising abroad. But in Ireland itself, the riots brought forth a propaganda bonanza to the south.[1] Irish pride had been high, entering into legend and song, over the heroism of Irish-born troops—such as Meagher's immortal Irish Brigade—fighting for the Union army. But Irish euphoria for the north—the democratic utopia, the emigrants' refuge from English tyranny—evaporated as the Irish-Americans emerged as cannon-fodder in an unwinnable war. Ireland was to become a Confederate stronghold until the end of the war. After peace, a convenient lapse of Irish memories occurred: the pacifism and rebel sympathies of wartime were dropped from the historical legend, as the Irish independence movement allied itself with supporters in the American northeast.

In London, news of Gettysburg and Vicksburg caused southern bonds to drop thirty-two points, and gave new drive to the propaganda war being waged by the Union and Emancipation Societies against Henry Hotze's southern lobby.[2] As the cotton industry showed signs of a leisurely, but encouraging, return to health, Richmond's pessimism about British intervention deepened. It became total when the ministry detained the Laird rams in early

---

[1]Joseph Hernon, *Celts, Catholics and Copperheads* (Ohio State U.P., 1968.) Also Adrian Cook, *The Armies in the Streets: The New York City Draft Riots of 1863* (Kentucky U.P., 1974).

[2]Hotze, one of the south's most successful agents & publicists, set up the *Index,* a weekly London newspaper, in May 1862. It became remarkably successful with "polite society," attracting the support of James Spence and employing at least seven writers from London newspapers. Hotze, in charge of Confederate propaganda in Britain, wrote leaders also for the *Morning Post, London Standard,* and Lord Derby's *London Herald.* See R. T. Smith, "The Confederate *Index* and the American Civil War" (Unpub. MA Thesis, Univ. of Washington, 1961.)

September. Historians once regarded the rams affair as the major crisis of the war.[3] It can no longer be seen in that light, but neither is it justly treated as a mere postscript to the momentous diplomacy of 1862, a phoney crisis. English policy-makers agonized until the last moment concerning the proper course of action to be taken over the Birkenhead ships. Had the decision gone the other way, the course of Anglo-American relations over the next generation would have been even stormier. The experts now doubt that the Laird ironclads, with dubious sea-going qualities, could have upset seriously the naval balance of the war. But their release by England might well have smashed the uneasy diplomatic balance of the postwar years.

When one of the Laird rams, the "294," launched for trials, Consul Dudley applied on July 7 for its detention by Liverpool customs. Adams took the case to Russell, although it was not watertight. The design of the ships was obviously warlike. On Secretary Mallory's orders the vessels had been planned specifically as blockade-breakers: 350 horsepower, 10 knot cruisers, armor-plated, with turret batteries that gave heavy firepower while permitting maneuverability and shallow draft for American coastal operations. Added to the prows were seven-foot iron piercers designed to sink wooden blockaders.[4] However the contention of the British crown law officers that a ship's warlike intention could be inferred from its structure had been brushed aside in the *Alexandra* decision. As the rams lacked arms, ammunition, or legal signs of Confederate ownership, the law office felt understandably dubious about its prospects of success in any prosecution. Bulloch—now in complete charge of the Confederate ironclad program abroad, a program at long last effectively backed by cotton bonds—had taken extreme precautions to disguise the rams' connections, and to keep the transaction with Lairds legal within the scope of Judge Pollock's ruling in the *Alexandra* case. Ownership was transferred to a compliant French firm, owned by Francois Bravay, who claimed to be buying the vessels for the

---

[3]James Ford Rhodes, *History of the U.S. etc* (N.Y., 1893–1906, 7 vols), Vol., 4; Brooks Adams, "Seizure of the Laird Rams," *MHSP,* XLV (1911).

[4]See Merli, *Great Britain and the Confederate Navy,* pp. 179–180. I have relied heavily upon Merli and W. D. Jones, *The Confederate Rams at Birkenhead* (Tuscaloosa, 1961) in the following account.

Pasha of Egypt. Customs officials and northern spies haunted Lairds' yards, where workmen worked overtime under gaslight to speed the project.

Seward had been pleased when the British government seized the *Alexandra*. He stopped threatening to issue letters of marque if Britain failed to end shipbuilding; and in August took Lord Lyons with him on a symbolic joint tour of New York State. Whether Seward believed the crisis settled, and the British "pledged" to suppression of "unneutral" ship construction, is a matter of debate.[5] In any case, from mid-August the anxious dispatches coming from Adams threw the whole matter back into the melting pot. Adams' diary, and the tone of his protests to the British Foreign Office, attest to his belief in the menacing seriousness of the situation. It was now only too likely that Russell would profess his government hamstrung by Judge Pollock's ruling in the *Alexandra* trial. The British government was caught in a fork stick: the prospect of the rams' escape became increasingly unpleasant, yet their stoppage could be effected only by an act outside the law. Respect for the rule of law, and the certainty of political embarrassment, made arbitrary action distasteful. On the other hand, if Britain dodged its international obligations by taking refuge behind inadequate domestic legislation, the United States might legitimately sue for reparations.

Adams sent a strong note to Whitehall on July 11 that spoke of active "malevolence" by Britain, but it had no apparent effect. Reports in late August suggested that the "294" was about to be towed to sea to have its turret fitted, perhaps, like the *Alabama*, never to return. Foreign Office enquiries had begun to unearth mildly suspicious, but legally useless, information on the Bravay connection. Russell wavered until September 3. He was, says Merli, "not fully satisfied with the advice of his legal advisers ... [but was] reluctant to override it, especially if by so doing he appeared to be responsive to foreign pressure." On September 1, Russell thought that the ironclads ought to be detained pending further investigation—but only "if sufficient evidence can be obtained to lead to the belief that they are intended for the Confederate States of America." The same day Russell, holidaying in

---

[5]Cf. *EDA*, II, Chapter 13, esp. pp. 141ff.

Scotland, wrote to Adams declaring the government's inability to interfere with the ships on existing legal grounds: Dudley's depositions depended on hearsay evidence; the ships belonged to Bravay; and nobody had been able to disprove their Egyptian destination. However by the time Adams received the note, on September 4, and sent off an angry and famous reply, Russell had already changed his mind. Arrangements were made to prevent the rams putting to sea until thorough investigations had been completed. This was acting on suspicion, not proof, but the Solicitor-General concurred in the measure "as one of policy though not of strict law."[6] The fact that the government determined merely on detention, and not yet on seizure, rendered the act less challenging to the law. Roundell Palmer, Vernon Harcourt, and the *Times* opposed repetition of government laxity as in the *Alabama* affair, pressure which possibly carried weight with Russell. Palmerston accepted Russell's move, and it was generally supported by officials and ministers although there were misgivings about its legality.

The matter would no doubt have stirred little historical dust had not Adams, unaware of the turn in events, made a desperate last minute play to stop ironclads on "hostile errand" against his country. Historians have superabundantly demonstrated that Adams penned his September 5 note two days *after* the critical British decision had been taken to detain the rams. It was not a case, as Americans once believed, of Britain caving in to a Yankee threat of war. Adams' note excoriated Russell's do-nothing approach, and in celebrated phrase stated: "It would be superfluous in me to point out to your Lordship that this is war." That phrase, ambiguous as it was, only repeated more provocatively what Adams had already said in his protest of July 11. There he accused the rebels of waging war from Liverpool to break a fully recognized blockade, and regarded British policy as "tantamount to a participation in the war by the people of Great Britain to a degree which ... cannot fail to endanger the peace and welfare of both countries." Palmerston reacted sharply: "It seems to me," he wrote to Russell, "that we cannot allow to remain unnoticed his [Adams'] repeated and I must say somewhat insolent threats of war. We ought I think

---

[6]Russell to Palmerston, September 3, 1863; q. Jones, p. 72.

to say to him in civil Terms 'you be damned'. . . ."[7] Honor was satisfied on both sides only after a choleric interchange of notes. England, said Russell, would not be induced by threats to overstep the limits of the law "or to propose to Parliament any new Law which they may not, for Reasons of their own think proper to be adopted." Adams denied being minatory, and submitted that the interests of the two nations "are of too much magnitude to be measured by the infinitesimal scale of the testimony permissible before a jury in a Common Law Court." The hot language should not be allowed to obscure the ultimately satisfactory outcome to all parties but that of the luckless Bulloch. Russell snubbed Adams by going over his head to Washington on the matter. But Adams won the larger battle of getting the rams stopped, a victory his son Henry dubbed a "second Vicksburg . . . the crowning stroke of our diplomacy."

Detention of the rams became seizure on October 8. By then the Pasha of Egypt had disavowed interest in Bravay's ironclads, while scare rumors spread of a conspiracy to free the vessels from navy surveillance at Birkenhead. The Foreign Office obtained a gunboat guard on the rams; and after hostile demonstrations by Lairds' dockyard workers, had the rams moored under the guns of a British warship in the Mersey. The ministry determinedly used legal procrastination to prevent the release of the rams, going to extraordinary lengths to build a cast iron prosecution case. For the court hearing (scheduled for May 1864) the British government proposed to subject the Viceroy of Egypt to legal cross-questioning, and sent a special delegation to Cairo. The Foreign Office fully mobilized its resources in order to unearth the truth behind the intricate rams affair. The task bristled with difficulties. Finally, when war loomed between Denmark and the German powers over Schleswig-Holstein, the government quietly dropped the case and purchased the rams from Bravay for the Royal Navy. With public opinion solidifying against a permissive stand on shipbuilding dangerous to British naval and marine insurance interests, the ministry easily survived a parliamentary debate on the Laird rams in the new year. The Conservative opposition confined itself to

---

[7]Palmerston to Russell, September 24, 1863, *PRO* 30/22/22; q. Jones, p. 77. For the battle of notes, Merli, pp 204ff.

scoring minor points off a government that it had not the resources to replace, and signally failed to call for a reversal of policy on Confederate shipbuilding. Bulloch & his colleagues felt let down when Napoleon III refused to press his British ally for the release of the ostensibly French ironclads. It seemed necessary to Bulloch by May 1864 to cut his losses, retrieve £188,000 from the sale of the rams, and to contrive other means of continuing the naval war.

In New York Senator Charles Sumner exploited the rams affair in an apparent effort to oust Seward from control of foreign policy. On September 10, 1863, at Coopers Institute, with the northeast seaboard almost hysterical at the prospect of the release of the Laird rams, Sumner denounced English neutrality. Unluckily for Sumner, he delivered the oration *after* Russell had ordered the rams detained. Seward, not Sumner, got the credit for browbeating the British and preserving peace, while England's retreat blocked Sumner from leading a noisy campaign for a war of revenge.[8] During the crisis, the northern press canvassed aggressive counter-measures, such as punitive raids by the Union navy to destroy the rams in British port, an embargo on British shipping, and seques-tration of British property in America. News of the rams' seizure was received with relief, and a good deal of cynicism. Horace Greeley alleged that "only in proportion as the Confederacy began to show the clearest indications of a speedy collapse, the [British] Government awoke to a consciousness of its duties as a neutral power."

In the Confederacy, Britain's policy was interpreted as covertly implementing the Union's ocean strategy, in order to maintain Britain's own naval predominance. Anglo-Confederate relations, poor for over a year, now broke down completely. Using his dis-cretionary power, as sanctioned by Richmond, Mason ended his London mission on September 21, and joined Slidell in Paris, which became the rebels' last foreign hope. Henry Adams thought it a cardinal blunder by the south: "Why should Mr. Davis aid our diplomacy by himself directing all our causes of alarm towards France, a nation whose power we have no real cause to fear, and away from England, with whom we have been on the very verge

[8]David Donald, *Charles Sumner and the Rights of Man* (New York, 1970), pp. 125–137. Greeley's comment below in *NYDT,* September 24, 1863.

of war?"[9] In October the Confederacy expelled all British consular agents. The fact that British consuls were still officially accredited to the enemy power, the United States, constituted a long-standing offense to southern patriots, made much of by the noisy anti-Davis newspapers. Davis and Benjamin, reluctant to press the issue with Britain and France, had claimed that exequaturs granted by the Union in the past under the foreign relations power retained validity, as the south honored constitutional obligations predating the rebellion.[10] In recent months, however, rancorous quarrels had broken out between the consuls, state governors, and Confederate officials, when the consuls resisted attempts by the states to conscript domiciled British subjects. Britain denied the Confederacy's right to ask military service of domiciled aliens in a civil war, although in normal wars this was a belligerent right sanctioned by international law. Russell advised that conscripted British citizens should throw down their arms in battle. Southerners read this as arrogant contempt for Confederate sovereignty. In June the British consul, George Moore, was expelled from his Richmond post, after protesting a new militia law in Mississippi (outside his jurisdiction) permitting conscription of aliens. Moore topped this by accusing the War Department of despotic behavior in cases involving Irish-born conscripts, and he provocatively disregarded the authority of Benjamin and the State Department. British agents in Georgia and South Carolina also offended by counselling Englishmen not to serve in the army of an unrecognized "rebel" state. But the final break with England came about less as the result of these pinpricks, than as the culmination of a year of bitter affliction and frustration for Confederate diplomacy. That Richmond's patience finally ran out is understandable, given British nonrecognition, Russell's hauteur and cynicism on the blockade, and the stoppage of southern ironclads.

As the opposing armies swept to and fro across huge areas of the southern homeland, devastating its resources, signs emerged of approaching collapse. Among the more desperate schemes of salvation broached after Gettysburg was one for a French alliance,

---

[9]Henry Adams to C. F. Adams, Jr., September 25, 1863; q. Worthington C. Ford, ed., *A Cycle of Adams Letters, 1861–65* (Boston, 1920), II, 87.

[10]M. L. Bonham, *British Consuls in the Confederacy* (New York, 1911).

made to Benjamin by the head of the Bureau of War, R. G. H. Kean. Kean spoke of sounding the French emperor on the basis of large commercial privileges, "a sort of protectorate guarantee of our territory, say 11 states" and entire rebel freedom in domestic administration: "This accepted would involve him at once in war with the United States but would give him control of cotton, abundance of ship timber and naval stores, and make France a first class naval power."[11] Benjamin balked at this deal, but was prepared to try another cotton bribe. How would Napoleon react (he asked Slidell) to a Confederate offer of eight million dollars worth of cotton at the bargain price of 8 to 10 cents a pound? The emperor showed no interest. But faith in the French died hard in the south. There was nobody else to turn to. Perhaps maturing events in Mexico would bring together the Confederacy and the Second Empire.

* * *

In June 1863—one more remarkable event in an *annus mirabilus* —French troops marched into Mexico City. Two years earlier, the outbreak of the civil war in the United states had provided Napoleon with the opportunity to exploit a situation of internal chaos in Mexico. When the liberal-republican regime of President Benito Juárez—strongly opposed within Mexico itself by clerical and conservative landowning factions—suspended interest payments on foreign debts incurred by its predecessor, France led the moves that resulted in the dispatch of an Anglo-French-Spanish expedition to Mexico in late 1861. According to the Tripartite Treaty of London (October 1861), the powers planned to exact reparations from Mexico, but were prohibited from acquiring territorial advantages or using force to prevent the Mexican people from freely choosing their form of government. From the beginning, it was patent that Napoleon had stronger ambitions to fulfill. Why Napoleon embarked upon the disastrous Mexican Intervention has intrigued, and exasperated, French historians. He was fascinated by the vision of a Catholic, Latin-cultured Mexican empire rivalling the Anglo-Saxon civilizations to the north. France

---

[11]Edward Younger ed., *Inside the Confederate Government: The Diary of R. G. H. Kean* (New York, 1957), p.82. Also p.42.

could provide a more urbane, humane, less racist, benevolent paternalism than that which the white North Americans seemed fated otherwise to impose upon the Mexicans. Moreover France was entitled to play a geopolitical role in the hemisphere, despite the efforts of Britain and the United States to corner markets there, control commercial routes, and leech upon the untapped resources of the area. From the 1840's, Napoleon foresaw that France could profitably exploit transit routes across Mexico or Panama, and tap the gold and other mineral resources of northern Mexico—France's new California. More specific pressures for French suzerainty came from speculative interests with investments in Mexico, powerfully applied by Napoleon's half-brother the Duke de Morny, whose business partner, the Swiss banker Jean-Baptiste Jecker, held $15 million in Mexican government bonds. Mexican emigres and monarchists assured the court that the Mexican populace yearned for French liberation from the anticlerical rule of Juárez. Moreover, humiliation of the United States would reduce its charismatic appeal as a democratic model for Latin American peoples, open the way for European-sponsored monarchies, and at the same time remove a disturbing revolutionary influence on Europe's masses.

Although the allies successfully occupied Vera Cruz they quickly split apart in early 1862, when the French army advanced on Mexico City to "seek our guarantees." General Juan Almonte, to all appearances a French puppet, accepted the Mexican regency, although Juarez' army put up dogged resistance to the invaders. The British and Spanish branded the French actions as contrary to the Treaty of London and pulled out from the expedition. Neither, at heart, objected to the French adventure, and their withdrawal gave Napoleon a free hand. Spain, no doubt, was repaying the French for their abstention from the San Domingo affair. The British won all round. They had appeared to act only to ensure their legal rights, washing their hands of the affair when Napoleon stood revealed as a faithless adventurer. France was intricated in Mexico, fettered in Europe and brought into collision with the United States; while Britain reaped goodwill in the north. Russell had even insisted that the United States be invited to participate in the intervention, an offer which Seward, predictably, declined. Privately Palmerston thought Napoleon's "monarchy scheme" a godsend that would stop the North Americans "in their absorption of Mexico": "If the North and South are definitely disunited and if at the same time Mexico could be turned into a prosperous monarchy I do not know any arrangement that would be more advantageous for us."[12]

On May 5, 1862, the Juáristas defeated the French at Puebla, thus frustrating Napoleon's hope of cheap victory and forcing him to tie up a large army too far from the European heartland. The "Cinco de Mayo" went down in Mexican history; it also dealt a severe blow to French military morale. The French army enjoyed hitherto a reputation as one of the world's finest. Napoleon, after Puebla, showed great reluctance to make any move that risked pitting his mercenaries against the battle-hardened Union troops. Napoleon persisted in Mexico, sending reinforcements to his army, but he did so not merely to restore French prestige. His sponsorship of the Habsburg prince Ferdinand Maximilian to sit upon the throne of Mexico had become an integral part of French European diplomacy. Napoleon's pledge to free Italy from the Alps to the Adriatic could be fulfilled only by detaching Venetia from the Austrians, who had held it in the face of French arms in the war of 1859. Napoleon planned a package deal with Austria: cession of Venetia to the Italians, in return for a Franco-Austrian alliance (giving the Austrians protection against their German rival Prussia), French guarantees against the complete unification of Italy, and—as this was not enough—the gift of the Mexican throne to a Habsburg prince.[13] The French defeat at Puebla only confirmed the Austrian court in its determination to keep Venetia; the Austrians dissociated themselves from the Mexican venture and advised Maximilian to do likewise. During the Polish crisis of 1863, Napoleon renewed his overtures to Austria, offering French friendship, the division of Italy, vaguely specified gains in Silesia and the Danubian provinces, and a crown for Maximilian, provided Austria supported his Polish policy. In such a deal Austria would pay heavily, losing Venetia to Italy and Galicia to a recon-

---

[12]Palmerston to Russell, January 19, 1862, *PRO,* G & D, 22:22; q. Bell, *Palmerston,* II, 313–314.

[13]Nancy N. Barker, "France, Austria, and the Mexican Venture, 1861–4," *French Hist. Stud.* (1963–4), pp. 229ff. Generally, see A. J. Hanna and K. A. Hanna, *Napoleon III and Mexico* (Chapel Hill, 1971).

CALIF.   N. MEX. TER.   TEXAS

El Paso

SONORA

CHIHUAHUA

•Chihuahua

COAHUILA

Rio Grande

Gulf of California

Monterrey

NUEVO LEÓN

TAMAULIPAS

Matamoros

Gulf of Mexico

DURANGO

•Mazatlán

San Luis. Potosí

Tampico

PACIFIC OCEAN

Mexico City

Puebla

Vera Cruz

Isthmus of Tehuantepec

Mexico

structed Poland—and on March 27, 1863, Austria rejected the terms. Playing its part in the Austrian decision was reluctance to be associated with the Napoleonic theory of nationalities (unsuited to the multinational Habsburg empire), or with Napoleonic designs to redraw the map of Europe. Mexican complications thus played a role in what historians now view as a fateful turningpoint in European history, one leading to the weakening of both France and Austria, and the rise of a Prussianized Germany. Ironically, as the reinforced French army under General Forey finally occupied Mexico City, relations between Paris and Vienna worsened and Napoleon lost incentive to continue an expensive, and electorally unpopular, campaign in Mexico that would gain no rewards in Europe. The emperor's unscrupulously pursued objective hereafter was to install Maximilian in Mexico with minimum

French commitments, and to leave the archduke to his own resources as soon as possible.

General Forey formed a handpicked provisional government for Mexico, which promptly offered the imperial crown to Maximilian. The United States refused to recognize the provisional government, and in August withdrew its minister Thomas Corwin to Washington. In the American view the existence of the Juárez government at the town of San Luis Potosí indicated the continuance of a state of civil war. Seward, as with the Polish issue, hewed scrupulously to a policy of nonintervention and neutrality, attitudes the Union expected overseas nations to observe on the American Civil War. Open support for Juárez would have been popular in the north, and with Hispanic Americans; but it might trip off French intervention in North America and create a Franco-Confederate alliance. Too soft a policy on Seward's part courted a complete French takeover in Mexico, and would be politically disastrous for the Republicans. Seward has been rightly praised for his skill in following a difficult middle path which preserved the forms of Franco-American amity, avoided diversions ("why should we gasconade about Mexico when we are in a struggle for our own life?" he asked Bigelow), while "compromising nothing, surrendering nothing."

From the start Seward made clear the position of the United States. While obliged to accept the right of the powers to coerce Mexico into observing its international duties, the Union stood behind the principles of republicanism and self-determination in the hemisphere. Seward devised a loan-treaty plan to stave off intervention, by which the United States assumed the interest on Mexico's foreign debts for five years; but the proposal expired in the Senate. As the war raged in Mexico, Seward accepted the patent fictions that France renounced territorial conquests for itself, and was engaged in mere police action. He deliberately refrained from invoking the Monroe Doctrine, but held out an implied threat of retribution in the future. A Mexican government headed by a "person alien to Mexico" would fall unless sustained by European alliances, while the return of the powers to the American continent was opposed to the historical trend of the century. Within this language, and northern anger generally, there was a quality of imperial resentment of a rival, for the idea of an

American mission to civilize, even conquer and colonize Central America, and to expel all foreign influence, was a long-standing one. The Union's Mexican diplomacy worried Napoleon, the more so after Gettysburg and Vicksburg. He did not know whether the north intended to go to war or not, when it was able, over the establishment of a French client state in Mexico. This uncertainty was Seward's trump card. What the south did not anticipate was the possibility that Napoleon might spurn Richmond, preferring to finesse a friendly Union into grudging acceptance of Maximilian's regime rather than provoke more overt northern aid for Juárez.

The infant Confederacy's first bearings towards neighboring Mexico had been predatory. Agents such as the roistering John T. Pickett hardly concealed their belief that northern Mexico's "boundless agricultural and mineral resources" were staked out for the south, or that access to the Pacific across the Isthmus was vital to their nation's future. Confederate officials held discussions with quasi-independent chieftains of the area such as Santiago Vidaurri, who was anxious to head a league of states allied with the south. The war forced Richmond to keep its Mexican ambitions in cold storage, partly out of an expedient desire not to upset the French, possible allies. But southerners shared with northerners the confidence that imperial success went to peoples who could colonize from short range, using emigration and commercial control to fasten an unchallengable grip on new lands. The French, for all their high phrases on Latin superiority, feared Confederate competition in Mexico. A Franco-Confederate alliance—which seemed an obvious step in Richmond's eyes—not only raised a host of domestic and diplomatic problems for Napoleon; it posed two other nasty possibilities: lasting enmity from the United States in the hemisphere; and a potential takeover bid for parts of Mexico by dynamic allies quite capable of penetrating local centers of power. Hence the attractiveness of the idea of containing the south by bartering for Union acquiescence in the Maximilian experiment.

Texas was an added complication. Persistent rumors flourished that France coveted Texas. Edward Everett, special adviser to the U.S. State Department, claimed publicly that France intended reviving the project of a "larger Texas" it had tried in 1844—it planned to join together in an independent league Texas, the New Mexico Territory, California, the northern states of Mexico, and possibly Louisiana.[14] Napoleon and Drouyn in fact considered a top secret plan to settle the American war on the basis of a four-state confederation. Discussed at the time of the French mediation plan of January 1863, the confederation would be administered by a diet (similar to that of Frankfurt), and consist of roughly equal states: the North, the South, the West, and Mexico. While the United States was to be completely dismembered, there were intimations that a French-controlled Mexico would be expanded to include Texas, and perhaps Louisiana.[15] Benjamin suspected that Napoleon wanted to resurrect France's old Texan policy of creating a client buffer state to obstruct southern expansion. He did not hesitate to expel, or suspend, French officials in the Confederacy (such as Theron, the vice-consul at Galveston, and Tabouelle, chancellor of the consulate at Richmond) suspected of conspiring to detach Texas from the south.

The Confederacy anticipated no hitch in exchanging ambassadors with the provisional government newly set up in Mexico City; and hoped then to exact recognition of the south from Napoleon. French officials and soldiers in Mexico, the regent Almonte, and Maximilian himself pressed Napoleon to recognize the south. In December 1863 Maximilian went out of his way to inform Jefferson Davis that he regarded Anglo-French recognition of the Confederacy as a precondition for his acceptance of the Mexican crown. But southern hopes of a quick break-through gradually evaporated. In January 1864, William Preston, a former U.S. minister to Spain who commanded a unit at Chickamauga, was named Confederate envoy to Mexico. But Preston and his entourage found official doors shut to them in Mexico, and later in Europe, where Preston and Slidell worked unavailingly to negotiate with Maximilian. Unbeknown to the southern agents, the fate of the Preston mission had been already doomed by European developments.

In November 1863 Austria refused participation in Napoleon's

---

[14] *NYT,* February 20, 1863.
[15] K. A. Hanna, "The Roles of the South in the French Intervention in Mexico " *JSH,* XX, No. 1 (February 1954), 9–10.

grand plan for a congress of nations which should settle Poland and other European questions. Napoleon was furious. Austria allied itself with Prussia in a joint invasion of the Danish provinces of Schleswig-Holstein, claimed by Prussia. In February 1864 the allies entered Denmark, alarming Napoleon and the rest of Europe. Vienna desperately feared that, while it was involved in Denmark, France might retaliate by moving against Venetia and other vulnerable provinces of the sprawling Habsburg empire. Austro-French talks finally resulted in a promise of French neutrality over Denmark. Maximilian negotiated the future of Mexico with Napoleon at this unlucky time. The Habsburgs found themselves in no position to extract cast-iron guarantees of French protection for Maximilian's new empire. Unable to resist the temptation of the throne, and too ready to take at face value Napoleon's vague talk of aid, Maximilian allowed himself to be maneuvered into a dangerous position. In the convention of Miramar, Maximilian got a guarantee that French troops would gradually withdraw from Mexico over a three year period, leaving a rearguard of 20,000 men in 1867. This fell far short of his earlier request for a joint Franco-British guarantee of the empire, a loan and a military occupation of up to 15 years. France promised not to fail the empire "however events in Europe turn out," but ominously did not undertake to defend Maximilian from a hostile United States. Mexico engaged to bear the cost of the occupying troops, and to indemnify France for the cost of intervention. Privately Napoleon was determined to liquidate the unpopular Mexican affair. He had no intention of allowing an impulsive Maximilian to tie his hands in the hemisphere. The archduke was informed that it would be inconvenient for France if he opened official relations with the Confederacy. Maximilian cold-shouldered Slidell at the time of the Mirimar signing (March 1864). Impatient and angry, Slidell and Preston tried veiled threats with Maximilian's Mexican advisers Estrada, Hidalgo and Arrangoiz; and also with minister Drouyn: France should beware lest a reconciled north and south enforced the Monroe Doctrine, and crushed the new monarchy. Such despairing threats were to become a feature of the south's final diplomacy.

Rumors flew in Europe that Lincoln and Napoleon had struck a bargain: Washington would recognize Maximilian if France abandoned plans of acknowledging the south. The southern lobby wrathfully accused Seward of inspiring the leak to sabotage the Preston mission. It now appears that the deception was Napoleon's.[16] He was floating a trial balloon. Even temporary northern tolerance of Maximilian's regime would ease Napoleon's problems: his objective was swift extrication from Mexico without losing face by appearing to act under Yankee pressure. For that he was willing to talk of troop withdrawals and an ultimate end to intervention.

Seward did not offer what the French wanted. But he took care to hold out some carrots for the emperor, while making sure that America's public policy had the stamp of firmness. Dayton duly protested that Maximilian's installation departed "very materially" from French assurances that the Mexicans would be given a free choice of institutions; nor, he made clear, would French-staged plebiscites give legitimacy to the regime. But subsequent silence from Washington indicated that the Union would take no more drastic action for the moment. Meantime Seward adroitly primed Mercier to hope for ultimate Union acceptance of Maximilian's *fait accompli.* As Mercier reported home, the United States had refrained from open protest at the establishment of a monarchy; Seward had damped down inflammatory tendencies in Congress (with the aid of Sumner, devoted to "one war at a time"); while Juárez was kept prudently at arms length by the State Department. Incensed that the French had assembled a large army and navy in the Gulf without complaint by the Union, Matias Romero (Juárez's active representative in Washington) protested early in 1864 that strict neutrality had not been observed in the Mexican Civil War.

Mercier, in behind-the-scene talks with New York financial interests, acquired the impression that business was not adverse to a *modus vivendi* with the French which should permit opportunities for American economic penetration of the area. American businessmen probably shared Seward's assessment that inevitable historical forces dictated the ultimately peaceful conquest of the continent by the North American race. As Seward told Bigelow in

---

[16]Owsley, pp. 526ff.

Paris: "... those who are most impatient for the defeat of European and monarchical designs in Mexico might well be content to abide the effects which must result from the ever-increasing expansion of the American people westward and southward."[17]

[17]Quoted, James M. Callahan, *American Foreign Policy in its Mexican Relations* (New York, 1932), p. 297. See also R. R. Miller, "Matias Romero: Mexican Minister to the U.S. during the Juárez-Maximilian Era," *Hispanic Am. Hist. Rev.*, XLV (1965), 228–245.

CHAPTER IX

The Last Phase

AS THE TIDE OF WAR TURNED AGAINST THE SOUTH, the focus of the powers changed from projects of interference to defensive strategies devised to protect national interests against a vengeful United States. Unavoidably, Canada and Mexico became major theaters in which were played out the dramatic tensions of the time. If they were still side-shows to the main stage, which featured Sherman in Georgia, Grant and Lee on the outskirts of Richmond, there seemed every possibility that the military spectacular would overflow into the new scenarios.

Between the battle of Gettysburg and the peace of Appomattox, Canada became a hotbed of wartime intrigue and a center of rival intelligence networks. The Great Lakes-St. Lawrence border became an armed frontier. The task of policing provincial neutrality steepened as Confederate bands plotted hit-and-run attacks into the north from neutral sanctuary, abetted by the numerous southern sympathizers within Canada. Close liaison between Seward and Governor-General Monck, helped by war-weariness among both Canadian and northern peoples, and burgeoning Canadian respect for the mighty Union army, were instrumental in heading off trouble. A "tip-off" from Monck to Seward in November 1863 enabled Union troops to frustrate a rebel plot to rescue Confederate prisoners of war held on Johnson's Island, off the Ohio shore of Lake Erie. The plotters were financed by the Confederate Treasury, a sign that Richmond, having broken with England, intended a more aggressive role in Canada, and one less respectful of British neutral obligations. Hopefully, the hated British and Yankees might be drawn into collision.

The south almost had its way in December, with the explosive *Chesapeake* affair. Posing as passengers, sixteen men led by the London-born adventurer John C. Braine captured the American coastal steamer *Chesapeake* on the high seas, killing the second engineer. Braine hatched the conspiracy in New Brunswick, intending to convert the ship into a rebel privateer under the dubious authority of a Confederate letter of marque applying to another vessel and issued to another person. However a Union warship cornered the short-of-coal *Chesapeake* in Sambro harbor, Nova Scotia, seized the vessel and captured a Nova Scotian raider, John Wade. On Secretary of Navy Welles' order, the *Chesapeake* was handed over to the Halifax authorities. Under the batteries of Halifax harbor, and with an angry pro-southern crowd on Queen's Wharf, Nova Scotian officials demanded the release of the captive Wade. Five Federal gunboats rode in the harbor poised for action, a combustible situation. Eventually Wade was taken ashore in chains, but onlookers prevented his arrest by county marshal, and Wade escaped.[1]

Seward and Lyons, remembering the *Trent* fiasco, handled the *Chesapeake* affair with restraint. Seward promptly denied that the United States had authorized any violation of Nova Scotian authority. In return he demanded more effective enforcement of the neutrality laws in British North America; and suggested that Britain withdraw the south's belligerent rights because of the hijacking of the *Chesapeake.* Otherwise, Seward made clear, he would have difficulty in restraining the House of Representatives from ending the reciprocity treaty. In February 1864 a New Brunswick magistrate ruled that Braine's raid was piracy, not an act of war (Braine was not legally a Confederate citizen, nor was his letter of marque properly issued according to British, or Confederate, law). A higher court then decided that if piracy was the offense, proceedings should have begun in a United States court. Those conspirators whom the provincial authorities had managed to arrest were discharged on the ground of incorrect processing of their arrest warrants. Seward did not press for extradition: to execute British subjects for piracy would needlessly have invited discord.

---

[1] Winks, *Canada and the United States, the Civil War Years* (Baltimore, 1960), pp. 244ff. Winks' definitive study is recommended for the Canadian theater.

Meanwhile the border remained tense. The rebels allegedly planned daring exploits against Yankee ships at sea and on the Great Lakes and canals, or harassment of Union military and civil targets from Canadian bases. Maine, Vermont, and Upper New York clamored for protection, and General John A. Dix, commanding the eastern military district, arrived to control the American side of the frontier.

Europe was embroiled in the Schleswig-Holstein emergency, and passive to the American question, a fact illustrated in the death-knell of the south's shipbuilding program. When he realized that the Laird rams project might collapse, Bulloch turned to France. By July 1863 he had contracted for the construction of six warships—including two ironclad rams—in Bordeaux and Nantes, under the auspices of the leading firm of Arman.[2] Napoleon allowed Slidell to believe that he would turn a blind eye to the armoring of the vessels and their secret delivery into Confederate hands. However, Arman's activities were revealed to the United States embassy by an employee in the Nantes shipping yard, who supplied original documents showing that Arman intended fraudulently to arm the ships and send them to the rebels. After prolonged diplomatic pressure by the United States—applied at a delicate stage in Napoleon's endeavor to obtain northern acceptance of Maximilian as emperor of Mexico—Napoleon was forced to crack down on the conspiracy. In May 1864 Minister Drouyn directed Arman and his agents, on pain of government seizure of the ships, to make a *bona fide* sale of the vessels to a neutral government. Arman managed, to Drouyn's anger, to spirit one ironclad, the *Stonewall,* to southern hands, after an attempted sale to Denmark had fallen through. Unseaworthy and poorly designed, it arrived in American waters too late to take part in the war. The *Alabama's* flamboyant career ended in June 1864 when it was sunk off Cherbourg by the U.S.S. *Kearsarge*—in twenty-two months it had logged 75,000 miles, taken some sixty-four prizes, and frightened from the oceans hosts of northern merchantmen. As other southern raiders were bottled up in neutral ports, including the *Rappahannock* at Calais, Bulloch and his team had few

---

[2] For the intricate story of the southern naval program in France see Case and Spencer, Ch. 13.

consolations left. One of them arose out of a brilliant coup by which the Confederacy purchased the graceful and deadly Clyde-built *Sea King,* which became the renowned *Shenandoah.* [3]

It was becoming clear that only through hemispheric events could Britain and France be stirred to blows against the north. In April 1864 Jefferson Davis set up a three-man commission to "crystallize anti-Northern feeling in Canada and mould it into some form of hostile expression." Led by Jacob Thompson, an able politician, once Buchanan's Secretary of the Interior, and including Clement C. Clay, an ill former Alabaman senator, the mission was instructed to lend aid to the anti-war movement in the north, and to promote opposition to Lincoln in the November presidential election. The Canadian situation seemed ripe to exploit. Tension over the future of Canadian-American trade rode high, not diminished by the abolitionist Joshua Giddings—the Union's dying and ineffectual consul-general at Montreal—who campaigned at Washington against the reciprocity treaty. The election of a Liberal-Conservative coalition under John A. Macdonald and Etienne Tache brought to power in the united Canadas a party dedicated to Canadian union. The stock-in-trade of the "confederationists" was fear of American expansionism, and the urgent need for a strong central government that could defend Canadians against the future menace of U.S. Grant's army. In the event the south underestimated the caution with which the coalition dealt with its giant American neighbor, while awaiting the movement for closer union to mature.

Thompson's mission, liberally backed by Confederate funds, soon became the focus of rebel activity in Canada. Placed under Thompson's wing was the Kentuckian Thomas Hines, sent by southern Secretary of War Seddon to Toronto to dispatch a marauding band of rebel soldiers into the north. With Thompson's blessing, the Virginian John Yeats Beall and a group of Confederates on September 19 took control of the lake steamer *Philo Parsons,* and scuttled another steamer, on the American side of Lake Erie. Beall planned to board the U.S.S. *Michigan,* key ship of the United States naval contingent permitted on the lakes under the Rush-Bagot agreement. In a stranger-than-fiction plot, the *Michi-*

---

[3]Merli, Chapter 11.

gan's captain and crew were to be drugged by an accomplice, the warship's eight inch guns then trained on Johnson's Island and its Confederate prisoners freed. The accomplice was discovered and Beall, realizing the scheme had miscarried, scuttled the *Philo Parsons* off Windsor. In December Beall failed to derail an express near Buffalo, intending to free Confederate officers aboard. He was arrested and executed for sabotage and treason. Protesting that Canada was becoming a base for Confederate subversives, the northern government unofficially—it hoped temporarily—suspended the Rush-Bagot arms limitation on the lakes. Armed tugboats were unobtrusively readied to patrol American harbor entrances, and another regiment sent to Detroit and Buffalo. Governor-General Monck ordered tighter vigilance on Canada's side of the border, and pressed a parsimonious British government to strengthen its forces on the lakes.

The need for vigilance was forcefully illustrated when on October 19 a twenty-strong group of Kentuckians led by a Conferderate lieutenant, Bennett H. Young, attempted to capture the town of St. Albans, Vermont, in the name of the Confederacy. The historic St. Albans raid was matured in Canada East, the brainchild of George Sanders, an unofficial member of the Thompson mission. Clement C. Clay, indifferent to British neutrality, authorized the provocative raid, which Sanders—an American consul during Pierce's presidency—viewed as a legitimate act of war. Clay and Thompson were on poor terms, and Thompson disapproved of the raid when he learned of it. The raiders robbed three banks, tried to fire the town, killed a townsman and wounded others during the melee. A Vermont posse pursued the rebels into Canadian territory, captured Young and some others, but delivered them over to the provincial authorities. On Monck's orders, provincial officials arrested fourteen of the raiding group by October 23. The full-scale border panic that ensued conditioned Canadian-American relations to the war's end, and after, providing heat to the quarrels over wartime compensations, Fenian retaliation against Canada, and Yankee annexationism.[4]

----

[4]See Brian Jenkins, *Fenians and Anglo-American Relations During Reconstruction* (Cornell U.P., 1969), and Leon O'Broin, *Fenian Fever, An Anglo-American Dilemma* (London, 1971).

The indiscretions of individuals threatened to throw the situation out of control. Hearing of the raid, General Dix—without consulting Washington—ordered Union troops in Vermont to pursue the offenders into Canada if necessary, and destroy them. When Montreal Judge Coursol discharged the prisoners on a technicality, Dix issued a second order: his troops were to chase future raiders into Canada, and either destroy them or bring them back to be tried by martial law. The London *Times* called this "a declaration of war against Canada." But Seward refused to lift such military pressure from the backs of the Canadians until he obtained watertight neutrality enforcement. The northern mood was truculent as Sherman speared north toward Richmond, after his army's shattering march through Georgia. From Cincinatti General Hooker blustered: ". . . in case a raid should be attempted from Canada I intend that somebody shall be hurt if I have to go into Canada to do it." More apparent to Seward was the risk of another St. Albans raid, Union retaliation, border violations, and war, thus springing an obvious Confederate trap.

The release of the St. Albans raiders converted a critical number of northern Congressmen against the reciprocity treaty, Justin S. Morrill in December carrying a House resolution calling for unconditional abrogation.[5] Such stormclouds were not lost on the provinces. Seward's policy blended public pressure, and private reassurance: he asked for extradition of the raiders, gave notice of American desire to end the Rush-Bagot agreement within the required six months, but unofficially proposed a review of the situation at the end of that time. If Canada failed to protect the lakes from rebel subversives, the United States would feel free to increase its naval arms there, and Britain would bear the blame for any future naval arms race. Seward added to the pressure by instituting a burdensome passport system to apply on the border as long as subversion continued to be a serious problem. At the right moment Seward made a peace gesture. On December 17 he obtained the revocation of Dix's warlike order from Lincoln. Monck responded by pressing the united provinces government for a more stringent neutrality law. In London Earl Russell, angered at

---

[5]On January 12, 1865, the Senate also called for abrogation, 38 to 8, with Zachariah Chandler and Charles Sumner strongly in support.

St. Albans, recommended stronger Canadian laws. Canadian opinion indicated mounting irritation at the south's abuse of provincial neutrality. The presence in Quebec of Preston King as Seward's troubleshooter helped coordination between Quebec and Washington. Cartier (Quebec's strongman in the cabinet) suspended Judge Coursol and disavowed his ruling. Young and other raiders were rearrested. Seward eventually obtained most of what he wanted: Macdonald's Frontier Outrages Bill proposed to expel foreign nationals suspected of engaging in hostile acts against a friendly nation; militia were mobilized for border duty and a secret detective force appointed to operate among Confederates on the Niagara and Detroit boundaries. The Thompson mission found itself almost totally neutralized. Seward also paid his debts. The last pieces of a complex diplomatic jigsaw fell into place in March 1865, when the State Department ended the passport system for the Canadas, and announced that the Rush-Bagot convention would remain in force.

* * *

Meanwhile the prospect of a Confederate collapse underlined Napoleon's monumental troubles in Mexico. The emperor's anxious attempts to withdraw with honor from a fatally weakening entanglement has its closest modern parallel, perhaps, in America's Vietnam debâcle. After the Mirimar convention, Napoleon's concern was to appease domestic criticism of the Mexican adventure, rife even in his cabinet. He tried to do so by squeezing the Mexicans dry for the profit of French creditors and sundry swindlers. Maximilian was to be kept on a shoestring, and French sons brought home as fast as decency permitted. The policy proved self-defeating. While the luckless Maximilian was stripped of the financial and military resources required for the pacification of the country, his helpless dependence on French support eroded his authority and popularity. The French goals of troop withdrawals and "Mexicanization" of the war (uncannily reminiscent of Indo-China in the 1970's) rested on assumptions of expanding imperial control of the countryside, growing stability, and prosperity. The patent reality was widespread Juárista control, perennial guerilla warfare, insurrection, an empty treasury, no organized national army, bickering between court factions, and an unavailing struggle by Maximilan to assert his authority over French generals such as Marshal Bazaine, whose first loyalty was to the Tuileries (or themselves.) There was another unspoken assumption underlying Napoleon's hopes—success for the south in the Civil War. With the Confederacy in its death-throes, the awesome probability had to be faced that Maximilian could only be shored up by an openended French commitment of massive proportions. That had never been contemplated and—in a context of utter French weariness with Mexico, resurrected Union power, and looming war in Europe—was destined never to be contemplated.

Napoleon trusted to luck to salvage something, hoping for the prolongation of the Civil War, for an exhausted north to forget about Mexico, for Anglo-French coordination to secure the *status quo* for colonial powers in America. Marshal Bazaine was plagued from Paris with orders plainly irreconcileable: he was to crush the enemies of the state and build a foundation of national unity and peace on which Maximilian should erect a lasting empire; at the same time he was to concentrate his forces, cut expenses, and prepare for ultimate evacuation. As large areas reverted to Juárista control, and loyalists were abandoned to the vengeance of the republicans, defeatism spread through the populace and government. Under the French spur, Maximilian began a draconian policy of reprisals which rendered very bitter the last phase of hostilities.

Had Maximilian conceded the full desperation of his position, he may have embarrassed Napoleon into giving greater help. But Maximilian clung to his delusions: that Napoleon would never desert him; that the people were loyal to him; that his liberal reforms would not alienate his conservative and clerical supporters; that he could raise the poor Indian-born without resentment from the Spanish-descended; that he could treat with Juárez; that, in the last resort, his good intentions were enough to win him the day. He was touchingly secure in believing that the powers would guarantee his empire, and even after the surrender of the Confederacy, persuaded himself that Washington could be cajoled from intervention, and even into recognition of his throne.

During 1864 "Defenders of the Monroe Doctrine" formed clubs in the north, made angry demonstrations, and shipped arms illegally to Juárez through New Orleans (proceedings winked at by the Union government). Andrew Johnson, the Republican nominee for vice-President, favored a punitive expedition into Mexico as a "sort of recreation" for northern soldiers after the rebellion had been crushed. Criticisms of Seward's caution on Mexico damaged his political stocks at home—they were not in any case particularly high in 1864 and he did not seriously consider himself a Presidential candidate—but strengthened his hand abroad. There the impetuous fire-eater now appeared the responsible statesman, curbing the chauvinist emotions of his countrymen in the interest of world peace. The gap between Seward and his Republican critics narrowed in June 1864, when a majority at the Baltimore national convention passed a resolution acceptable to the administration. The Radical wing had favored a sweeping condemnation of antirepublican governments anywhere on the continent. Avoiding this trap, the convention viewed as menacing to American independence any European efforts "to obtain new footholds for monarchical governments, sustained by foreign military force in near proximity to the United States." As General Grant made his final sanguinary onslaughts on Richmond in the new year, it seemed that the politicians might be placed under insuperable popular pressure to mobilize a grand army which should drive the French invaders into the Gulf of Mexico.

As 1864 ended reports circulated that Maximilian had ceded to France the north Mexican states of Sonora, Sinaloa, Chihuahua, Durango, and Lower California. William L. Gwin, ex-senator from California and long interested in developing the Sonora mines, was said to have been created a Duke of Mexico and Napoleon's Viceroy over the new colony. The French (who had in fact abandoned plans to exploit Sonora in November) officially denied any cession in February. To northerners, it all smacked of a last-ditch try by the French to complete a vital link in their supposed schemes for world commercial supremacy. Napoleon was known to have placed a high priority on construction of a transit railroad across the Isthmus of Tehantepec. By forestalling the Anglo-Americans, with their plans for a canal across Panama, France would gain a strangle-hold on interoceanic trade in the western hemisphere. When the Suez canal was completed under French auspices, control of the world's major trade routes would pass to France. More immediately, Napoleon's assertiveness in northwest

Mexico could be construed as a flank movement on California, and preparation for the establishment of a large French naval and commercial base on the Pacific coast. North Mexico continued to be a turbulent area, inviting to the rapacious: at varying times late in the war it promised to be a new base of Confederate resistance, the possible nucleus of a larger Texas, and the subject of a Yankee takeover masterminded by business and army interests.

* * *

The Confederacy, in its moment of extremity, made a desperate last-minute bid to wring action from Europe, and thus to avoid the humiliation of having to palaver with the Yankees at a peace table. Duncan Kenner, Louisiana politician and gambler—a symbolic choice—headed a mission whose job was to dispel two disabilities that had plagued the south in Europe: the prejudice against slavery, and belief in the inevitability of the rebellion's success without outside aid. Kenner's task was to make it crystal clear that his country stood on its last legs. If the powers failed to act, a reconstructed United States would bestride the hemiphere, evicting the British from Canada and the French from Mexico. On slavery, Kenner had the go-ahead to test his long-held conviction that emancipation of southern slaves must be a precondition for foreign recognition or aid. The south proposed to abolish slavery if that was the barrier to British or French recognition. Friends of the south in London, including the Southern Independence Association, and in Paris, including Persigny, de Lesseps, and court officials, had plied Davis and Benjamin with advice on the need for "some promise for prospective emancipation." Within the south itself survival triumphed over racial dogma, when plans were made to arm and enlist blacks in the army, despite warnings of slave uprisings and economic chaos. Why refuse complete emancipation of the slaves, when the alternative was emancipation by the conquering Yankees?

By the time Kenner reached Europe, north and south had already met at the Hampton Roads peace conference. Driven to seek a respite from hostilities, Confederate representatives met with Lincoln and Seward in February, 1865, aboard the U.S.S. *River Queen*. Kenner's goal of forestalling American peace talks was thus lost before he started. But leverage might yet be applied upon the powers; for the *River Queen* discussions were known to have raised the possibility of north and south forming an alliance for a divertive war against either Britain—over St. Albans and the *Alabama* claims—or France over Mexico. Crying "America for the Americans," the Richmond *Enquirer* asked why, if the European powers allowed the Confederacy to sink, the south should not join the Union in vengeful retaliation against them? Such threats proved to be of little avail, and the promise of Negro emancipation irrelevant. An emancipation gesture made at the flood of the Confederacy's fortune may conceivably have worked; but its chances of appearing at such a juncture seem historically negligible. Now the south was beyond salvation. For European countries, recognition would be a legal absurdity and a political blunder of gigantic proportions: at the simplest it would bring upon the offender the wrath of the world's most formidable army, and with no corresponding recompense to be won from the south.

Slidell broached Kenner's offer to Napoleon on March 4, but was gently rebuffed: France could not move without England; England had so decisively rejected previous French overtures on recognition that Napoleon felt disinclined to risk another snub. The Hampton Roads talks genuinely alarmed Napoleon. Geofroy, the French *chargé* in Washington, warned that "alliance against a foreign power will be the pivot of reconciliation" between the sections; if attained, "we would, within the next six months, see the war transplanted to the borders of Mexico and Canada."[6] Seward reassured Paris that the United States intended to maintain its neutrality on Mexico—Napoleon's chief worry—and entertained no aggressive designs after the war's end. But Geofroy's reports of a rift between Lincoln and Seward kept up the uncertainty. Napoleon ordered a military appreciation from his experts. It was gloomy. The French navy was not competent to convey 100,000 troops to Mexico, and carry on naval warfare single-handed against the north. Success was possible only by an Anglo-French combination. As that was hardly in the cards, French policy toward the Union thawed perceptibly as the war ended. In London, Mason fared no better with Kenner's deal. Palmerston fathomed

---

[6]Geofroy to Drouyn, January 24, 1865, q. Case and Spencer, p. 561. Mercier had returned to France in December, 1863.

with difficulty Mason's circumlocutions on the tabooed topic of Negro emancipation; then bluntly discounted slavery as the cause of British inertia. Her Majesty's Government, he said, had not been satisfied at any period of the war that rebel independence "was achieved beyond peradventure, and did not feel authorized so to declare when the events of a few weeks might prove it a failure."[7]

The Civil War was indeed almost won for the north. At Hampton Roads Lincoln dismissed the idea of a north-south "war of liberation" in Mexico. He wanted, above all, a peace that achieved full restoration of the Union and abolition of slavery. The conference collapsed, and the war dragged on until April 9 when Lee, his decimated army trapped by Union columns, surrendered to Grant at Appomattox Courthouse. Jefferson Davis and his ministers were already in flight. An exodus of Confederate soldiery took place into Mexico from the devastated south, threatening to embroil Maximilian with a triumphant United States over breaches of neutrality. The State Department kept alert for southerners carrying arms across the Rio Grande, for mass enlistments in Maximilian's imperial army, and continuing Confederate operations against the north from Mexican bases. Nor was Maximilian enchanted by the prospect of men like Kirby Smith's battle-hardened veterans carving out a new Texas for themselves in north Mexico. At Puebla in June, 1865, Maximilian indicated to his advisers, including the new French minister Dano, that he hoped to reach agreement with the United States on the delicate issues of Confederate emigrants and the resumption of commercial relations.[8] He rejected plans—proposed by the southern agents Gwin, Soule, and Maury—for Confederate soldier settlement in the northern provinces: "What will happen when a compact Anglo-Saxon group is established on the frontier? They will become rich and will they follow our rule or want to be independent?" The rebels would be allowed only into Central Mexico where they must blend with the indigenes. Matthew Maury, appointed impe-

---

[7]Mason to Benjamin, March 31, 1865, q. Owsley, p. 540.
[8]Dano to Drouyn, June 11, 1865, q. K. A. Hanna, "Roles of the South in the French Intervention in Mexico," *JSH*, XX, No. 1 (February, 1954), p. 18. Also R. L. Kerby, *Kirby Smith's Confederacy: The Trans-Mississippi South, 1863–5* (Columbia U.P., 1972).

rial commissioner of colonization in September 1865, visualized the settling of 200,000 southern families on plantations in Mexico. Only a few thousand arrived, but a land office was set up, land surveys initiated, and a Confederate newspaper started. Maximilian permitted the southerners to bring their former slaves on an apprenticeship basis, a blunder. Juárez' minister Romero protested to Seward, Bigelow applied pressure on Drouyn, and Maximilian was persuaded by Dano to drop the colonization scheme. So petered out the Confederacy's variant version of American mission.

* * *

After Appomattox the world waited for the United States to take hemispheric revenge against the despised great powers. "After Mexico will come Canada, and after Canada will come Cuba. The crash will be heard, like Horace's thunder, from a clear sky." So predicted the *New York Herald* (August 1, 1865). It was a classic misprediction. Why did an expansionist outburst await postponement until 1898, when unexampled scope existed in 1865 for making a *fait accompli* fulfilling at a stroke the master design of the geopoliticians? Grant's Juggernaut awed the world; Welles' navy was among the top three; and Europe's distractions on the eve of the Austro-Prussian war matched those of America in 1861. Yet the Canadians were allowed to create their nonrepublican Dominion, in Van Alstyne's phrase "the great surprise of North America," which "while still in swaddling clothes ... placed a permanent barrier against the American northward advance."[9] And the French were driven out of Mexico by "the un-American plan of matching diplomacy with diplomacy."[10] Seward's superbly pacific strategy restored the Mexican republic, even kept up formal friendship with the French, without gaining America an inch of territory. This extraordinary restraint determined the essential contours of the modern United States.

There is no easy explanation for it, and the whole question warrants more thorough discussion in the current debate on American expansionism. I shall return to the subject in my concluding chapter. It may suffice here to say that warweariness, and a desire for

---

[9]Van Alstyne, *Rising American Empire,* p. 176.

[10]*NYH,* August 1, 1865.

economic and social recuperation, played a large part in the opposition to territorial annexations. The expansionist vision persisted, but the American nation seemed psychologically unprepared yet to accept the full implications and responsibilities of imperialism. It seemed enough for the moment within the hemisphere to expel the invaders, preferably by persuasion, and to reestablish the regenerative principle of republicanism. Americans would have to be satisfied, for a time, with a role of tutelage in the hemisphere. White supremacist ideas also discouraged the incorporation of lesser breeds within the American sphere. Reconstruction promised a surfeit of racial troubles within the existing Union. Why add to them? Ultimately, if inferior peoples failed to fulfill republican expectations, they risked being supplanted by the expanding, more dynamic populations of North America. Underlying racial attitudes often surfaced with respect to the Mexicans. The *Herald* sneered at them as "not up to the mark"; "they need policeing . . . and if we choose we can do it just as well as France." "Marshal Bazaine and his soldiers . . . have done much good to Mexico, more, in fact, than all the native governments since the country became independent."[11] Such comments indicate the difficulty, often unconscious, which Americans experienced in repudiating their European heritage for a philosophy more appropriate to a "good neighbor" foreign policy. Despite the shock caused by the "perfidy" of the powers to the United States during the Civil War, Americans continued to share European racial and cultural values.

Triumphant Union generals such as Grant, Lew Wallace and others favored a decisive strike against the French in Mexico. Grant posted a powerful army of observation under Sheridan along the Rio Grande. The presence of Sheridan's army, eager to invade, makes nonsense of claims that military exhaustion would have precluded American intervention. With Juárista assistance, Sheridan could justly expect to overwhelm opposition in quick style before French reinforcements arrived across the Atlantic. In Washington Seward and the Marquis de Montholon, the new French minister, worked for a diplomatic settlement, against the Francophobe clamors of Republicans like William M. Evarts, John A. Dix and the Blairs. Seward blocked a provocative move inspired by Grant, Romero, and General John M. Schofield and backed by

---

[11]*NYH,* August 26, 1865.

Andrew Johnson and Stanton. Schofield planned to take leave, cross the border into Mexico, and gather together an army of ex-Confederate and Union soldiers who had emigrated. Men and materials would then be funnelled across the Rio Grande to fight the French. Seward diverted Schofield to Paris as a special agent with instructions "to get your legs under Napoleon's mahogany and tell him he must get out of Mexico."[12] By the time Schofield arrived in December Napoleon had no need of such persuasion.

Lincoln's assassination, which evoked an extraordinary outburst of grief from world opinion, caused Maximilian especial depression. Lincoln had promised no more wars under his Presidency; Andrew Johnson might prove a creature of popular passion. Maximilian sent an emissary, Felix Eloin, to see Napoleon and King Leopold of Belgium on a bootless quest for great power protection. He also sent Mariano Degollado to Washington with condolences and an offer of negotiations on border problems. Johnson refused to receive Degollada. However the new President continued to give Seward his head in foreign policy, backing Seward when he gave notice to the French of rising American impatience for an early end to their occupation of Mexico. In return for French withdrawal Seward offered restoration of the ancient friendship between the two nations, hinted at support for French claims to the Rhineland at an international congress, and promised that America desired no aggrandizement by conquest or purchase of land in Mexico. This last was also designed to reassure the Juáristas, who were not fighting their guerilla war to pave the way for a Yankee takeover: hence the vested interest of Juárez in a diplomatic settlement. He wanted to appear as the real saviour of free Mexico, not a puppet brought in the baggage of a conquering army. His ambivalent attitude toward the Americans was to become characteristic of Latin American nationalists. Juárez of course, posed a massive stumbling block to any annexationist designs on Mexico: it would have been transparent hypocrisy, as bad as French behavior, to shoulder aside the Juáristas, to impose Yankee rule at the bayonet point in Mexico. The pure theory of American mission, after all, required the consent of the subject peoples in new acquisitions by the Republic.

---

[12]Van Deusen, *Seward,* pp. 489–490. Schofield never saw Napoleon, but interviewed government officials.

Seward spoke to the French about the future in Mexico in studied nonspecifics. After the French withdrew, the United States was prepared to allow the Mexican people to "be the arbiter" on Maximilian's monarchy. The United States stood for nonintervention in the hemisphere; but it also stood for the republican system of government there. Seward did not intend the French to rule out the chance of armed American resistance to their Intervention. Seward's new minister in France, John Bigelow—Dayton died of a stroke in December 1864—almost sabotaged American strategy when, believing that "it is hardly worth our while, under pretext of defending republican institutions, to get ourselves into a war with one and perhaps several of the most powerful states of Europe," he set up a package deal with Drouyn: France would evacuate Mexico in return for an American guarantee to recognize Maximilian as soon as he proved self-sustaining.[13] Washington squashed the idea in November 1865.

Monographs have been written on the circumstances leading to the French evacuation of Mexico. What emerges is that Napoleon understood the minatory basis from which American pressure was unyieldingly applied, and was alarmed by it. That is why he tried, in November 1865, to arrange a mutual assistance pact with Britain, to be invoked if the United States tried aggression against either partner. It was not an irresistable proposition as far as London was concerned. The French were offering a highly dubious contribution to Canadian security in return for probable British embroilment in Mexico. Britain's rejection of the plan underlined the other key factor compelling Napoleon to cut his losses in Mexico: France's diplomatic isolation in Europe. At a time when forecasts of European conflagration were heard on all sides, the restoration of good relations between Paris and Washington, and the concentration of French troops where they were needed, in Europe, were obvious insurance policies for Napoleon.

There was, of course, nothing new about the intrusion of European considerations into the Mexican question. It had been, all along, one piece in a complex international mosaic. It would be no more extreme to contend that the abandonment of Maximilian

---

[13]Callahan, *American Foreign Policy in its Mexican Relations,* pp. 309–310; Clapp, *Bigelow,* pp. 247–248.

had been ordained in 1863, with the failure of Napoleon's design for an Austrian alliance, than to declare that it was decreed by the looming Austro-Prussian war of 1866. The French decision to announce a staged withdrawal from Mexico was made *before* the Austro-Prussian feud had moved from the serious to acute stage. And in practice the withdrawal program differed little from that envisaged in the secret provisions of the treaty of Mirimar. On February 22, 1866, Napoleon publicly promised evacuation (the decision had probably been taken the previous November); on April 5 a dispatch to Montholon in Washington specified return of the army in three detachments (November 1866, March 1867, November 1867). Mirimar had proposed no more than a three year occupation (1863–1867).

Nevertheless it would be ludicrous to forget that Napoleon's retreat took place while Europe was enduring what A. J. P. Taylor calls "the lesser revision" of the old balance of power. The Prussian victory over Austria in 1866 paved the way for German unification; and the resultant cession of Venetia to Italy completed Italian unification. Napoleon, it is true, saw no immediate danger in a stronger Prussia (nor did London and St. Petersburg). He allowed the the war to occur because it assured Venetia to the Italians—his old obsession—and promised possible pickings on the Rhine. But he needed domestic unity, and peace with America, to exploit (even to cope with) a very uncertain situation. Hence elimination of the divisive and costly Mexican issue. As Blumenthal shows, Bismarck in 1865 worried that sudden resolution of Napoleon's American difficulties might dispose the Emperor to interfere in the German question. Diseased and depressed, the emperor showed signs of being distinctly rattled over Mexico. Bismarck also feared French humiliation at American hands, for "Napoleon might seek to recover the prestige he lost in the New World by troubling the Old."[14] Prussian diplomacy hence aimed

---

[14]Blumenthal, p. 176. For a perceptive analysis of the effects of European power politics, p. 175 and following. See also Corti (which shows Napoleon's real anxiety on Mexico and Prussia); C. A. Duniway "Reasons for the Withdrawal of France from Mexico," *American Historical Association Reports,* I (1902), pp. 315–328; Count Otto zu Stolberg-Wernigerode, *Germany and the United States during the Era of Bismarck* (trs. Reading, Pa., 1937; original, Berlin, 1928); Perkins, *Monroe Doctrine, 1826–1867,* pp. 515–518 takes exception to explanations based on European considerations.

to keep France embroiled with America, maximizing the chances of French neutrality in any Austrian war. Whether Prussian intrigues had any effect is another matter.

The February promise to evacuate French troops followed intense pressure from the United States, leading to a near-crisis in Franco-American relations in the last months of 1865. Napoleon's bitterness derived from his inability to obtain a face-saving *quid pro quo* for French submission. He would have settled for an "amicable attitude" to Maximilian by the Americans; and he offered them economic concessions. But Washington refused to give official assurances of nonintervention. They were needless, went the argument; America had always been noninterventionist. Late in November Drouyn was flatly told that the United States "still regard the French effort to establish permanently a foreign and imperial government in Mexico as disallowable and impracticable." Drouyn bridled at this. Seward's language, according to Drouyn, "practically claims that the whole American continent belongs to the United States, and that governments and institutions there must correspond to your wishes. . . . If you mean war why not say so frankly?" Bigelow was dutifully evasive in response, but riposted that the American people opposed "a government founded on our borders for the avowed purpose of limiting the diffusion of the Anglo-Saxon race on the American continent." He reported that Drouyn spoke with warmth but "seemed to imply that, if we insisted, it would be the end of their Mexican experience. . . ."[15]

It seems that Napoleon, unbeknown to Drouyn, had already accepted the inevitable. In a long interview with Union General James Watson Webb (November 10), Napoleon declared his readiness to withdraw over a two year period.[16] An old acquaintance of the emperor's, Webb had learned in a letter of 1863 that Napoleon was tormented by his Mexican albatross. Webb looked up

---

[15]Quoted, Callahan, *American Foreign Policy in its Mexican Relations,* pp. 310, 315 and following.

[16]For Webb's unofficial diplomacy, Blumenthal, p. 177 and following; R. B. McCormack, "James Watson Webb and French Withdrawal from Mexico," *Hispanic American Hist. Review,* XXXI (1951), pp. 274–286. Webb alleged that Napoleon offered to sell Cayenne (in the West Indies) to the United States for 50 million francs, as part of his policy of liquidating the French colonial system. Webb, who wanted a string of coaling stations for the American navy, approved.

Napoleon on his way home on leave of absence from Brazil, where he had been Union ambassador. He later claimed that he had persuaded the emperor to accept a timetable for evacuation; and he promised to sound President Johnson on the proposal, which left unresolved the question of Maximilian's recognition. (Napoleon, we know, was actively considering extracting more material consolations for a retreat—his ideas included selling Sonora to the United States, and securing, belatedly, American guarantees on the French debt in Mexico. These terms were suggested to Seward in January 1866, and turned down.) It is not known if Johnson's favorable reply was passed back to Napoleon by Webb; in any case the French had received abundant diplomatic indications that a genuinely peaceful settlement was on offer. But Seward knew henceforth that the game was won, and could pile on pressure for a swifter withdrawal.

It is now legend that Maximilian proved unable to hold Mexico without French troops, which were withdrawn ahead of schedule under the demands of the European crisis and American pressure. The American army of observation was conspicuously maintained on the Rio Grande during Maximilian's decline and fall before the Juáristas. Maximilian tried to enlist Habsburg help, in the form of regiments of Austrian volunteers raised for Mexican service, but was stymied by an unexpected American threat of war against Austria. Vienna backed down with nervous alacrity to prepare for the more imminent issue of war with Bismarck's Prussia. Maximilian's fall vindicated the view, asserted throughout the Civil War by the United States and the Latin American republics, that the imperial monarchy had been imposed against the will of the Mexican people. Maximilian's execution, at the hands of a republican firing squad on June 19, 1867, was a deliberate slap in the face by Juárez to Europe's monarchs. It was perhaps his harshest gesture of independence. Not only did he spurn appeals for clemency from the old powers of Europe, but even from Garibaldi, and the world's newest (perhaps only newly restored) great power, the United States. For Maximilian's release Seward was ready to join the Prussians and other European states in a pledge guaranteeing Mexican independence.

As an act of vengeance against Napoleon, the execution was incalculably successful: the "betrayal" of Maximilian (for which the Habsburgs never forgave Napoleon), the depressing futility of the entire Mexican escapade, became the scandal of the Second Empire. The grand design had become grand folly, and Bismarck (as he aspired) took the spoils. When Prussia crushed France in 1870, few North Americans lamented the emperor's ruin. Prussia had earned credit for its pro-northern sympathy during the Civil War, and for contributing emigrants to the Union armies. But Napoleon III was remembered as one who had, with cynical disregard, placed in hazard the mythical Gallic alliance—and all for the silver of Sonora and the "white gold" of the Confederacy. Consistent with their civil war faith in the fundamental soundness of the French people, and their belief in the need for an international fraternity of democrats, Americans welcomed the Third Republic.

CHAPTER X

Verdicts

THE RESTRAINT OF THE GREAT POWERS during the American Civil War was too clearly the product of contingency, cynical self-regard, and moral hesitations to impress as a piece of generous and lofty statesmanship. And that was the judgment of the time. In retrospect the distractions of European power politics helped materially to save the Union. The powers did not meddle because they were unable to subdue their rivalries or find a mutually acceptable basis for intervention. Reduced to essentials, the powers, in particular France, would not intervene without the cooperation of Britain, still the world's top dog nation. As has been always recognized, British nonintervention was the key to civil war diplomacy. Even British sanction for unilateral action by France, or others, was inadequate: indeed to Napoleon III British coaxing was highly suspicious, a trick to get him involved in yet another eroding commitment and to weaken France in Europe. The time for a joint move by France and Britain, a serious and risky intervention, had probably passed by the time Poland exploded, and it became more remote as the European situation worsened over the vital "German Question." Napoleon spoke still of joint recognition of the south and titillated southern hopes; but to further his European policies he was willing to cut his losses in Mexico (a policy arrived at during, not after, the war) and to maneuver for northern friendship. War might conceivably still have come between the north and one of the powers, had the diplomats been clumsier, had questions involving national honor and face been pressed to extremes—for there was ill-will and in plenty on all sides—but war would have come against the European realpolitik interests of the participants.

Britain was certainly subject to these restraints. Despite its power, Britain was finding it difficult to have its say on Europe's future, partly because of its military weakness in Europe and partly because—after Poland and Schleswig-Holstein—it had lost control of some key diplomatic pressure points. A war with the United States would have meant having no say at all in Europe, would have sacrificed its precious freedom of action on the major theater of international politics at a vital period of change. As it was, Britain's American distractions prevented it playing the role in Europe it might otherwise have essayed. Thus America was saved, as Horace Greeley hoped it would be, by "the unprincipled egotism that is the soul of European diplomacy." Fortunately for the Union, the Civil War coincided with the first major revision of the European power balance which had lasted since the Napoleonic wars.

It is not enough to argue that Britain stayed neutral because of the profits of neutrality: booty from munitions; the spoils of blockade-running; the monopoly of the Atlantic shipping trade through transfer of the American merchant marine to the British flag; the bonanza which wartime demand brought to a range of industries (offsetting cotton unemployment). Nor is it enough to urge the more vigorous proposition that intervention spelt war, and war spelt certain economic pains and only uncertain gains: the destruction of an integrated Atlantic economy, disruption of British maritime trade, economic unrest, and social divisiveness at home, etc., for the distant attractions of a southern alliance, cotton and markets. (Had there been general awareness that the cotton famine was a largely artificial crisis, and one offering opportunities for development of India's colonial economy, even the King Cotton thesis could have been weakened.) These were powerful deterrents to adventurism, particularly powerful at the height of the "doveish" free trade era, but they were capable of being overwhelmed by considerations of strategy, national interest and imperial security. What is crucial to an understanding of British neutrality is the fact that the latter factors never unequivocally demanded war and disruption of America. Ambiguity at this level permitted economic, humanitarian, moral, and domestic political forces to exert their sway upon the American question.

Englishmen debated the prospects of a war with the north at length, but there was a consensus that it would be a difficult, expensive, and in certain circumstances, an unpopular war. There is no need to rehearse the warnings that were constantly made concerning the vulnerability of Canada to the Union army, of the far-flung and exposed British possessions to naval attack, of the British merchant marine to commerce-destroyers. Again the Union was lucky, for the Civil War coincided with a time of rapid modernization in naval technology, and the north's industrial strength would have enabled it to build an effective striking force, partly neutralizing British superiority in traditional ships, and forcing Britain in any war into an expensive naval program.

What international objective could justify taking such a grisly gamble? Unfortunately the documents are elusive on this vital subject. It may well be that it was never thoroughly discussed by British policy-makers, either because it was ruled out as a live issue or because they followed a pragmatic course of meeting American problems as they arose from day to day amidst a welter of other demanding questions. Even when war was seriously con- templated, at the time of the *Trent,* preservation of national honor was the only cogent and consistent motive for hostilities urged by ministers. The cliché about England wanting a breakup of the Union for realpolitik reasons, to destroy a rival in the hemisphere, to pave the way for an expansion of British hegemony in the hemisphere, was much paraded by northerners during the war, and has been paraded by many writers since. One might assert, with greater plausibility given the record of Anglo-American rela- tions in the latter 1850's, that the British ministry took account of an opposite view: that British interests better flourished in a stable hemisphere based upon United States power.[1] A balkanized America could engender threats by a revanchist north against

---

[1]Palmerston made some utterances to cabinet colleagues (Russell and probably Gladstone) on the gain to England of separation, but such sentiments were uncom- monly rare from government members, and, in Palmerston's case, uttered in anger at Union navy high-handedness with British ships. Bell, *Palmerston,* p. 315. Wilbur Jones, in his study of the papers of prominent Conservatives, was unable to find any expression of desire for a permanent split of the Union. W. D. Jones, "British Conservatives and the American Civil War," *AHR,* LVIII (1953), pp. 535, 542.

Canada, and a wave of Confederate imperialism to the south; while the hemisphere might become a cockpit of European rivalries, open to all sorts of fishing in troubled waters. Even Napoleon, who did not scruple when advantage was offered for French aggrandizement, saw danger as well as opportunity in any breakdown of American unity; for southern ambitions threatened any client state he might set up in Mexico, while the extinction of American maritime power deprived France of a counterweight to Britain. The British were already a giant imperial power, unenthusiastic about further territorial commitments and expense. If Napoleon stood (at least nominally) for revisionism of boundaries, Britain stood instinctively for a settled international order and minimal change in the balance of power.

Nor was the generation of men who controlled British destinies in the sixties cast in adventurous mold, willing to gamble for high but frighteningly uncertain stakes in America. For most of them it was a matter of keeping out of trouble and playing safe, balancing immediate neutral interests against long-term naval interests, preserving face against Yankee bluster but avoiding a "partisan" interference which would divide the English nation. The long-term problem for England must have seemed not how to exploit American weakness, but how best to face up to the international results of the rebellion's inevitable success. Whether desirable or not for Britain, separation was going to occur. The mediation suggestions of 1862, although also spurred on by humanitarianism and a supposed need for cotton, proposed accepting this inevitability. They by no means necessarily endorsed the strategic implications of an American breakup. Gladstone personified this ambiguity, wanting an armistice to save the remnants of American liberty but believing that a unified Republic best suited British interests. When the north insisted that the struggle was still in doubt, and rejected mediation as intervention in favor of the south, the steam behind mediation dissipated. It evaporated completely as the war became chronic, and as parallel attempts by the powers to mediate in Poland crumbled because of quarrels between the participants. Harcourt saw to the heart of the matter when he listed the reprehensibilities in Russell's peace proposals. The implications of a settlement to the war had simply not been thought through. A scheme which was forcibly imposed upon the north, and which never came to grips with the issues dividing America (including slavery and states' rights), lacked moral validity. It would appear merely a pretext for sealing the fate of a rival power. And a mediation which offered prospects of interminable jealousies between Britain and France, jostling for position in an American power vacuum, lacked statesmanship.

Britain ended the Civil War despised by both sides. Victor and vanquished complained inconsolably that Britain's neutrality had favored their opponent, an indication of the problem of neutrals in extended warfare. In war, powers demand sympathy from their friends, not calculated self-interest or cool correctness, and even less a detached appraisal of the issues at stake. The war illustrated the potential for emotional crisis embedded in the Atlantic connection. It showed the extent to which intimacy of cultural contact could embitter and complicate ordinary power relationships. France's expediency and notorious disposition to intervene, if safe, was not as deeply resented in the north as Britain's more circumspect behavior. Resentment would have been greater toward France, one suspects, if a republican regime had been in power. Ungenerosity from a Napoleonic autocracy was to be expected; from kith and kin it was unforgivable.

To regard the recrimination which marked Anglo-American relations in the postwar generation as a mere temporary misfortune, to be rectified with the Great Rapprochement of the 1890's, appears to me misguided. The Civil War marked the end of a distinctive, and probably the most intimate, phase in Atlantic history. The war markedly accelerated a process of social and economic disengagement which was taking place inevitably as the result of American national maturation. Cultural and economic emancipation from the old English metropolitan center were natural features of this transformation. The war added immeasurably to the incubus of bitterness and rejection which Americans carried as an historical legacy from the Revolutionary period. The war disrupted, brutally and almost beyond repair, the integrative bonds of the Atlantic connection, just as it tore asunder the fibers of the body politic in America itself. What has been perhaps insufficiently recognized is the rapidity with which the Anglo-American relationship was impoverished, and reduced to the stark essentials of power. Peace demanded a reconstruction of America's major foreign relationship as well as of American society. Both processes proved to be acrimonious, divisive, and ultimately disappointing.

Canada raised difficult questions concerning the nature and strength of American expansionism. The whole subject of American imperial concepts and forces during the Civil War and the following decade is in need of intensive research. The fate of ideals of external expansion during a time of pathological internal development may well bring into relief the critical social values underlying the debate on American destiny, both in mid-century and later. At the moment, only generalizations may be hazarded. Here are some: There was a strong expansionist undercurrent in mid-century America, despite the distractions of the sectional debate —and they were literally distractions and an irrelevancy to those intoxicated by the broader vision—and it was not extinguished by the war. Rather, anger against the powers was channeled into demands for the evacuation of all European influence (except white North American republican) from the hemisphere. America's might, having been mobilized by the rebellion, would come into its own after the south's suppression. The arrogance of northern language (one might hypothesize) was sharpened by the primitive emotions of wartime; and was unrestrained by considerations of feasibility, because everybody except a dwindling band of "foreign war panaceaists" agreed that such vendettas and adventures were to be shelved until peace. Idealist arguments justified the conferring of republican independence upon peoples still enslaved by the imperial powers of Europe; and the hope was held out that such peoples might freely join the United States, the "citadel of freedom," on terms of equality with its present inhabitants. The ideological justification for expansion was presented the more forcibly because the war had reawakened a sense of America's missionary revolutionary role in world affairs. Although the idea was quickly abandoned after Appomattox, northerners spoke violently during hostilities of launching an international movement which would unite the submerged masses of the world in a democratic jihad against oligarchic oppression.

But the war produced full measure of less edifying American self-centeredness. Greed for the possession of new economic resources and control of strategically placed trade routes and communications featured in discussions of hemispheric change. Ideas of white racism and global power considerations underpinned the debate. James Gordon Bennett's suggestion that Russia and the United States divide the world between them, Russia dominating Europe and Asia while the United States ruled the "Western World," was merely an extreme expression of "brute realist" sentiment.

Peace however brought the expansionist debate back to earth, and resurrected all the old national divisions on the subject. Conventionally the latter 1860's are regarded as antiexpansionist, and it is a measure of the failure of the annexationist school that neither Canada, Mexico, nor Cuba were harvested for America, as had been freely predicted in 1865. Traditional preferences reemerged for American sponsorship of continental freedom without territorial acquisitions; for annexation only on the earnest request of colonial peoples; for American racial purity and thus the exclusion of racially-mixed states (e.g. Cuba and Santo Domingo); for concentration on the development of existing frontier lands. To these considerations must be added a profound emotional reaction throughout the nation against more wars. Top priority was given to the restoration of peace, and to the problems and politics of reconstruction. While expansionism was approved in the form of informal commercial "empire," expensive military adventures were anathematized as adding to a colossal war debt. As peace brought industrial dislocations and agricultural difficulties, the hallowed cry of government retrenchment became strong. Congressional opposition was powerful even to the purchase of strategically valuable bases such as the Danish West Indies, plausibly but unsuccessfully urged by Seward as a bargain at 7.5 million dollars. Even the purchase of Alaska, which admirably suited American geopolitical and strategic interests, was pulled off by Seward only after some skillful Russian bribery of Congressmen. Alaska, "Seward's Folly," was acquired, instructively, amidst general public indifference.

But to characterize the postwar years baldly as antiexpansionist is to oversimplify. There were apostles and theorists of empire aplenty, even if the public was less responsive than they wished; and their ideas were to bear fruit as war memories faded, economic conditions changed, and escape was desired from the aridities and corruptions of domestic politics. Seward's restrained case for ac-

quiring strategically important outposts on trade routes vital to
American interests—for example, St. Thomas and San Domingo in
the Caribbean, Hawaii on the way to Asian markets—might have
succeeded in less bitter political times. Congressional opposition
to Seward's projects was essentially a method to abash the hated
Andrew Johnson rather than a considered judgment on empire.
The emotive politics of Reconstruction were to cut across and
confuse the issue of expansion in myriad ways during the Johnson
and Grant administrations. Jealousy between executive and legis-
lative killed Grant's Santo Domingo project as surely as suspicion
of sordid speculators. The nation came close to intervention in the
Cuban rebellion, but Grant and a strong force of Congressional
warhawks encountered the restraining influence of Sumner's radicals, and the Federalist caution of Hamilton Fish at the State Department. The hostility of Congress to the lame duck Johnson
government killed Seward's hasty efforts to reach rapprochement
with Britain, when the Johnson-Clarendon convention was rejected by the Senate 54 to 1. There can be little doubt that in this
case Congress prevented the administration stifling deep national
resentment over the *Alabama* claims. The outcome opened the
gates to a flood of expansionist designs upon Canada. Some of the
rhetoric on the annexation of Canada was hot air, directed by
parish-pump politicians at the Irish and other immigrants; but
much of it was genuine. While the "cede Canada or fight" school
was a small, vocal minority, the hope of acquiring Canada peacefully—perhaps in a deal over wartime claims—penetrated even to
the State Department. Zach Chandler, senator for Michigan, was
not talking practical politics when he declaimed:

Great Britain owns a little land up north of us and I, Sir, am willing to
consider this a first mortgage on the little debt that Great Britain owes.
I do not want arbitration. I want to let it rest until the time comes to
foreclose that mortgage. This North American continent belongs to us and
ours it must be.[2]

But Chandler's "spread-eaglism," uncomplicated by sophisticated
economic theorizing, had wide appeal. What confounded the an-

---

[2]Quoted Doris W. Dashew, "Story of an Illusion: the Plan to Trade the *Alabama*
Claims for Canada," *CWH,* XV, No. 4 (December, 1969), p. 338. See also LaFeber,
New Empire, pp. 28–39; Van Alstyne, *Rising American Empire,* p. 176.

nexationists, ultimately, was miscalculation concerning Canadian eagerness for joining a mammoth American republic. The expansionists had interpreted the Canadian Confederation movement as a symptom of the disintegration of the British connection, and as prelude to a Canadian stampede into the Union. Instead the Dominion became established fact, permanently confining the American homeland south of the 49th parallel. Alaska was left in frozen abeyance, the top arm of a pincer originally designed to squeeze the British from the lands of the Hudson Bay Company and the crown colony of British Columbia.

The legacy of the Civil War to European politics was curiously meager, especially so considering the gargantuan events and intense debate which had occurred. Perhaps the war was simply too horrible to remember. Even the military lessons it flaunted to the world—the destructiveness of modern firepower, evoking the answer of defensive trench warfare and foretelling the horrors of World War I—were quickly forgotten as Prussia's campaigns against Austria in 1866 and France in 1870 illustrated new offensive patterns.[3] Politically, the triumph of the north gave only short-term impetus to democratic movements in Western Europe. Moreover that triumph was cruelly ambiguous.

The Civil War contributed to the passing of electoral reform in Britain in at least two ways: the outcome encouraged a climate of opinion conducive to change; while the war forged a fighting partnership between middle class and trade union radicalism on behalf of the north, an experience which smoothed the path for their cooperation in the campaign for the 1867 Reform Bill. The verdict of arms at Appomattox gave a crushing answer to those who claimed that transatlantic democracy was incapable of surviving as a workable system. After Lincoln's apotheosis, it seemed capable even of producing heroic statesmen. Moreover Gladstone was not alone in his joy that the distressed cotton operatives had acted reliably and responsibly during the war. During the reform debates much was made of this point as an argument for conferring the vote on the artisan and mechanic class. Nevertheless the major franchise changes wrought in 1867 were the product of

---

[3]See Jay Luvaas, *The Military Legacy of the Civil War: The European Inheritance* (Chicago, 1959).

complex forces: the legislation was shaped by political contingency and expediency, it was engineered by a parliamentary elite within a largely parliamentary context, and it owed its form to hierarchic reasonings rather than to democratic doctrine. The second Reform Bill, like the first, aimed to perserve the balance of the constitution—and the predominance of the country's natural rulers—by permitting a limited infusion of healthy new blood into the political system. The vote might be safely extended to include steady workingmen, likely to be deferential and adhere to current social values. Disraeli's bill, he freely admitted, was a "bulwark against democracy" and would strengthen the conservative character of Parliament by founding it "on a broad popular basis." Population pressures and expanding industrialization rendered some such adjustment inevitable. The significance of American events was as one more sign that the world was going in much the same direction. In France, the victory of the north was more damaging to the existing regime, for it magnified the prestige of Napoleon's republican opponents, the men who were to come to power with the creation of the Third Republic.

In retrospect, however, the Civil War may be seen to have occasioned the last great liberal evangel on behalf of American democracy. The great rallying which accrued to the northern cause in the war's latter years was perhaps to prove less prophetic than the doubts and hesitations which beset liberal consciences in the opening phase. As America entered the age of Big Business and the robber barons, it became easier to interpret the Civil War as a success for capitalism, political centralism and force. Those were very appropriate themes for Europe in the Age of Bismarck.

Suggestions for Further Reading

THE LIST BELOW EMPHASIZES IMPORTANT RECENT WRITINGS AND SPECIALIST ARTICLES. For a detailed critical bibliography, dealing particularly with primary sources, see: Norman Ferris, "Diplomacy," in Allan Nevins, et. al., eds., *Civil War Books: A Critical Bibliography* (Baton Rouge, 1967), I, pp. 241–278. Many of the works cited below have excellent bibliographies, while the journal *Civil War History* includes material on diplomacy in its annual "Bibliography of Civil War Articles." For more detailed treatment and documentation of the themes treated in the present work, see D. P. Crook, *The North, the South, and the Powers, 1861–1865* (Wiley, New York & London, 1974.)

E. D. Adams, *Great Britain and the American Civil War.* 2 vols. (New York, 1925), and F. L. Owsley, *King Cotton Diplomacy: Foreign Relations of the Confederate States of America* (Chicago, 1931; revised ed. by Harriet C. Owsley, 1959) dominated the field until recently. Written at the time of the "great rapprochement" between Britain and the U.S., Adams' work de-emphasizes the antagonisms which developed in Anglo-American relations during the Civil War; events are carefully recounted but are viewed from the meridian of London, Union diplomacy receiving little analysis. Owsley's monumental research in the Confederate archives will remain of permanent value, but southern partisanship and an imperfect awareness of European power politics limit the book's value.

Recent monographs which have spectacularly widened our knowledge of affairs include: Lynn M. Case and Warren F. Spencer, *The United States and France: Civil War Diplomacy* (Philadelphia, 1970), a massive treatment illuminating Napoleonic policy, Union and Confederate intrigues for French sympathy. The authors confirm the traditional view that French freedom of action on America was severely limited by the alliance with Britain. The omission of the Mexican affair from the book imposes difficulty upon the reader seeking a broad view of French strategy. Frank J. Merli's *Great Britain and the Confederate Navy, 1861–1865* (Bloomington, London, 1970) now provides the best account of southern shipbuilding abroad. His portrayal of a jittery British ministry, beset by the traditional problems of a neutral power, and meshed in the web of circumstances, offending all parties, is more convincing than the image of a malevolent anti-Yankee nation which was generated at the time. Another side of the maritime war is conveyed in Stuart L. Bernath, *Squall Across the Atlantic: American Civil War Prize Cases and Diplomacy* (Berkeley and Los Angeles, 1970), showing that the Union Navy's efforts to stifle trade with the south were made at the serious risk of an Anglo-American war. Concern for national interest, on both sides of the Atlantic, caused a retreat from the brink.

There is still no definitive study of Union diplomacy, but the gap is partially filled by Glyndon G. Van Deusen's admirable, if highly compressed, biography, *William Henry Seward* (New York, O.U.P., 1967). Seward's role as a theorist of empire is discussed in Walter LaFeber, *The New Empire* (Ithaca, New York, 1963). Students may profitably consult the rich literature on Manifest Destiny and the expansionist impulse to gain deeper insight into both Union and Confederate foreign policy. Other writings on Seward and the Lincoln administration are listed in Van Deusen's bibliography. David Donald, ed., *Inside Lincoln's Cabinet: The Civil War Diaries of Salmon P. Chase* (New York, 1954) and H. K. Beale, ed., *Diary of Gideon Welles* (New York, 1960), are sometimes useful, as is John Niven, *Gideon Welles* (Oxford University Press, 1974.) David Donald, *Charles Sumner and the Rights of Man* (New York, 1970), exposes Sumner's efforts to undermine Seward and take his place. Allen Nevins's ample volumes on the Civil War contain well-researched chapters on foreign policy and international opinion. Jay Monaghan, *Diplomat in Carpet Slippers: Abraham Lincoln Deals with Foreign Affairs* (New York, 1945) is lightweight and exaggerates Lincoln's role. Martin B. Duberman, *Charles Francis Adams* (New York, 1961), Margaret Clapp, *Forgotten First Citizen: John Bigelow* (Boston, 1947) are competent, but not detailed, biographies of Union diplomats. Norman B. Ferris, *Tempestuous Mission, 1861–1862: The Early Diplomatic Career of Charles Francis Adams* (Unpub. Ph.D. thesis, Emory University, 1962) is a valuable pioneering study which deserves publication. See also N. B. Ferris, "An American Diplomatist Confronts Victorian Society," *History Today,* XV (August, 1965), pp. 550–558, and other articles. S. A. Wallace and F. E. Gillespie, *Journal of Benjamin Moran, 1857–1865* 2 vols. (Chicago, 1948), is a delightfully informative record of people and events by Adams' waspish secretary of legation. John Bigelow, *Retrospections of an Active Life* (London, 1910); Brainerd Dyer, "Thomas H. Dudley," CWH, I (1955), pp. 401–413; La Fayette C. Baker, *The U.S. Secret Service in the Late War* (Philadelphia, c. 1889, Lost Cause Press microcards, 1957); R. D. Saltvig, *Charles Francis Adams and Special Missions to England, 1861–1865* (Washington, Unpub. M.A. thesis, 1959); A. E. Taylor, "Walker's Financial Mission to London on Behalf of the North, 1863–1864" *J. Econ. & Business H.,* III (1931), pp. 296–320; H. C. Owsley, "H. S. Sanford and Federal Surveillance Abroad" *MVHR,* XLVIII (1961), pp. 211–228; D. H. Maynard, "The Forbes-Aspinwall Mission" *MVHR,* XLV, No. 1 (June, 1958), pp. 67–89 provide information on Union agents, espionage and missions abroad. P. Van Doren Stern, *When the Guns Roared: World Aspects of the American Civil War* (New York, 1965), is mainly for the general reader.

Specialist articles on the *Trent* affair are listed in Chapter 3 of the present volume, but mention may be made here of: N. B. Ferris, "Lincoln and the *Trent* Affair," *Lincoln Herald,* LXIX (1967); V. H. Cohen, "Charles Sumner and the Trent Affair," *JSH,* XXII (1956), pp. 205–219; Gordon Harris Warren, *The Trent Affair, 1861–1862* (Unpub. Ph.D. thesis, Indiana, 1969), with a useful discussion of the literature.

Owsley's work, mentioned above, is still the main authority on Confederate diplomacy, but a refreshing short reappraisal is contained in Henry Blumenthal, "Confederate Diplomacy: Popular Notions and International Realities," *JSH,* XXXII (1966), pp. 159–167. James Morton Callahan, *Diplomatic History of the Southern Confederacy* (New York, 1901; repr. 1964) is dated, but puts southern aims within a proper hemispheric context. Southern expansionism in the antebellum era is dealt with in Robert E. May, *The Southern Dream of a Carribean Empire, 1854–1861* (Baton Rouge,

1973.) Robert D. Meade, *Judah P. Benjamin, Confederate Statesman* (New York, O.U.P., 1943) is a competent short biography of the south's best Secretary of State. R. W. Patrick, *Jefferson Davis and His Cabinet* (Louisiana State University Press, 1961) treats relations between Davis and Benjamin. Van Mitchel Smith, "British Business Relations with the Confederacy, 1861–1865" (Unpub. Ph.D. thesis, Texas, 1949) may be used in conjunction with Martin P. Claussen, "The U.S. and Great Britain, 1861–1865: Peace Factors in International Relations" (Unpub. Ph.D. thesis, Illinois, 1937), summarized in Claussen, "Peace Factors in Anglo-American Relations, 1861–1865" *MVHR,* XXVI (1940), pp. 511–522. That the south miscalculated the nature of conditions within the British cotton industry is revealed by Eugene A. Brady, "A Reconsideration of the Lancashire 'Cotton Famine'," *Agric. H.,* XXXVII (1963), pp. 156–162, which cites the existence of ample reserves of raw cotton in England and claims that Lancashire was suffering an overproduction crisis. For the controversy over the relative importance of southern cotton and northern wheat within the British economy, see my account in Chapter 6 and statistics in Robert H. Jones, "Long Live the King?", *Agric. H.,* XXXVII, No. 4 (Oct., 1963), pp. 166–171. Jones' assertion that the British did not worry about "King Corn" may be treated with caution. Confederate financing is considered in Richard Lester, "Confederate Finance and Purchasing in Great Britain during the American Civil War," (Unpub. Ph.D. thesis, Manchester, 1962). That the Erlanger loan, with a bad press from historians, elicited vital funds in 1863–1864 is contended by Judith F. Gentry, "A Confederate Success in Europe: The Erlanger Loan," *JSH,* XXXVI, No. 2 (May, 1970), pp. 157–188. There is supplementary material in C. S. Davis, *Colin J. McRae: Confederate Financial Agent* (Tuscaloosa, 1961); Charles P. Cullop, *Confederate Propaganda in Europe, 1861–1865* (University of Miami Press, 1969) and "Edwin de Leon, Jeff Davis's Propagandist," *CWH,* VIII, No. 4 (1962), pp. 386–400; Robert T. Smith, "The Confederate *Index* and the American Civil War," (Unpub. M.A. thesis, University of Washington, 1961); Louis M. Sears, *John Slidell* (Durham, 1925). Works on Civil War Mexico (see below) provide a vital dimension on southern territorial ambitions, too often neglected by scholars.

The international wrangles which arose over the maritime war and Confederate attempts to build a navy abroad are skilfully studied in monographs by Merli and Bernath, mentioned above. Readers are urged to consult Merli's exhaustive critical bibliography for further references. On the Union blockade, see articles by Marcus W. Price in *Am. Neptune,* VIII (1948), pp. 196–237; XI (1951), pp. 262–290; XII (1952), pp. 229–238; XV (1955), pp. 97–131; proving that impressive numbers of small craft broke the blockade. John B. Heffernan, "The Blockade of the Southern Confederacy," *Smithsonian J. Hist.,* II, No. 4 (1967–1968) indicates that the blockade achieved its major strategic objectives. Richard S. West, Jr., *Mr. Lincoln's Navy* (New York, 1957) and Joseph T. Durkin, *Stephen R. Mallory: Confederate Navy Chief* (Chapel Hill, N.C., 1954) discuss the naval objectives of both sides. Confederate shipbuilding is dealt with in: Wilbur D. Jones, *The Confederate Rams at Birkenhead: A Chapter in Anglo-American Relations* (Tuscaloosa, 1961), with intriguing insights into official thinking at the British Foreign Office and Admiralty; Douglas Maynard, "Union Efforts to Prevent the Escape of the *Alabama,*" *MVHR,* XLI (1954), pp. 41–60 and "Plotting the Escape of the *Alabama,*" *JSH,* XX (1954), pp. 197–209; Rupert C. Jarvis, "The *Alabama* and the Law," *Trans. Historic. Soc. Lancashire and Cheshire,* (1959), pp. 181–198, plausibly arguing that the British government was legally justified in not stopping the *Alabama's* departure; D. Maynard, "The Confederacy's Super-*Alabama,*" *CWH,* V, (1959), pp. 80–132, describing efforts to build the C.S.S. *Pampero.* D. Higginbotham, "A Raider Refuels: Diplomatic Repercussions," *CWH,* IV (1958), and Frank L. Owsley, Jr., *The C.S.S. Florida: Her Building and Operation* (Philadelphia, 1965) deal with one of the early rebel raiders. James D. Bulloch, *The Secret Service of the Confederate States in Europe or How the Confederate Cruisers Were Equipped,* 2 vols. (New York, 1883; repr. 1959) is a valuable original source, written by the south's greatest agent abroad. Britain's concern to maintain her long-term interests in strong belligerent rights at sea qualified her attitude to Union naval operations: see James P. Baxter, "Some British Opinions as to Neutral Rights, 1861–1865," *Am. J. Int. Law,* XXIII (1929), pp. 517–537, "The British Government & Neutral Rights, 1861–1865," and "Papers Relating to Belligerent and Neutral Rights, 1861–1865," *AHR,* XXXIV (1928), pp. 9–29, 77–91.

British diplomacy is surveyed generally in Kenneth Bourne, *The Foreign Policy of Victorian England, 1830–1902* (Clarendon Press, Oxford, 1970), while Bourne's *Britain and the Balance of Power in*

North America 1815–1908 (London, 1967) examines Britain's historic naval and military policies in that theater. The chapter on the *Trent* affair is essential reading on British strategy, giving London's blueprint for an all-out Anglo-American war. Britain's European and hemispheric diplomacy is often neglected in civil war studies: see A. J. P. Taylor, *The Struggle for Mastery in Europe* (Oxford, 1954, repr. since), and *The Trouble Makers: Dissent Over Foreign Policy: 1792–1939* (London, 1957), especially chapters 2, 3, on Cobden and Gladstone, for Britain in Europe; and Richard W. Van Alstyne's articles on Central America: e.g. "British Diplomacy and the Clayton-Bulwer Treaty, 1850–1860," *J. Mod. Hist.,* XI, No. 2, (June, 1939), pp. 149–183. Van Alstyne's *The Rising American Empire* (Oxford, 1960) gives a brilliant account of the clash of British and American imperialisms in the C19. H. C. F. Bell, *Lord Palmerston,* 2 vols. (London, 1936) is probably still the best biography, with more detail on the civil war years than more recent works. Bell shows that Palmerston's reputation for showy aggressiveness was belied by his concern for pragmatic British interests. Donald Southgate, *The Most English Minister* (London, 1966), and Jasper Ridley, *Lord Palmerston* (London, 1970), although excellent studies, are not revealing on civil war diplomacy. Further reading on British politics and society may be obtained by consulting Geoffrey Best, *Mid-Victorian Britain, 1851–1875* (London, 1971).

An understanding of "Atlantic history," of the cultural, economic, and political links between Britons and Americans, is essential if the war's impact abroad is to be appreciated. Frank Thistlethwaite, *The Anglo-American Connection in the Early C19* (Philadelphia, 1959), and D. P. Crook, *American Democracy in English Politics, 1815–1850* (Clarendon Press, Oxford, 1965) may serve as guides to the ante-bellum years. J. Potter, "Atlantic Economy, 1815–1860, etc." in A. W. Coats and R. M. Robertson, eds. *Essays in American Economic History* (London, 1969) illustrates the strong economic bonds between industrial Britain and a developing northern economy. Such views (including Claussen, above) give much needed corrective to the southern-oriented emphasis upon cotton's "kingly" sway within Atlantic trade. Brady (above) reappraises the nature of the "cotton famine." See also: Amos

Khasigian, "Economic Factors and British Neutrality, 1861–1865," *Historian,* XXV (1963), pp. 451–465.

Max Beloff, "Great Britain and the American Civil War," *History,* XXXVII (1952), pp. 40–48, and H. C. Allen, "Civil War, Reconstruction, and Great Britain," in H. Hyman ed., *Heard Round the World: The Impact Abroad of the Civil War* (New York, 1969), are provoking general essays. Wilbur D. Jones, "The British Conservatives and the American Civil War," *AHR,* LVIII (1953), pp. 527–543, is a fine study which illustrates the Tory hierarchy's disinclination to meddle in American affairs. Case studies of international crisis points include: N. B. Ferris, "The Prince Consort, the *Times* and the *Trent* Affair," *CWH,* VI (1960), pp. 152–157; J. Wheeler-Bennett, "The *Trent* Affair: How the Prince Consort Saved the U.S.," *Hist. Today,* XI, No. 12 (Dec., 1961), pp. 811–816 (includes rare archival extracts); Frank J. Merli and T. A. Wilson, "The British Cabinet and the Confederacy: Autumn, 1962," *Maryland Hist. Mag.,* LXV, No. 3. (Fall, 1970), pp. 239–262; E. W. Ellsworth, "Anglo-American Affairs in October of 1862," *Lincoln Herald,* LXVI, No. 2 (1964), pp. 89–96; K. J. Brauer, "British Mediation and the American Civil War: A Reconsideration," *JSH,* XXXVIII, pp. 49–64.

For the historiography of the vexed issue of British public sympathies during the Civil War, see Joseph M. Hernon, "British Sympathies in the American Civil War: A Reconsideration," *JSH,* XXXIII (1967), pp. 356–367, claiming that historians writing with hindsight of Federal victory exaggerated the influence of Union supporters in Britain during the war. D. Jordan and E. J. Pratt, *Europe and the American Civil War* (1931, repr. New York, 1969) helped to create the view that English bourgeois and nonconformist opinion was partisan for the north. Their array of evidence still commands respect. The most telling recent blow against the legend of proletarian support for a democratic north is struck by Mary L. Ellison, *Support for Secession: Lancashire and the American Civil War* (University of Chicago Press, 1973). Bradford leaned to the north, according to D. G. Wright, "Bradford and the American Civil War," *J. British Stud.,* VIII (May, 1969), pp. 69–85. Joseph M. Hernon, *Celts, Catholics and Copperheads: Ireland Views the American Civil War* (Ohio State University Press, 1968) shows that the slaughter of Irish-Americans caused progressive Irish disillusion with the north. Scots opinion is treated in Robert Botsford, *Scotland and the American Civil War* (Unpub. Ph.D. thesis, 1955, Edinburgh.) D. P. Crook, "Portents of War: English Opinion on Secession," *J. American Studies,* IV, No. 2 (Feb. 1971), pp. 163–179 shows how initial journalistic sympathy for the plight of the north was eroded by events (p. 163 for review of the literature). A. Whitridge, "British Liberals and the American Civil War," *History Today,* XII (Oct., 1962), pp. 688–695, illustrates the dilemmas the war posed for liberals, the theme also of C. Collyer, "Gladstone and the American Civil War" *Proc. Leeds Philosophical Soc.,* VI, part 8 (May, 1951), pp. 583–594. Royden Harrison, *Before the Socialists: Studies in Labour and Politics, 1861–1881* (London, 1965), Chapter 2 "British Labour and American Slavery," shows the early wartime influence of a small group of labor editors with southern sympathies. Sheldon Van Auken, "English Sympathy for the Southern Confederacy: The Glittering Illusion" (Unpub. D.Phil. thesis, Oxford, 1957) is dogmatically pro-Confederate, but assembles much useful material; he claims that nonintervention by Britain was a sign of complacent belief in the inevitability of rebel independence. Biographical works of relevance include: H. Ausubel, *John Bright: Victorian Reformer* (Wiley, New York, 1966); Donald Read, *Cobden and Bright: A Victorian Political Partnership* (London, 1967); M. Churchman, "Bagehot and the American Civil War" in N. St. John-Stevas, ed., *Collected Works of Walter Bagehot,* (London, 1968), IV, pp. 179–194; see pp. 195–425 for Bagehot's articles on the war; J. O. Waller, "Thomas Carlyle and his Nutshell Iliad," *Bull. New York Pub. Libr.* LXIX, pp. 17–30; J. O. Waller, "Dickens and the Civil War," *Stud. Philol.,* LVII (1960), pp. 535–548; W. D. Jones, "Blyden, Gladstone and the Civil War," *J. Negro H.,* XLIX (1964), pp. 56–61; Elisabeth Wallace, *Goldwin Smith, Victorian Liberal* (Toronto, 1957); F. L. Bullard, "What Goldwin Smith did for Uncle Sam during the Civil War," *Lincoln Herald,* LII (Dec. 1950); J. Saville, *Ernest Jones, Chartist* (London, 1952); N. F. Adkins, "Thomas Hughes and the American Civil War, etc.," *J. Negro H.,* XVIII (1933), pp. 322–329; J. O. Waller, "Charles Kingsley and the American Civil War," *Stud. Philol.,* LX (1963), pp. 554–568; R. Greenleaf, "Marx and the St. James Hall Meeting," (with reply from R. Harrison) *Science and Society,* XXVIII, pp. 323–325; also Karl Marx and F. Engels, *The Civil War in the U.S.*

(Citadel Press, 3rd ed. 1961); G. N. Ray, *Thackeray: the Age of Wisdom 1847–1863* (Oxford, 1958). W. M. Rosetti, "English Opinion of the American Civil War," *Atlantic Monthly,* XVII (Feb., 1866), pp. 129–149 is an interesting contemporary analysis. See also C. E. Shain, "English Novelists and the American Civil War," *Am. Quart.,* XIV (Fall, 1962), pp. 399–421, and Oscar Maurer, "Punch on Slavery and Civil War in America, 1841–1865," *Victorian Studies,* I (Sept., 1957), pp. 5–28.

Further reading on Franco-American relations may be located in the bibliography to Case and Spencer's authoritative account of the topic (above). Henry Blumenthal, *A Reappraisal of Franco-American Relations, 1830–1871* (Chapel Hill, N.C., 1959) is a brilliant short analysis, giving proper weight to European power politics. Daniel B. Carroll, *Henri Mercier and the American Civil War* (Princeton, 1971) is an excellent biography of the French minister in Washington. Carroll clears Mercier of the charge of excessive partisanship to the south. Serge Gavronsky, *The French Liberal Opposition and the American Civil War* (New York, 1968) traces how Napoleon's liberal critics reinforced their domestic program from principles enunciated by Lincoln. Harold Hyman, ed., *Heard Around the World: The Impact Abroad of the Civil War* (New York, 1969), has essays upon Britain, France, Central Europe, Russia, Canada, and Latin America. Vatican diplomacy has attracted much attention: e.g. Anthony B. Lalli, S.X., and Thomas H. O'Connor, "Roman Views on the American Civil War," *Catholic Hist. Rev.,* LVII, No. 1 (April, 1971), pp. 21–41. See also Jordan and Pratt, (above). Albert A. Woldman, *Lincoln & the Russians* (New York, 1952); J. W. Wieczerzak, *A Polish Chapter in Civil War America* (New York, 1967); J. Kutolowski, "The Effect of the Polish Insurrection of 1863 on the American Civil War Diplomacy," *Historian,* XXVII, pp. 360–377, are informative. For the "Russian fleet myth" see writings listed in Wieczerzak, *ibid.,* pp. 177–178. See also H. I. Kushner, "The Russian Fleet and the American Civil War: Another View," *Historian,* XXXIV, pp. 633–649.

Canada and Mexico were important theatres in which international tensions were played out. Robin Winks, *Canada and the United States: the Civil War Years* (Baltimore, 1960) is a definitive study. K. Bourne, *Britain and the Balance of Power in North America, 1815–1908* (London, 1967) is vital for British defense policy.

Alfred J. Hanna and Kathryn A. Hanna, *Napoleon III and Mexico: American Triumph Over Monarchy* (Chapel Hill, N.C., 1971) narrates the rise and fall of Napoleon's "Grand Design." Their exhaustive bibliography includes recent writings on Mexico and Latin America. Arnold Blumberg's *Diplomacy of the Mexican Empire, 1863–67* (Philadelphia, 1971) uses a wide variety of archival materials and argues that Maximilian's empire was not a puppet-regime of France. See also LeRoy Fischer, and B. J. Chandler, "U.S.—Spanish Relations during the American Civil War," *Lincoln Herald,* LXXV, 136–147. Nancy Nichols Barker, "France, Austria, and the Mexican Venture, 1861–1864," *French Hist. Stud.,* III, No. 2 (Fall, 1963), pp. 224–245, fits Napoleon's Mexican intrigues into the mosaic of his Austrian-Italian strategies.

Index